An Epitaph for German Judaism

HTV 04, a Jewish sports club, on May 18, 1924. Its president, Curt Lewin, is in the dark suit. To his right is Otto Wurche, a gentile sports teacher. To Lewin's left is the *Vorturner*, my father, Julius Fackenheim; an unidentified boy; my older brother, Alexander Fackenheim; two more unidentified boys; I, myself; and my younger brother, Wolfgang Fackenheim. Lewin and my father had founded the sports club twenty years earlier and this picture is of a celebration of its founding.

An Epitaph for German Judaism

From Halle to Jerusalem

Emil L. Fackenheim

THE UNIVERSITY OF WISCONSIN PRESS

This book was was published with generous support from
the LUCIUS N. LITTAUER FOUNDATION and
the CHILDREN OF EMIL FACKENHEIM.

The University of Wisconsin Press
1930 Monroe Street
Madison, Wisconsin 53711

www.wisc.edu/wisconsinpress/

3 Henrietta Street
London WC2E 8LU, England

5   4   3   2   1

Printed in the United States of America

Library of Congress Cataloging-in-Publication Data
Fackenheim, Emil L.
    An epitaph for German Judaism : from Halle to Jerusalem /
    Emil Fackenheim
        pp.   cm.—(Modern Jewish philosophy and religion)
    Includes bibliographical references and index.
    ISBN 0-299-17590-1 (cloth : alk. paper)
        1. Fackenheim, Emil L.   2. Jews—Germany—Halle an der Saale—Biography.
3. Jews—Germany—Intellectual life—20th century.   4. Germany—Ethnic relations.
5. Refugees, Jewish—Canada—Biography.   6. Jews, German—Israel—Biography.
7. Holocaust, Jewish (1939–1945)—Influence.   8. Jewish philosophers—Israel—
Biography.   9. Judaism and philosophy.
I. Title. II. Series.
DS135.G5 F244   2002
296'.092—dc21   2002004638

To the memory of my wife,
Rose

and the future of my grandchildren,
Daniella, Benji, Dan, Adam, Gideon

and to Professor Mike Morgan,
former student, colleague, and friend of thirty years,
without whose labors this book would never
have been published

Contents

Foreword: To Mend the World, to Mend a Life

Michael L. Morgan

Emil Ludwig Fackenheim was born in Halle, Germany, on June 22, 1916; he died in Jerusalem, Israel, on September 19, 2003. At the time of his death, these memoirs and reflections on German Jewry had been in progress for about a decade. The book was in proofs, but the proofs had been in Emil's hands for a year. When he passed away, he had made many corrections, some minor but some substantial, including replacing the epilogue and adding a new essay, but fortunately the corrections were very close to being completed. What is published here is as near to what he wanted as I could determine from these corrections and various notes.

The book is a very unusual document. It is personal but at the same time public, narrative at times, but also reflective. At first glance, it looks like a memoir of a life, a man's surveying of his past, his experiences, family, friends, and acquaintances. But it is more than this. As you read and reread these pages, as I have done many times, over years, in the course of the difficult, halting stages of their composition, you will see that this document is more than a memoir and less, that it is something different.

Biographies are stories of lives, shaped by the biographer's sense of what is important, memorable, and in the end the message or point of that life's story. After all the details are unearthed and the context researched, the bits and pieces of evidence are constructed according to a design, and the life examined and told becomes a story. Many autobiographies are like this too. The author sets about to tell his or her life story, to recall events and people, with an eye to giving the life a certain look; memoirs can be more episodic, but they often have this look too.

It is tempting to pick up this book in the light of these expectations. For years, I did. As Emil first decided, only after a great deal of personal struggle and uncertainty, to write them, I was encouraging. I saw this as an opportunity for him to bring to light the details and development of a life I knew had been fascinating and important. Over the years, Emil had written various pieces that shed light on his experiences. Here was an excellent way for him to fill out those pieces and to share the whole of his life, as he recalled it. Once I even spent a week with him, at his home in Jerusalem, taping hours of recollections and asking him questions, probing, prodding, gently (I hoped) encouraging him to remember details—chronology, events, people, relationships, on and on.

Now, as I reflect back on that decade or so, I realize that all of my prodding, and all of the details, and my growing delight as Emil would return again and again to the book, all this was not a failure on my part, but it was based on much too narrow a view of what Emil was doing and what the book was and was becoming. I certainly realized all along how much its pages meant to him, how cautiously and sometimes painfully he took each step, and, as time went on, how the importance of the work became greater and greater. And I realized too—I knew—that Emil was living through a great deal in those years. But, until recently, I did not put together the pieces. Now I have started to do that; let me share some of these thoughts.

Writing books involves all kinds of acts, and I do not mean this in the trivial sense. Perhaps it would be more helpful to say that writing can *be* many kinds of acts and that the work of thinking, imagining, remembering, and crafting the words and sentences—all this can be many things at once. We are more prone to reflect on these rhetorical matters with poets and novelists than with philosophers and academics, and especially we are attentive to these rhetorical matters when we read diaries, letters, sermons, and such things. Even though Emil was a philosopher and a Jewish theologian, and indeed just because he was a philosopher and such a careful writer, we cannot forget these matters here. I would venture to say that Emil was more attentive to language and expression, to the union of form and content, since about 1985 or so, than he was even before, and here, in these pages, more than ever. He pored over these words and sentences. The rhythm of the sentences, the order and placement of the words, the precise terms, the content and the way it is conveyed, the weaving of events and personalities with ideas—everything has painstakingly and painfully undergone scrupulous reflection. At one level, then, we should read these pages with due attention to the cadence, the tone, the impact, and the order of thought and word.

But this is only the beginning. The sentences are often very fragmented. In many cases they do not flow. They are chopped up, interrupted constantly, qualified and intruded upon, halting. These pages record steps of memory—some of them forced, others opportune—taken slowly and not smoothly and easily. Qualifications, pauses, abrupt interruptions. Over the years, I would receive versions and at times make my own revisions to smooth out the accounts, making the episodes and transitions more seamless; I—like many of Emil's friends—heard many of these stories and recollections dozens, even hundreds of times. Why, I thought, could they not be told more artfully? Why was Emil slightly refashioning them and jumping from one to the other? Why was Emil not using the wonderful literary skills I knew he possessed? I did not realize: he was.

This is a very personal book that is also a theological and philosophical book. It engages in philosophy and is a way of life, both at once. It is an effort of remembering, dealing with the past, with the traumas of the past and the present, and more. We ought never to forget that it took Emil nearly thirty years after leaving Germany to engage the events of Nazi Germany and the Holocaust. Then, in the years between 1966 and 1982, he shaped intellectually, philosophically, and theologically a strategy to expose oneself to those events in all their particularity and to go on living. In 1983, he, Rose, and their family made aliyah and moved to Jerusalem—an utterly extraordinary, complex, anxious, exhilarating, and, I think, heroic decision. In 1982 he had published a book, *To Mend the World*, that was philosophically deep, but it was also demanding: it arrived at a call—to mend, to repair—but what? The world, yes, but for each of us and for him also, our lives. For Emil, the challenge—he himself had discovered it and

set it—was to mend his life. As we read these pages, we cannot
forget this necessity, this momentous obligation, that probity required Emil not just to tell Jews, Christians, and others about
mending but also to do it.

These memoirs are both an *expression* of Emil's mending his
life during his last decade and also a major *vehicle* of that mending. Here he is literally writing his life. In the course of the
decade, as the memoirs grew, were revised hundreds of times,
supplemented and deepened, they became the instrument and
the location of Emil's effort to mend his life and his world. More
and more, as age and memory and the events of his personal life
and of his world progressed, mingled, and clashed, the memoirs
became the site of this act of repair and recovery, of return and of
settling affairs. The fractured, disrupted, joyful, painful, episodic, and reflective character of these pages expresses this process. But it does so not only for personal reasons. It also says
something about this process for German Jews, for Germans, for
Jews, for others too.

To Mend the World is Emil's magnum opus. But even it is a book
that already begins to show that mending is a profoundly complex and discontinuous process. Even there Emil begins to show
that mending is not always smooth and easy. For example, the
book has both endnotes and footnotes. There are sources and
citations, but there are also digressions and qualifications. And,
if we read the text carefully, we can see that the same sentence
structure so clearly evident in these memoirs is already beginning to appear there: long sentences—broken into pieces, clauses,
phrases—qualifications, interjections, parentheses. The thought
there has a deep, philosophically controlled character. But the
tempo and rhythm, if overall continuous, is countered by the discontinuous, fragmentary quality of the sentences and the writing.

And then there are the prefaces. The book *To Mend the World*
has been issued three times. Each time Emil provided an additional preface or introduction. This of course is not unusual. But
the character of these prefaces is unusual. These are not formu-
laic, brief, or casual. Each is new, substantial, and yet of a different type, not always clearly connected with the volume itself,
certainly not *as* an introduction or preparatory set of remarks.

Here in the pages of these memoirs, we can see how complex
the process of mending was for Emil. Why has that been so? There

are many reasons and layers—philosophical and personal. He, after all, was a philosopher and theologian who was torn from Germany by the Nazi government and whose career struggled to cope with the reality of the Nazi persecution and the death camps. How often did he argue that these events are a unique manifestation of radical evil and a rupture that requires us to recover and reconstitute our lives thereafter.

But as powerful and important for Emil were the personal reasons. He began to write these memoirs when two things happened in his life. First, he received an invitation in 1993 to return to Halle, his birthplace and hometown, from which he had fled in 1939 after his incarceration in Sachsenhausen, and he decided to accept, to return home to Germany. It was to be his second trip to Germany since flight but the first to Halle and one that opened the door to many others and to a decade of rethinking Germany, German Judaism, and his Germanness, his family, his loss. Second, Rose, Emil's wife since 1957, began to manifest symptoms of Alzheimer's, a disease which progressed, and which he, she, and Yossi had to live with at home, leading to her placement in a home and finally to her death in 1998. Rose had been the driving force behind their aliyah; she was politically and theologically passionate, a person of extraordinary energy, and a major influence on Emil's life and work. One can imagine the daily burdens—physical and psychological—on Emil as he cared for Rose and yet watched her decline and fall into the strange seclusion of her disease. Friends watched his stoic efforts and marveled at his ability to cope with her suffering and all the domestic and bureaucratic complications attending it. But underneath the surface of control, surely there was deep turmoil. These events, the return to Germany and Rose's illness, stimulated the memoirs, framed the mending process, and mark it as a project of great complexity and struggle and depth.

Israel too. We must never forget Israel. It is fair to say that Israel and the state played no special role in Emil's thought or in his life until 1967. Then, after the Six Day War, everything changed. Israel became a centerpiece in his philosophical and theological account of response to Auschwitz, of his commitment to Jewish survival, and of his thought and his actions regarding Jews and Christians together. One need only look at his essays and books after *God's Presence in History* to see this. Israel came to

play a central role in Emil's and Rose's lives—first with prominent lectures in 1968 and 1970, then with regular summer visits,
later with aliyah, with friendships, and with increasing emotional and intellectual involvement in Israel's political life. In
some ways, however, the road to Israel was easier than the dwelling in Israel. Emil started these memoirs a decade after making
aliyah, and the decade, with all its sense of fulfillment, was filled
with frustrations and difficulties. For a few years, he had split his
time with the University of Toronto, until he could retire; then, as
emeritus, he found himself with a teaching position in Jerusalem
different from what he had expected. Surely this was cause for
frustration. Upon aliyah, friendships that were longstanding became fragile; some broke off completely; others were strong and
new ones began. But never was Emil located in Israeli academic
life and Jewish culture or even in the Israeli world of philosophy
as he had been in North America and as one might have expected,
given his reputation and prominence. His eager, passionate engagement with political events and his strong commitments made
him vocal and energetic; he wrote a great deal—letters, columns,
articles—both in Israel and in Canada; he gave interviews and en-
gaged in public debates, encouraged, aided, and in some ways
motivated by Rose's own passionate commitments. But in many
ways he was on the margin, and one can easily imagine that he
knew it and found it painful and deeply wounding. He was taking his own words and bringing them to life and into life, and the
results were anything but what he would have expected. They
were hard, and life was hard. He persevered, with pride in his
Israeli life and yet with doubts about whether he had done the
right thing.

Then, there was his German past. In 1970, when he and Rose
went to Bergen-Belsen on the way to Israel, the significance of the
visit was diminished with the focus on Israel. But in 1993, Halle
acknowledged him and he returned. From 1939 to 1993 he en-
gaged in virtually no intellectual or psychological or physical return to Germany or to his German past; then a crescendo. Here
Emil overcame a great deal of resistance that lay deep within him.
But in Israel he had met German Christians and taught German
students of theology; he had made friends and found that he
and his work were known in Germany. Obviously he found a
way to return, in memory and in person. But every step was slow

and deeply upsetting, the result of enormous struggle. Every new memory was unearthed, isolated, clarified, examined, mulled over; bits and pieces, some fit together, some did not. And, as Emil returned in memory, he was filled with regrets. Yet he grasped the past of his German and Jewish life to gather his life together, to place it in the world that was lost and to think about what it meant for him and for our understanding of what German Judaism was and what the Nazi destruction of it meant.

At first, and I recall this vividly, Emil had resisted the very idea of writing his personal memoirs as something unworthy and of little interest to others. When he finally decided to engage in the project, it was because he became convinced that his life, when recalled in a certain way, might say something about German Judaism and its character and about what the Holocaust had destroyed. But, as time went on, no matter how often he would reiterate this task, the excavation of his past in Germany, in flight, in Canada and beyond, became more complicated and harder to piece together. Early on in the writing, the chronology of the life was subordinate to the overall plan: to reflect, through an interweaving of philosophical reflection and particular memories, on the Nazi destruction of German Judaism and the world that was destroyed. But there was no grand narrative of a life. There was an overall progression—from Germany to Aberdeen, to Toronto and finally to Jerusalem—but there was no coherent story to tell. Rarely did a memory contain a great deal: a feature, an utterance, a term or word, a glimpse, and no matter how often repeated, no more was recalled. Each memory captured some point, which Emil could unearth, brush off, and illuminate, but that was it.

In Germany Emil received attention and honors and even was received as representative of the exterminated world of German Judaism. Every encounter generated more thoughts about the present and the past, more distress, and more reflection too, as he placed each memory within his thinking about the Holocaust, Germany, Judaism, philosophy, and life. Each speech in Germany during these past several years added to the attempt, by offering another opportunity to confront this past and what it meant. He was invited to teach in Germany, spent three months in Kassel, and received an honorary degree in Bochum. As time went on, he began to use more and more German in his conversation and in his writing, to recall and use terms, expressions, and to quote from his prodigious and remarkable memory of German poetry, literature, and philosophy. A very deep layer of himself was being bored into and each new entry released German language, literature, and tone, to be placed into the life he was living and the life he was trying to reclaim.

Emil, for the nearly thirty-five years that I knew him, worked and thought by verbalizing his thoughts. Ideas, connections of themes, insights, and ways of framing and articulating were slowly built up in his mind, turned over and over, and at every opportunity—whether in personal conversation or public lectures—were repeated again and again, then written, rewritten, crafted—all of this continually. This process had not changed since 1993; indeed it intensified. Each vignette, each account or description, each picture and remembrance in these memoirs underwent this process. Each is a glimpse of Emil's past, his life, projected on the screen of memory and then turned over and over before being formulated.

But the final years were often relatively solitary ones. There were conferences, speeches, events, but there were also the years of Rose's advancing illness, and the eventual end to his teaching. There were excellent, devoted research assistants, but there were also long periods alone with Rose, and with the silent process of recollection, thinking, shaping, writing, rewriting. Solitude, for a philosopher, is never quiet; indeed, it may not be quiet for any of us. Thoughts after all are noisy companions. The work of collecting and mending the life did not proceed smoothly and efficiently. It was often a relatively solitary life, and it could hardly have eluded Emil's grasp that his immersion in memory, with all its successes and frustrations, was going on in solitude from Rose, whose own life was increasingly sinking into its own isolation, bereft of nearly all memory.

Part of mending, very clearly for Emil, was about mending fences, as he often put it. The memoirs are filled with people. Generally Emil does not have more than a word to say about someone; sometimes a single fragment of a memory, or a single comment. There are innumerable reconciliations with the dead that take place in these pages. And many too with the living. Whatever the estrangements that occurred largely in the years after 1967, the effort to reach out and to mend is present everywhere. No one who is a friend should or can go unmentioned;

and, as he tries in life to mend broken fences and reestablish old friendships, each one must receive its moment, some notice. When a story leads to such an old friendship, Emil is drawn to follow the road to reconciliation, and while these strands of attention to mending broken relationships and acknowledging longstanding ones trail off, no effort is made or could be made to recover the flow of the text. Emil abruptly returns or moves on or back. The point of these acknowledgments and this attention to people is not to contribute to the story in any narrative way; it is to acknowledge them and to incorporate them into the life that is being written.

Stories may have main characters and secondary ones. In mending one's life and gathering its pieces into one place, both the dead and the living share pride of place, and all are important. And, when all are to be included and no one forgotten or neglected, it is impossible or at least unlikely always to say something dramatic, fascinating, interesting to the reader. What makes and has made people important to Emil are often beyond his grasp, or they are little things or simply the depth of the relationship. Or the person is important even if no telling episode, story, or reason is available to explain why. Here characters come and go for little, occasional reasons, in ways that a constructed plot would avoid or exclude. But Emil has no such plot; his life has much to do with gathering people around him, both the living and the dead, some with an easy joy, others with great pain and inner turmoil.

Equally, people come to mind and are recalled in such a way that they become central features of Emil's making an important philosophical point. His uncle Adolf, who had lost his leg in World War One, is such a person, as is the family friend, whose neighbor was Heydrich and who, Emil believes, must have been protected by this diabolical Nazi SS officer. And there is Emil's childhood friend, who was a German and who lost his life in the war, and Emil's revered high school classics teacher, Adolph Lörcher. Each one of these figures is recalled, sometimes with a modest vignette and sometimes with less, but each is placed at the center of a philosophical reflection about Germany, the Nazis, and German Jewry.

Rose and Michael; here the story is different. Both tell us a great deal about how the philosopher's decision to write a philosophical memoir about his life as a lesson about German Jewry has become a long, halting, traumatic process of the personal mending of his life. For years Emil would say that two things he would not write about were Rose, her Christianity and her illness, and Michael and his autism. These were intimate personal matters that had no place in his memoirs, his epitaph for German Judaism. In the late 1990s, however, his decision changed. There may be and doubtless are many reasons for this change of heart, but it is extraordinarily significant. For there can be no collecting of memories and fragments that is a genuine mending that does not confront all the joys and sorrows, even the hardest and most personal, as well as the most public and well-known.

About Michael, Emil's and Rose's oldest child, he says what he wants to be said and perhaps as much as can be said. Autism is still a great mystery and when Michael was diagnosed, in the sixties, a greater one. Emil and Rose went through the denial and the coping, and there is no telling the extent of the toll it took, as they saw to him, his care, and worried about their family. Did they face all of this without strain, anguish, and perhaps guilt? Hardly. But one can imagine Emil, in those years wholly invested in the depths of Hegel's system and in the work of reason, at the very same time exposed to his own child's descent into unreason, fragmentation, and one knows not what. What was the toll?

And Michael's story is part of the larger one of Emil and Rose. To all of us who knew her, Rose was a cyclone: brilliant, mercurial, passionate, intense, and relentless. When I think of her today, I cannot get out of my mind William Blake's song: "Tyger, tyger, burning bright in the forests of the night; what immortal hand or eye dare frame thy fearful symmetry?" Dare indeed? And little did one know, in those years, what those "forests of the night" would turn out to be.

The poem is appropriate. In Toronto, Rose studied once with the great Blake and Romantic scholar Northrop Frye, whose famous book on Blake is entitled *Fearful Symmetry,* and with whom Rose argued about the Bible and how to interpret it. Rose was indeed a fiery personality—sophisticated about literature and theology, religiously and politically intense, and a sojourner on the border between Judaism and Christianity. Rose and Emil were a team, a pair; to many people, Fackenheim meant Emil-and-Rose. They were always together, and, I am sure, given their separate intensities, their experiences, what they lived through in the present and in the past, their daily life was often turbulent and volatile. Certainly the house on Briarhill in Toronto was—a place filled with activity, forever welcome to guests, but in many ways unable, like that "immortal hand or eye" to contain Rose's "fearful symmetry."

Emil's mending means facing Rose's Christianity in a public way and talking about it and then her Alzheimer's, finding words and ways to bring the two into the mending of his life. Emil is one of those whose writings and experiences make him an especially important figure in the encounter between Jews and Christians. Part of this comes from his German heritage, where philosophy and theology brought Jews and Christians together and, of course, also set them apart. But a large part, and perhaps its passionate intensity, comes from Rose, for whom Christian honesty and self-examination, antisemitism and the guilt for the Holocaust, meant so much. In Toronto, Emil fought with figures like A. C. Forest. He wrote often on Christian self-understanding and responsibility, the Holocaust, and Israel, and during the past decade his relationships with German Christians have been continuous and deep. Among his oldest friends and intellectual and religious partners—people like Franklin Littell and Roy and Alice Eckardt—were vigorous Christian theologians and outspoken critics of the church's neglect of its responsibilities. Rose was so involved in all of this that we may never be able to isolate and appreciate fully what was her contribution, what his.

Eventually, in New York in 1983 (just prior to their aliyah), Rose did indeed convert to Judaism. Walter Wurzburger, a prominent Orthodox rabbi and philosopher, an old friend from Toronto days, arranged the conversion. The event was private. For twenty-five years of marriage, she lived a more committed and involved Jewish life than most Jews and had remained a Christian. What all of this meant to Emil he tells us—in his way, his words, for his reasons. It probably registered in all kinds of negative reactions from people who never understood what was involved and never knew Emil and Rose well or even at all. Close friends, knowing Rose's sense of integrity and Emil's, accepted the situation unquestioningly. But mending requires looking at all of this too, and if the mending is a public act of writing, then that means exposing bits and pieces, with a comment to bring this part of life into the process.

The Alzheimer's, so private a struggle, also has a public dimension. This mental deterioration is painful and sad, but what made the tragedy sadder still was Rose's relative youth. When Rose was diagnosed, which took some time, Emil was over seventy-five. Rose was twenty years younger. Emil and Yossi, then very young, had to go on at first with Rose at home, her symptoms getting worse and worse, a danger to herself and an increasing hardship for them all, and then on their own when Rose was placed in a care facility. Rose, once so vibrant and intense, still young. But here too Emil came to realize that the memoirs required confronting the darkness and speaking of it publicly. Indeed, today, with so many living to advanced age and suffering from Alzheimer's or other dementia, others could appreciate, understand, and perhaps benefit from some reflections on Emil's life in these hard times. In a strange and difficult sense, living with and through the loss of memory, the enclosing of the self, is now so public and frequent an experience that there is no reason or need to keep it to oneself. But even more, in Emil's case, to mend required never denying the significant, no matter how painful and traumatic.

Epitaph, then, is a book of mending, of *tikkun.* This is, after all, the term that Emil himself appropriated from the Talmudic and Kabbalistic traditions and refashioned in his magnum opus. A comparison with Franz Rosenzweig is appropriate: just as *The Star of Redemption* and its system ends with the words and the charge, "Into life," so *To Mend the World* and its "systematic labor of thought" that attempts to confront honestly and seriously the Nazi Holocaust ends with the mandate to *teshuvah* [return] and to *tikkun olam* [to mend the world], to return and to mend, to repair. I do not want to suggest that Emil lived through a period like Rosenzweig's eight-year struggle with ALS. What I do mean to call attention to, however, is the existential and imperative outcome of the two works. Both are achievements of thought that issue in mandates to action, to life. Moreover, in Emil's case, the outcome and the mandate are about reconstituting the world and one's life after Auschwitz, and for him, as for so many others, in Germany, Israel, America, and elsewhere, that is a personal matter of great difficulty and inner conflict. Furthermore, the repair or mending, while framed by the enormity of Nazism and Auschwitz, also requires facing all the ruptures of one's own life and returning to all the memories to carry out the task. Mending is no simple summing up or taking stock or pulling together. It is slow, laborious, interrupted, and forever incomplete.

All of this is reflected in the composition and character of these pages. Some day someone will study the literary qualities of Emil's work, from his earliest essays and articles in the 1940s to these late writings. His philosophical and theological essays and books, from an essay like "Self-Realization and the Search for God" in 1948 to the essays collected in *The Jewish Return Into History* of 1978, are marked by extraordinary philosophical clarity, an elegant use of texts and images, and a powerful, controlled cadence. These works have engaging literary virtues; they are genuine works of art. As I mentioned, *To Mend the World* already begins a transition—to a style that is more fractured and atomized, condensed, and disrupted. The book is filled with careful, probing philosophical analysis and discursive argumentation and analysis. But it has these other qualities as well. In a way too, the style that emerges in these later works is a more associative and Midrashic one that is not as philosophically discursive and flowing as in earlier periods. These memoirs extend these stylistic changes and dramatically so, in part because they call so regularly on memory, which is partial and fragmentary, and in part because they *are* the working out of a process of mending that is neither seamless nor complete.

At the end of the preface to the second edition of *To Mend the World*, published in 1989, Emil comments on a saying of Hegel's in a way that tells us something about his own style in writing-as-mending his life:

Hegel once said that the wounds of Spirit heal without leaving scars. He could no longer say this today. To speak of a healing has become inappropriate. Scars of the wounds of Spirit remain and will continue to remain. But a mending is possible, and therefore necessary.

The scars must remain. They cannot, even in a mending, be eradicated, ignored, or denied. And there are scars at all levels, to be acknowledged and attended to—philosophical and literary as well as psychological and personal. Emil's epitaph for German Judaism and for the intellectual and philosophical world that nurtured him—and so many others—is for a world, historical and personal, filled with pain and despair, with hope and refusal, with joy and love. He does not overindulge the positive or neglect the negative. For, as Emil was fond of saying, quoting Hegel, "Happy pages in the book of history are blank pages."

Note on the Text

Emil began to write his memoirs in 1993. The text was sent to the University of Wisconsin Press in 2001, and the proofs which he received in 2002 were dated September 27, 2002. They were due to be returned on October 21. When Emil passed away in the early morning of Friday, September 19, 2003, the process of correcting and revising the proofs was not yet complete. During that year Emil had made numerous minor corrections to the text, replacing words or phrases and making many small additions. He had also replaced some paragraphs and made more substantial corrections. Chapter 20 was completely rewritten; the present epilogue is substituted for an older one; and he added an essay as Appendix F. In addition, he had organized various sets of documents to be reproduced in the book, in addition to the album of pictures and the occasional pictures and documents that appear in it. He had written a new preface and also collected a group of additional pictures.

It was a year before Ben Pollock and I, at the request of Emil's family and his legal executor, Zvi Ehrenberg, spent a week in his apartment, during which time we organized his library, to be donated to various institutions, and his papers, to be sent to the Canadian National Archives in Ottawa. At that time, we set aside all the papers that seemed relevant to the preparation of *Epitaph;* this included a number of versions, stacks of printed versions of materials, packets of documents and pictures. The material was not organized in any way. I also received a copy of all the files that were on Emil's computer, dating back about four years from his death; the material on the hard disc was also, by and large, not organized.

When I turned to the proofs, I found several copies, but one, which was completed before March 26, 2003 (which I determined from evidence elsewhere), had numerous corrections, and each page was initialed by Emil. There is evidence that Emil had not ceased making corrections and working on the proofs until mid-July before he died, and I used later notes when I could verify their accuracy. I began to prepare a corrected set of proofs, basing myself on this last initialed copy. I also organized all the copies, drafts, etc. that I had from Emil's apartment, and copied from the computer disc everything in his files relevant to the memoirs and dating from August 2002 to his death. I organized copies of corrections according to the date they were last revised on the computer. The proofs I submitted to Wisconsin are the result of my best judgment of what was Emil's last correction or revision. I also made some editorial modifications, generally for clarity.

The documents and pictures were more complicated still. Together with the proofs, I found a packet of captions for documents labeled "Cluster B." On the computer I found files with captions for documents, called clusters, separated into five groups: Clusters B, C, D, E, and an additional cluster. From what I could gather, all of these captions were typed versions of notes that were taken orally from Emil's descriptions of the documents and that had not been reviewed or corrected by him. Fortunately, in the materials from his apartment, there were various batches of documents or copies of documents. I was able to match up many of the captions with documents. The result was five clusters, organized roughly by periods of his life: cluster B, 33 captions and all 33 documents for them; cluster C, 14 captions and 11 documents; cluster D, 12 captions and 10 documents; cluster E, 7 captions and 2 documents; additional cluster, 9 captions and 9 documents. Not all of the captions, especially in cluster E and the additional cluster, are more than a title or identifier, but most of them are several sentences. In a few cases, a document is in fact two or three related documents.

It has not been feasible to include all of these documents, nor did it seem to me that all would be equally valuable additions to the book. I have therefore taken the liberty of selecting several documents from these clusters, and we have printed them at the end of the book, roughly in chronological order. I have edited the captions for clarity.

On the computer there was also a set of very brief captions for an additional album of photos, but the photographs in Emil's apartment were scattered in many places and in no order, many with no way of identifying them exactly. It has not been possible to include any of these additional photographs.

‡

The book could not have been completed without Ben Pollock's help during a memorable week in Jerusalem in June 2004. I thank Zvi Ehrenberg for his devotion and commitment to seeing the book through to publication and David, Suze, and Yossi and their families for their friendship and confidence in me to carry out the work in these final stages. Gwen Walker and Adam Mehring at the University of Wisconsin Press were vital to the project's completion. Special thanks to Lawrence Tapper of the National Archives of Canada, Ottawa, Ontario, for providing copies of the many documents included in the volume. Emil has always had a special place in the hearts of my own family—Aud, Deb, and Sara. Like myself, they are very pleased that these memoirs are finally appearing.

MICHAEL L. MORGAN

May 22, 2007

Preface

This epitaph is not an autobiography, nor is it a biography of my father, my mother, or my brother Alex, who was left behind in Nazi Germany; it is not even an epitaph of German Jewry as a whole. Rather, it is the story of German Judaism and how it ended, with men such as Leo Baeck, Martin Buber, and Franz Rosenzweig, the last named perhaps the greatest Jewish thinker in modern Judaism—a tragic end, perhaps incomparably so in history, surely so in the history of thought.

If this epitaph also includes my own story, it is largely because I have tried to follow these thinkers, and since it includes my own, it includes also the stories of friends, teachers, and, of course, my family.

Speaking of family, I never asked my father if in the Great War he had any "Aryan" *Kameraden,* nor did I check my mother's Schopenhauer volumes (which I have inherited) for sentences or chapters she may have marked. Schopenhauer hated women as well as Jews, the latter because their optimism was too "superficial." Frankly, these omissions occur to me only now; and, of course, I have written much too little about my older brother.

An autobiography about me in particular would have interested few, my friends and grandchildren, and an account of German Jews in general may have interested many. But I am no historian or sociologist; rather, after a lifetime as both a general and a Jewish philosopher, I wished to make a reckoning with my life within the context to which it belongs.

I could have written this epitaph soon after 1939, after most of my immediate family fled Nazi Germany, first my younger

xxvii

brother Wolfgang, last my parents—*really* last, just four days before the war—I between them, on May 12, but then it would have
contained only one part, about Germany, not also parts about
Canada and Israel. Also, while I would have remembered the
past more vividly then, I would have done so less sensitively: the
young think of the lives of their elders as dull, of not much happening in them; but when I began to write in my seventies and
concluded in my early eighties, I was sensitive to the troubles my
parents must have had: the Great War, of course, and then Hitler
so shortly after, with Weimar hardly counting. Should I have
waited even longer to write? But I could not.

About one person in my family I had no time to think at
greater length, for only four or five years ago did I learn how
Uncle Adolf Goldberg, left behind in Germany, had died. An upright German, Volkhart Winkelmann of my *Heimatstadt* (hometown), found out for me. My uncle had been my father's partner,
both of them lawyers; I knew him well, for we were together regularly on Sunday for coffee and cake at our home and on Friday
night for dinner at my grandmother's. Uncle Adolf had volunteered in the Great War and lost a leg in it: he was *schwer verwun-
det*, "heavily, permanently wounded." I was especially impressed
with how he confronted the two SA men who boycotted their
law office on April 1, 1933. "Tell your superiors you are boycotting a man who lost his leg for Germany while you were shitting
in your diapers." Not till Winkelmann found out for me did I
learn when, where, and how the SS had murdered him. Bernburg
had long been a *Heil- und Pflegeanstalt* (sanatorium and asylum).
In 1940 it was that still, but the Nazis converted part of it into an
institution for mass murder. They gassed my uncle, but in what
category? "Insanes and Cripples," subcategorized as "political."
In what respect was my uncle political? That he had dared to volunteer in the Great War for Germany, happened to lose a leg?
This was too absurd, even for the Nazi Weltanschauung, so they
lied in the death document: he died of a heart attack.

If I live to 120—as everybody wished for me on my eighty-fifth
birthday—I will continue to spell out what few theologians and
philosophers want to hear: that the Nazi Weltanschauung was
not just a radically evil "ideology," which, like all ideologies, is
only historical, but an *antitheology*, an *antimetaphysics*, with a

führer fancied as philosopher, both by himself and countless others. Unless we recognize the Holocaust not only as radically evil but also as philosophically, theologically unredeemable, neither philosophy nor theology has a chance. By just walking with his wooden leg and cane across the Halle *Marktplatz* (marketplace), Uncle Adolf could have smashed the whole Weltanschauung: this is why they had to murder him the way they did and, afterward, to lie about it, even to themselves.

In the years between 1933 and the outbreak of the war, no country would accept a one-legged immigrant whose profession as lawyer, moreover, was useless outside his native country. Uncle Adolf was no Zionist, but had there been an Israel, with its monumental Law of Return, it would have welcomed him.

I have asked that my book be published without change, but I have made one exception. Some readers of the manuscript questioned why did I not mention my Toronto Ph.D. dissertation, completed in 1945 when I was rabbi in Hamilton. Perhaps when writing the chapter about that period, I thought of the Holocaust, then raging at its worst, while some committee or other huddled together almost every night, solving trivial problems but helpless to address the big one, saving Jews. Thus I failed to describe how I spent most of my days, writing a thesis on Arabic philosophy. So I have added, in my chapter about my time as rabbi in Hamilton, a brief synopsis of my thesis on Muslim philosophers, written, even then, in the hope that Jews could share again, as once they did, philosophy with Muslims, should they return to Jerusalem.

‡

When I studied Jewish theology in Berlin, from 1935 to 1938, our philosophy professor, Max Wiener, asked the class how, when Christianity and Islam seek to convert all humanity, Judaism, which can be as universal as either, can yet keep its Truth to itself. Wiener asked us to think about it for next week's class, but I have thought about it all my life.

In a way, I already knew the answer, from a Bar Mitzvah lesson of our rabbi, Albert Kahlberg. Kahlberg had once been Wiener's fellow student: Christianity and Islam are the "daughter religions" of Judaism. But that was before 1933. The story that follows was completed in 2000. But this is 2002, after September 11, 2001, also after the Second Intifada, and I must ask, more urgently than ever: why are the "daughters" indifferent or more often so nasty to the "mother"?

Introduction

I began this epitaph in 1993 and completed it in 2000: it has taken me a long time. I needed those years to reflect on the one-thousand-year history of German Judaism or, more precisely, on its end. This end occurred more than sixty years ago, was simultaneous with the Holocaust, the end of nearly all Europe's Jewry. But it is still worth an epitaph, by itself. Sometimes I think it is still too soon.

We have begun to face the Holocaust worldwide, profoundly, only now; I say "face," "worldwide," "profoundly," because an acknowledgment—historical, psychological, "psychohistorical," not to speak of philosophical and theological, Jewish, Christian, even Muslim—will always evade us; or, if not always, for a long time. Philosophy escapes into universalism, theology into resistance, the wrong kind—that nothing has happened to faith, Jewish or Christian.

But the Holocaust may also be forgotten. It was not enough for the perpetrators to rely on the German proverb "It was so long ago, it is no longer true": even though they predicted that, with the last survivors gone, their own actions would also be gone, they wanted to make sure their deeds would be forgotten. (The stories of the victims—those who survived—were past belief: such a thing could never have happened.) But they tried to wipe out traces, were good at it, but—as fifty years of scholarship have shown—not good enough; more and more archives are still becoming accessible, only in the 1990s.

The Holocaust was planned, organized, executed by a legally elected German government, and a complete account of it is too much for these memoirs; but if my story did not include its first victims, German Jews and their Judaism, I would not be writing merely personal memoirs.

An Epitaph for German Judaism is also *From Halle to Jerusalem,* my own story. Born in Halle/Saale in 1916, I was raised, like most German Jews, a "German Citizen of the Jewish Faith." But I became a convert to Zionism and—many years after my flight from Germany—acted: in 1983 we moved to Jerusalem, my wife, Rose, two children, and I.

This would hardly have happened had I been born ten years earlier. If, say, 1906 had been the year, I might have gone to Marburg or Freiburg, wherever Martin Heidegger was, to study philosophy with him. But my matriculation was in 1935, after two years of unprecedented assaults on German Jews and insults to Judaism. Hence—unlike Hans Jonas, memorable for philosophy, German and Jewish—I went to Berlin rather than to Freiburg, to study in person with Leo Baeck and to read the books of Martin Buber, Leo Strauss, and others, all of whom were trying to cope. Baeck and Buber were still in Germany; Strauss had already left. At the time lies about Jews and Judaism were shouted from the housetops; but the ninety or one hundred of us in Berlin wanted, minimally, *Wissenschaft,* truth—"the facts."

In 1935, the thinkers I just mentioned were alive; Franz Rosenzweig had already died. His death occurred in 1929, less than four years before the *Machtergreifung,* the Nazi seizure of power. Few of us in Berlin understood much that Rosenzweig had written, even fewer his *Star of Redemption,* but nearly all of us were inspired by how he had lived and died.

He lived just a little over forty years, experienced a personal crisis between Judaism and Christianity, recovered his Judaism just before the Great War; he began in its trenches, then completed and published in 1921 possibly the greatest work in modern Jewish philosophy. Afterward he initiated a postwar Jewish renaissance. As if these accomplishments were not enough in forty years, for the last ten years of his life he was paralyzed, badly enough to give up on everything, but he continued to think courageously and stoutly to his Jewish death.

Minimally, we wanted *Wissenschaft;* but what most of us wanted, maximally, was a Jewish faith that could be believed, was credible, could endure.

In Rome stands the Arch of Titus, recalling an emperor's victory over the Jewish state, the Roman destruction of Jerusalem. The arch is not the original, merely a replica; but its inscription is still the old one, saved and brought up to date. The Christian Middle Ages wanted to preserve the ancient pagan victory over the Jews, above all over their state.

Jews would not walk past the arch and were prepared to pay a fee for passing elsewhere. After the 1967 Six-Day War, someone scribbled three words underneath the arch: *"Am Yisrael Chai"* — "the Jewish people lives": this time, the Jewish state had not perished, as had widely been predicted or feared.

The unknown Jew who wrote these words surely was not familiar with Hegel's "Owl of Minerva," about historians rising to flight when the day of action is done. But he wrote as if he knew Hegel's comments on Romans and Jews. As a well-established Berlin professor, Hegel said of Romans that they had died bravely, but this they shared with criminals condemned to death; of Jews—Job in extremis—that they were "stubborn in faith," even through medieval times, and this had been "admirable."

If historians cannot go beyond rising to flight when the day of action is done, neither can philosophers. (The "Owl," after all, is "Minerva's.") Hegel comprehended the Roman Empire's conquest of the Jewish state, its destruction of Jerusalem, but as a person and, even more, as a philosopher, he would have been confounded by the Holocaust: Jews, first, singled out by the Star of David, then branded and murdered; this was done in the twentieth century.

Hegel's *Weltgeschichte* needed Jews, stubborn in faith or not, alive.

But he would have known how to respond to the rest of the century. From the point closest to despair in four thousand years, the Star of David was "raised" to the national symbol of a new Jewish state, and Jerusalem was rebuilding: Hegel would have recognized a page in *Weltgeschichte,* "world history."

But his "Owl" would also have limited him: he would not have known the future—of rebuilt Jerusalem, of the Jewish state, of *Weltgeschichte.*

These memoirs are written by a Jewish philosopher who has spent much time and thought on Hegel; they also contain thoughts on other philosophers, including Heidegger, who was also not Jewish. But much of this commentary on philosophers, in chapter 13, in the epilogue, to a lesser extent in chapter 20, and in some notes, is for cognoscenti and can be skipped by other readers.

Of these others, some must feel apprehension—as I did in the years of writing—for they know that Hitler is gone but are not sure if his shadow too is gone.

But they wait with hope, as do I, for a time when the visitation is past.[1]

Part 1

Germany

1

Childhood and Youth in Halle

1916–1933

The date was May, 24, 1924, the occasion: the twentieth anniversary of the "HTV 04." The Hallische Turnverein was a Jewish sports club my father had founded, or cofounded, in 1904, and of which, together with his friend Curt Lewin, he was the guiding spirit still. Nearly a decade later, in 1933, the HTV 04 was to become critically important. My father remained at the helm to the end. That end, for him and my mother, was flight to England on August 27, 1939, four days before the outbreak of the war. For Jews left behind, trapped, the end was catastrophe. My parents got out on the last plane.

The 1924 anniversary was celebrated with a *Schauturnen*, an exhibition of athletic skills and prowess by the young for the benefit of the old, such as parents—those less athletic than my father, who was a participant—uncles, aunts, others. Since the weather was clement that Sunday morning, the *Schauturnen* was held out of doors, in the courtyard of the school rented for the purpose. I still have the photograph that was taken on that occasion. My father, the perpetual *Vorturner*, is in the middle; behind him in the middle is Curt Lewin, his friend and the perpetual president, the only one in a suit. The picture shows the athletes in a *Riege*, a row, arranged, as was the German custom, according to height. My twelve-year-old brother Ernst Alexander is in the front row, close to the middle. My brother Wolfgang and I are at the end. At age eight I was the second youngest. He was the youngest at six.

The *Schauturnen* was well underway when two Nazis stopped at the gate, and one made an anti-Semitic crack. My father walked over and gave him an *Ohrfeige,* slapped him. The other Nazi ran off but reappeared shortly with about fifty others, all armed with clubs. In the turmoil that ensued everybody there for the *Schauturnen* fled helter-skelter into the school building, children, parents, others, everybody, that is, except Wolfgang and me. We had been told to stand at attention and nobody had said "at ease." I still remember the Nazi standing in front of us, not knowing what to do with his club and us kids. Our mother, having looked frantically inside the building and not found us, came running out and pulled us—struggling, for there still was no "at ease"—to safety. The police were called, and they duly arrived. Also, no less duly, they confiscated the Nazi clubs. That, however, was all. Nobody was arrested. No names were taken, with a view to charges in court of assault and battery. Thus I had an early experience of the Weimar Republic presenting, as philosopher Leo Strauss was to put it, the "sorry spectacle of justice without a sword or of justice unable to use the sword."[1]

This inability of the Weimar government to enforce justice was especially noticeable in its treatment of the Right, which included not only generals and Junkers (whose loyalty to the republic was dubious, to put it mildly) but also the street-brawling Nazi thugs, who made no secret of their intention to destroy the Weimar Republic and all it stood for. One year prior to our HTV 04 episode, Hitler, charged with sedition after his 1923 putsch, had been allowed to turn his trial into a circus. Jailed for an absurdly short time, he had been permitted streams of admiring visitors and also a secretary, the future Deputy Führer Rudolf Hess, to whom he dictated, in all the leisure and comfort prison could provide. A few years later, but still in the Weimar period, our school class used a history text in which the 1923 Hitler putsch was described. A very short time later, the führer would destroy Weimar itself. Yet our Weimar text described him as a *Heissporn,* a "hothead"—not a traitor or a criminal but simply a chap a bit hasty to try a Good Thing.

There were other examples of such haste in my school. Once a principal declared that at least one good thing had come from the Versailles Treaty: the Weimar Republic was more united than the

Kaiser-Reich had been; soon it would be more so—*ein Volk, ein Reich, ein Führer.*

At age six and eight, respectively, Wolfgang and I considered the *Schauturnen* incident a lark, for it ended with the rare treat of a taxi ride home. But now, more than seventy years later, I ask: Why did our father not take his young family out of Germany, then and there? Still young himself and a man of energy and ambition, he was at the beginning of a promising career, until it was interrupted abruptly in 1933. He would have done well, starting anew anywhere.

Why do I feel compelled—almost overnight—to dig into my long-buried German past? Why does that past feel like a close-up in the movies, with seemingly long-forgotten incidents, even names, flooding back into memory, some in vivid detail? If I go on with these memoirs, I shall have to ask this question more than once or—at least with as much depth and truthfulness as I can muster—toward the end. One answer is old age, apparently catching up with me; but this is not all.

In February 1993, just a few months before beginning to write, I returned, for four days, to Halle/Saale in the former East Germany, the city in which my ancestors are buried, where I was born and raised, the place that once was home. I was still under the impact of that return when I started writing. It was my first return to Germany in fifty-four years.

Just one month later, in March 1993, I had to place my wife, Rose, a victim of Alzheimer's, in a nursing home: after years of caring for her at home, Yossi and I could no longer manage. (Yossi, our youngest, then fourteen years old, was the only member of my family still with me.) I also was and will remain under the impact of that event, a rupture after thirty-five years of marriage.

Thus it should not surprise me that I am in need of a reckoning with my life, looking to the future but also, and especially, to the past and, more especially still, to the distant past. But am I writing for publication? I have published for over half a century, but mostly on philosophy and theology and—except for a few short pieces more recently—not about my personal life. That, I have always felt, is private, of interest only to family and friends. Has anything changed?

A change has been developing for some years, but the crucial event seems to have been that four-day visit to Halle. My private

life in and of itself still rarely seems of interest. But what if it is
intertwined with something larger?

The "something larger" is the last German Jewish generation
or, to be more specific and personal, my parents, my maternal
grandmother, one uncle, and one aunt, as well as my two brothers
and myself. Our generation was last in the unique history of German Jewry and its Judaism; but just as unique was its end. The
generation prior to ours was still part of German Jewish history;
and for the generation after mine, my own children included, it is
only a pale, secondhand memory. My generation, in contrast, still
had enough of a share in the German Jewish experience to call it
their own: but they lived to see—if live they did, rather than
being murdered—its utter annihilation in a storm of fire, rage,
and groundless, meaningless, incomprehensible hatred.

German Jews who have had this experience cannot get over it.
If they survived and forgot, they lived remarkably normal lives;
but this, I now think, has been because of a protective numbness:
there has been no real forgetting. I also detect that numbness in
myself. Hence writing these memoirs is an act of shaking it off
and remembering, a self-liberation, even at the cost of reopening
old wounds, but doing so is necessary—*out of simple honesty, but
also philosophically, theologically—for the sake of truth.* Thus these
memoirs may become an epitaph—very late but not too late—for
a modern German Judaism that began with Moses Mendelssohn
and ended with Franz Rosenzweig, Martin Buber, and Leo
Baeck. But also for ordinary folk among German Jews—I call
post-Holocaust Jews *amcha*—among them my own family, their
friends, and mine.

I should explain the term *amcha*. When the Nazis "combed"
(their term, as for lice) occupied Europe for the last hidden Jews,
these last Jews ran into others also in hiding, but did not know
who they were. They found the word "Jew" too dangerous;
amcha, "your people," was enough. For me, all Jews today are
amcha, for while Hitler is gone, his shadow is not.

American Jews, less so Canadian Jews, may disagree, and my
view may be personally exaggerated. But at a 1967 New York
symposium, important for me, on "Jewish Values after the Holocaust," a sober American participant, Professor Richard Popkin,
asserted that what happened in Germany *could* happen in America: no nation would let one group become too prominent. At

least a quarter of a century after the Holocaust, Hitler's "shadow" was not gone.

I should also make two points about memoirs: First, it is said that a person may be a scoundrel and still, in his memoirs, a great poet or mathematician. But in the case of memoirs written *by philosophers,* I strongly disagree. As "lovers of wisdom," their thought must be judged by their lives: Socrates would have been even greater if, before drinking the hemlock—and instead of talking with other philosophers—he had comforted his wife and children; Heidegger's silence on the Shoah is not irrelevant to his philosophy.

My second point is just as essential: Of the old it is often said, they write memoirs when they have nothing more to say. But philosophers in their eighties who have nothing more to say have no business writing memoirs. True, they relate past events and their own thoughts from earlier times; *but they must also think again.*

To return to the shaking off of numbness: it is not new to me. It began in 1967, with confronting the Shoah; until then—for the sake of Judaism—I had avoided/evaded it. (I will relate this experience in the proper place.) But having stressed ever since its uniqueness, I must now focus on one aspect that is "uniquely unique." (Thus one of the few Christians who takes this view of the Shoah as a whole is the late American Protestant theologian Roy Eckardt.) The Jews of Poland, Holland, France, Hungary were humiliated, robbed, deported, starved, tortured, murdered by enemies. All this happened to German Jews, not at the hands of enemies but of men and women with whom, so to speak, they had sat on the same bench at school.

That this fact should be overlooked, belittled, trivialized, forgotten simply cannot be allowed. Yet what is "not allowed" is happening all the time, for it is impossible to do the Holocaust justice. The world cannot, nor can well-intentioned Germans or Christians (who have "identity problems" of their own) or German Jewish survivors. These memoirs will not do justice to it either.

"On the same bench at school": these words have haunted me for some years. But, having used the expression metaphorically, not until that 1993 return to Halle did I realize how close it was to being literal. I was visiting my old school, the *Stadtgymnasium,* and the teachers were chatting, recalling how in 1918 there had been a musical celebration, conducted by Bruno Heydrich. *Heydrich? Did his son Reinhard*—next to Hitler and perhaps Himmler, the worst murderer of Jews, the one they say who, had he not been assassinated, could have taken Hitler's place—*attend my school?* (According to Hitler, none of the Nazi leaders were "artists," with two exceptions: he himself, who, though inspired by Wagner, was really an "architect," and Heydrich, who was a violinist.)

I discovered to my relief—absurd, as if *that* mattered—that Heydrich had gone to school elsewhere. Yet perhaps it was this shock that made the past come back to me, like a close-up in the movies.

What the shock disclosed was itself shocking: in addition to their other crimes, did they succeed in creating barriers between Jewish survivors and other Jews, perhaps even within families? When survivors came back, few of us wanted to listen; now we wish we *had* listened, but most survivors are gone.

Because my Aunt Trude's husband was blinded in the Great War, the Nazis had taken him, my aunt, and her stepdaughter to Theresienstadt, a "luxury camp" for "important" and war-wounded Jews; they survived and came to New York. I remember Louis Stern, unshaken in an orthodoxy, which his wife, Trude, had come to share; he never complained, was always cheerful, always helping others, cheering up everyone. He died long ago, but Aunt Trude died just a few years ago, at age ninety-six. She wrote me once, on a postcard, that she had escaped death three times. *On a postcard*!! She must have known that as a child I had loved her, but even as an adult I could not bear the details. Later I guessed what must have happened: the Nazis had wanted to deport her but backed off when her husband said he would go too if she went: thus the blind man, helpless though he was, had protected his wife. I wish I could talk to her now. Once she told me that disasters one misses must be viewed as a blessing.

I have called *all* present-day Jews *amcha*, although I know that even survivors, as well as many sensitive people, including Jews who were not yet born, feel guilty. Under the unique circumstances, this Jewish feeling of guilt may be natural, but it is, nevertheless, mistaken. And Jews should watch lest they make it a posthumous victory for Hitler. Jews were killed like vermin,

but vermin are not tortured. Primo Levi has written that Auschwitz *Sonderkommandos* "were deprived even of solace and innocence."[2] Surely *these "guilty ones" could not be robbed of it!* But
when at Auschwitz, as Levi writes, some Jews were kept alive
for the special purpose of disposing of the Jewish dead, the
Nazis wanted just this. Surely these people, if any, are innocent!
Only the perpetrators are guilty, directly; the guilt of others, if
any, is derivative. Nobody is as clear on this point as Auschwitz
survivor Primo Levi.

But let me return to the HTV 04. Traditionally Germans seem
unable to have a *Verein*, a club, without endowing it with a purpose. We in the HTV 04 used to sing about the purpose of our
Turnen, for we belonged to the Deutsche Turnerschaft, which had
a theme song—theirs but also ours—that included the phrase
höheres Ziel (higher purpose). The Deutsche Turnerschaft had
been founded in the nineteenth century and was inspired by the
Turnphilosophie of *Turnvater* Ludwig Jahn (1778–1852) in the wake
of Prussia's defeat by Napoleon. Jahn's higher purpose had been
German nationalism, and the higher purpose of that—although
we did not know it, had forgotten it, or thought it no longer
mattered—included violent hatred of the French and rabid anti-
Semitism. Our own higher purpose in the HTV 04, as shown by
my father when he slapped the Nazi, was to fight anti-Semitism
and to acquire physical strength and moral stamina. In our view,
it was a good fight, on behalf of both *Deutschtum und Judentum.*
Few of us had heard of the essays by that name, in which the
Jewish philosopher Hermann Cohen had asserted a kinship
between the "essence" of the two, on an exalted philosophical
plane. But we all held, on a more ordinary plane, that our fight
was on behalf of *Deutschtum* as well as *Judentum,* that anti-
Semitism was a blot on the "German essence" and un-German.
But in 1933 the HTV 04 was expelled from the Deutsche Turnerschaft: Ludwig Jahn had won after all.

When in 1983 our son David on his eighteenth birthday applied for Israeli citizenship, I told him: "If your grandfather were
still alive he would say 'My boy, I fought the same battle as you
but on the wrong front.'"

The wrong front included the HTV 04, but the sports club was
only a small part of it. My father had served in the Great War; my

Uncle Adolf, husband of my Aunt Erna, volunteered at age seventeen before being drafted at eighteen and lost a leg in the war; and my Uncle Willy, my mother's brother, had been killed in it. (I never knew him; he fell before I was born.) In order to refute anti-Semitic lies generated in the middle of the war and spread again in the 1920s, the Reichsbund jüdischer Frontsoldaten (Reich association of Jewish soldiers at the front; RjF), the German Jewish veteran's organization, published a book that contained the names of the twelve thousand Jews who had fallen for Germany. President Hindenburg, the wartime field marshal and hero, had endorsed the book. But Hindenburg or no Hindenburg, Josef Goebbels advertised his own number of Jews fallen in the war. I do not remember the number. It does not matter. 331 or 423? Goebbels knew that for a lie to be believed, the liar had to be brazen and his lie exact.

In 1914 the kaiser had declared a *Burgfrieden*, that is, from now on he "knew no parties, only Germans." Pacifist socialists gave up their pacifism; Jews must have believed him too, which is why one uncle of mine fell in war and another volunteered. But for Jews the *Burgfrieden* did not last: in 1916 the Prussian government ordered an inquiry into whether Jews serving in the army compared adequately to the rest of the population or whether many were *Drückeberger* (shirkers). As I noted, the RjF had published the names of the twelve thousand Jews who had fallen for Germany and got President Hindenburg to endorse it. But I was shocked to discover, in 2000, that they had been forced to act in self-defense as late as 1932, for the government *had not published the results when they were not what the government expected, perhaps hoped for.*

This belief, founded in the war itself—not merely, as widely believed, the stab-in-the-back legend *after* it—is the *real* beginning of Nazi Jew-hatred, encouraged, moreover, by the government: one need go no further to explain that, although Hitler admitted that "Jews had fought bravely," his hatred and that of his followers began in the Great War *itself*.[3] ("My Jewish pal Joe Cohen is a good soldier, but I believe the government that the Jews are *Drückeberger*.")

I wish I could ask my father now whether, during the war, he had "Aryan" *Kameraden*. But he died in 1970.

German Jews, then, were good Germans. Were they better Germans than the Germans, but worse Jews than the Jews? With one exception—a serious one, however—that widespread opinion is a calumny. The exception was lack of solidarity with, or even understanding of, the grandeur and plight of East European and, in particular, Polish Jewry. A few great thinkers, among them Hermann Cohen and Franz Rosenzweig, came to understand that Polish Judaism had preserved a Jewish vitality that German Judaism had largely lost. Ordinary folk, among them the Jews of Halle, had a more limited vision. They themselves were law abiding citizens who lived—so they thought, and did at the time—in a *Rechtsstaat*, a state based on law, whereas for Polish Jews the state had been an enemy and remained one even after their escape from Poland into Germany. In my own, admittedly limited experience, this cultural gap between German and Polish Jews was never bridged. But I wish that just once in my life—during my Scottish interlude—I had acted like a Jew who never left Poland or Czarist Russia, saw himself persecuted by every state, and had used all means for his family's survival.

How Jewish were the Jews of Halle? The historian Simon Dubnow has written of the "baptismal epidemic" among German Jews, of conversion to Christianity viewed, as Heinrich Heine put it, as the Jewish entrance ticket to German society. (Heine himself was the greatest of these converts; I view him as such, because, unlike most others, he remained torn about his apostasy.) But that "epidemic" had occurred around 1800, had long since passed, and had largely been confined to big cities and visible intellectuals, among them, in addition to Heine, Abraham Mendelssohn Bartholdy, the father of Felix, and Heinrich Marx, the father of Karl. Both had their sons baptized so as to ease life for them, and they themselves were also baptized.

But Heine's conversion was not genuine, and he remains my favorite poet. He wrote beautiful poems such as *Princess Sabbath*, which, like Marx, admits that in week-time Jews deal with business such as selling secondhand pants but says, unlike Marx, that on the Sabbath the Jew becomes a man.

Recently someone remarked in a book written in Hebrew that Heine was the first Zionist; the author may have had in mind

Heine's poem *On Edom*, considering it addressed to anti-Semites, telling of the Jewish anguish of a thousand years that flows southward into River Jordan.

Since Heine's time, the position of Jews in the German *Rechtsstaat* had been consolidated, with the state recognizing legitimate religions and, indeed, collecting taxes on their behalf. A dubious arrangement in American eyes, this practice had its virtues, one of which was that the Jews of Halle had no "identity crisis": their identity was defined for them by the state. In an old joke a German sergeant major registers recruits and records their religions. Protestant? Fine! Catholic? Fine! Jew? Fine! Agnostic? What is that? "Sir, I do not believe in a higher being." "*Quatsch*, next week you report with a decent religion!" In pre-Hitler Germany, Judaism was a decent religion.

But while there was no separation of church and state, one could create such a separation for oneself, by having oneself registered as *konfessionslos* (without religion), a step that also saved religious taxes. In large cities like Berlin there must have been a lot of *konfessionslose* Jews. In Halle only one Jewish family had legally opted out, and in the Jewish consensus, this simply was not decent. As for Jewish converts to Christianity in Halle, opportunistic or genuine, I never heard of even one in my youth. (The philosopher Edmund Husserl, a professor at Halle University before he became famous, was a convert to Protestantism; but he had left Halle fifteen years before I was born.)

As I write these lines, Franz Rosenzweig's dissent occurs to me. As a young man Rosenzweig considered conversion to Christianity, but became a *Ba'al T'shuvah* (one who returns) and thereafter arguably the greatest modern Jewish philosopher. While still in the turmoil of his religious crisis, he once wrote to his mother that there was nothing Jewish in their lives except "religion: Jewish" as the "empty notation at the registry office." For me, that registration, even if nothing religiously Jewish had been in my life, would not have been "empty": the HTV 04 presupposed Jewish solidarity and, if only as such, minimal religious content. (Even my father's *Ohrfeige* was part of this Jewish identity.) But our postwar Jewish Halle was probably better than Rosenzweig's prewar Jewish Kassel. My paternal grandparents lived in Kassel, and we visited at times. I remember meeting the rabbi once or twice. I also remember being unimpressed.

Our own rabbi, Albert Kahlberg, did have an impact on me. The Jewish education he was in charge of didn't seem much, but, rob us though it did of a free afternoon, it was a fact of life and thus accepted. With instruction for just two hours, plus occasional youth services on Shabbat afternoon, it may seem astonishing that this Jewish education stayed with me. But I can think of two reasons why it stuck. There was no hunting after "relevance" and no frills, only substance—Torah, prophets, siddur, history, Hebrew. And after a fashion, the teachers were professionals. I say "after a fashion" because only Rubenstein, the Hebrew teacher, was a professional, employed full time by the community. He was also the only Polish Jew I knew more than slightly in my youth. He was pretty bad at maintaining discipline, and we did not help by poking fun at his poor German; but nobody questioned his command of the subject, and I still remember grammar as he taught it. (Hebrew grammar is as exact a subject as Latin and Greek, and this experience cured me of the notion often leveled at after-hours Jewish schools—that they are not "real" school.)

But one cannot learn much Hebrew in one hour a week. And the fact that the Halle community imported a Jew from Poland to teach Hebrew speaks volumes.

Who were the other teachers, and in what sense were they professionals? There was the rabbi, of course, but also Kaufmann the cantor and Heymann the *shammes* (beadle), and since different classes would meet on different afternoons these four were enough. Kaufmann and Heymann were professionals, in that Judaism was not for them a part-time but a full-time job—a lifetime vocation—and it was good that teaching was part of it. (What if the caretaker of an American synagogue also had to teach?) I have fond memories of Cantor Kaufmann, a lovable person with an excellent—I would say, devout—voice, sincere and devoid of cantorial mannerisms, and a knowledgeable teacher also. As for Heymann the *shammes*, I remember him with affection. He was a huge man, or so he seemed to us children, with a formidable handlebar mustache. Once I came home announcing I would get a pretzel from Heymann next time. Actually it was a prize, a Pesach Haggadah. (The words pretzel and prize are similar in German.) Heymann was a natural teller of stories for the young. From the biblical stories, I remember how the wicked Jezebel was thrown out of the window and eaten by dogs.

Heymann also taught elementary Hebrew grammar, but he didn't do it very well, for in reciting "my song, your song" and so on, everybody invariably got stuck, and Heymann would call the delinquent a sheep. Once he forgot, so I reminded him: "Herr Heymann, this one is a sheep too."

Then there was Rabbiner Kahlberg himself. He also taught several grades; and, since he did not preach every Shabbat, had few weddings and funerals, and did not, except for holidays, have much else to do, teaching took up most of his professional time, not a bad thing for a rabbi. True, there was no adult education, for there was no demand for it, and this may have soured him on his rabbinical life in Halle. But later, when in preparation for Berlin I studied with him privately, I was amazed by his knowledge. I had only an inkling of this knowledge before, such as in bar mitzvah classes when he taught us about Spinoza on freedom and determinism. Later I learned that at seminary he had been the equal of Max Wiener, my future philosophy professor in Berlin.

Such as it was, our Jewish education had substance. More importantly, it conveyed the idea that Judaism itself was substantial rather than ephemeral and prey to fashion: it had to be respected even when it was boring. And boring Kahlberg's major sermons—for Rosh Hashanah and Yom Kippur—may often have been. But they were solemn, for they dealt with verities.

The solemnity of Judaism I experienced even more strongly in the synagogue liturgy. Ours was not orthodox but liberal Judaism, yet, except for omissions in the lengthy services and a few prayers in the vernacular, the liturgy was traditional. Nearly everyone in the congregation knew enough Hebrew to read the prayers and understand some, if not all, of them. (That few knew Hebrew really well resulted in the worst feature of the services: almost nobody listened to the Torah reading, nearly everybody talked during the reading, and the rabbi's requests for silence were never heeded. The sensible custom of supplying the *T'nach* with a translation and having copies in the pews had yet to be invented.) Still in my view it was good that the liturgy was not tampered with: keeping the text pristine gave authority to its content (which attracted my attention early) and also to the services as a whole. A good many of Halle's Jews may have attended services just three days a year, for Rosh Hashanah and

Yom Kippur. But the authority of these three days was powerful, and I still cannot imagine Halle Jews staying away from the synagogue on these days.

The one truly original liturgical creation of German liberal Judaism was in music. Rosenzweig once suggested that Bach be brought into the synagogue, but Händel, the most pro-Jewish Gentile among the great composers (born, incidentally, in Halle, although he soon moved to England), was much more suitable. To sing the *Hallel*, the classical hymn of praise ordained for festivals (Psalms 113–118), to the tune of the great hymn from *Judas Maccabaeus* was a moving experience in my childhood, and moves me still on the rare occasions I hear it.

But German Judaism also produced composers of its own, among them Solomon Sulzer and Louis Lewandowski. When my brother Wolfgang, the first in the family to leave Germany and presumably lonely, visited a London synagogue, he found the music different and concluded that the German experience had been, after all, only aesthetic, not religious. When he remarked so to me he may have wanted a response, but I said nothing. You don't explain things to your brother, let alone lecture him. We never discussed it. Unfortunately.

For me the music was ministerial to the liturgical content. The awe that belongs to the Days of Awe would fill me musically, religiously, when Kaufmann recited the *U'nethane Tokef*, the great account of the Day of Divine Judgment. A shofar is blown. A small voice is heard. The angels in heaven quake with fear, declaring that at hand is the Day of Judgment, on which even they are judged. This is the prelude. It is followed by a stern, fiercely realistic catalog of what is written on Rosh Hashanah, sealed on Yom Kippur, and decided for the year to come—who will live and who will die, who in old age and who in their prime, who by fire, by water, by the sword, by a beast, by hunger, by thirst, by earthquake, by the plague. But this catalog is followed by a redemptive affirmation: "But repentance, prayer, and good works avert the evil decree."

Much later, when reciting these words, I would think—could *not but* think—of Dr. Josef Mengele. The Auschwitz doctor was fond of choosing Jewish festivals for conducting the "selections" that separated Jews fit for work from the unfit, for deciding which Jews—for the time being—would live and which would die, thus arrogating unto himself the role of God. But as a questioning youth in Halle, I had a much easier although not entirely simple problem, and I took it to the rabbi. What if repentance, prayer, good works are performed, all in utter sincerity, yet the evil decree is not averted? Kahlberg answered by translating *"roah ha-gezerah,"* not as "the evil decree," but as "evil *of* the decree": the decree is no longer evil if it is borne with unfaltering faith. At the time Kahlberg's spiritualizing translation, grammatically possible though it is, failed to satisfy me. Now it does, provided—a big proviso—that his translation does not replace but supplements the customary one, with the two in dialectical relation. A Jew who prays, say, for a sick mother, most decidedly prays for her recovery, not merely for steadfast faith in case she does not recover. Yet, if she dies a few days later, this same Jew, standing at her graveside, will, like the Biblical Job, render praise to the Judge of Truth. For me as an adult, this view of Jewish prayer still satisfies. But it does not deal with Auschwitz and Dr. Mengele.

The Days of Awe do not exist in isolation but are the climax of the Jewish liturgical year. With the approach of Rosh Hashanah an air of expectancy would come over our home. As the day arrives, the "gates of repentance open," to stay open until, ten days later at the end of Yom Kippur, they "close." In Judaism any time is good for that "turning" to God that is the essence of *t'shuvah*, and tradition urges us to repent one day before death, on—since no one knows the day of his or her death—every day. Yet as the Yom Kippur liturgy becomes ever more urgent, ever more compelling the nearer it comes to the "closing" of the "gates," the realization becomes ever more inescapable that the time for *t'shuvah* is not next week, or in twenty years, or at any time and therefore at no time, but here and now, that is—after ten days of increasing intensity—before the gates are closed.

In later years I became involved with existentialism. Perhaps more than anything else, the Yom Kippur experience was the *existenziell* matrix of my later *existenzial* thought. The cognoscenti will recognize the Heidegger allusion, *existenzial* referring to the thought and *existenziell* to the experience.[4]

Be that as it may, the "here and now" of existentialism does seem close to the Yom Kippur experience.

If the "existential" Days of Awe ranked first with me in our home, the Passover Seder was a close second. Its memory— better, its reenactment—of the Egyptian Exodus in prayer, story, song, and a festive meal, all must take place at a precise time, just as, according to tradition, the Exodus itself did: not too early (before Pharaoh let the people go) nor too late (when he changed his mind and summoned the charioteers). During the Seder night, Jews go out of Egypt all over again: it may well be described as *the* "existential" experience in Judaism, more so even than Sinai, for if Torah in Judaism is everything, without existence— vouchsafed by the Exodus from Egypt—it would be nothing. (One must not forget the event at the Re(e)d Sea: had the "miracle" not happened, the beginning of Jewish history would also have been its end. A song once sung in Adolf Stoecker's Christian Social Party, "praying" for the "drowning of the Jews, so the world can have rest," comes as close as I recall among German Christians to suggesting the Holocaust.)

The Seder is observed in the home by the family. My grandparents on both sides had been Orthodox, and my maternal grandmother, who lived in Halle, still was. (My grandfather, after whom I am named, had died before I was born.) If Shabbat observance in our home was lax, Shabbat dinner for the whole family at the home of my grandmother, nicknamed "Ozi," was strictly observed. (In our Jerusalem home, it still is or, perhaps more accurately, is again.) My parents, while not Orthodox, were both religious, albeit in different ways. Busy lawyer though he was, my father never failed to use tefillin, or phylacteries, and recite the lengthy morning prayers. Also, despite the annual migraine, he would not dream of breaking the Yom Kippur fast or even leave the synagogue for a bit of fresh air. And he would always conduct the lengthy Pesach Seder in full, only omitting asking God to "pour out His wrath" on nations not knowing God, for they have "eaten Jacob and laid waste his dwelling."

I have restored that prayer, not as a "regression" to outmoded "Old Testament-vengeance," but in honesty to the present age.

Even so I have problems with the Seder, for those four hundred years of slavery were much too long; and I have come to dislike theologies arguing that because those generations "got it" they must have deserved it. But as a youth, still with my own simple piety, I once wrote an essay, as a Pesach gift for my father, in which God "considered the End." Even then I was moved less by my father's piety than by its simplicity: he knew enough Hebrew to read the prayers, but not enough to understand them. What impressed me permanently was this: what treasures they contain, for one who understands.

My mother's piety was different. Cantor Kaufmann's devoutness would reach a climax, during Shabbat-eve services, when he recited the *Hashkivenu*. This prayer implores God to protect his people from enemies, pestilence, famine, grief, and, summing it all up, urges him "to shelter (his people) in the shadow of his wings." This was my mother's favorite prayer, or so I always assumed. I put it this way, because she communicated this much of her piety, but not much more. Hers was not a simple faith. Women did not attend university in her time, but she would have fit naturally in any philosophy or literature seminar. When I fled Germany in 1939, I took little with me except clothes, a pair of Shabbat candlesticks, and books, among them some of my mother's: a set of Nietzsche, several volumes by Schopenhauer, Spengler's *Decline of the West,* and Franz Rosenzweig's *Star of Redemption*. My mother wrestled with Judaism, with Germany, with modernity, with all these things in the light of the Great War. My father had a copy of Kant's first *Critique* (which I have inherited), but there was never any doubt she was the thinker in the family.

As I try to reconstruct what she may have thought, I am glad I did not write these memoirs earlier in life. The young know they have hopes and despairs, joys and sorrows, but think that their elders' lives are uneventful and dull. My mother's books tell a different story, for their dates and donors are carefully inscribed. The earliest is Schopenhauer's *Aphorisms on Wisdom for Living,* dated November 29, 1917. Next is Schopenhauer's *On the Vanity of Existence,* dated December 1, 1917. Thereafter is Schopenhauer's magnum opus, *The World as Will and Representation,* dated December 16, 1917. That permanently depressed and depressing philosopher must have struck a chord with her, and she herself must have been depressed; no wonder. Her father had died young, her sole sibling, Willy, was killed in the war, and, with my father presumably at the front, she must have bought the Schopenhauer—which was unsigned by a donor—herself. During that time, she was, except for the inevitable maid, alone with Alexander, aged five, and me, aged one and a half, and pregnant with Wolfgang. The Nietzsche set, dated September 30, 1920 (her birthday), was a present from my father, and the Rosenzweig volume was probably acquired on a visit to Kassel. But the Spengler work tells the most revealing story. Volume one, bought for Easter 1920, looks read and reread so much she had to have it rebound. Volume two, acquired in June 1922, in contrast, looks hardly read at all. In 1920 there was still political unrest. But by 1923 Stresemann was almost in power, peace seemed assured: perhaps the West was not "in decline" after all. Not to mention that my father was back at his profession—which he had always loved—and, with Alexander ten years old, myself six, and Wolfgang four, we were a happy family.

Alex, though only four years older then I and six years older than Wolfgang, continued telling us stories. Wolfgang and I had sibling rivalry, but it was not serious: once I pushed him into the fireplace, and he was rewarded by permission to go to the movies; but he would go, only if I came along.

I should mention the wider family. My mother's brother had fallen in the war, and, as I have said, she had no other sibling. But in addition to Aunt Erna, my father had three other siblings, Willy, Harry, and Trude. Willy lived in Hannover, Harry in Mönchengladbach, and they only visited for bar mitzvahs. We saw Trude more often, for she was in Kassel looking after my grandmother. (My father once told me that Trude had the hard job and he the soft one. He merely paid to help his mother, but she took care of her. When he told me that, he did not yet know the hardest: she would be stuck in Nazi Germany.)

So in practice "family" meant just the eight of us in Halle, my parents, Aunt Erna and Uncle Adolf, my father's legal associate, Grandma Ozi, and the three of us.

Why didn't my mother discuss philosophy with me? Perhaps when I began to study philosophy, her days with it were over. But now a grimmer possibility occurs to me: when Jewish existence reached darkness again—something undreamt of in Schopenhauer's purely general, widely advertised, and, for both reasons, cheap "vanity"—she may have thought philosophy was useless, but didn't want me to know.

I have read Schopenhauer and Nietzsche, of course, but never "Nietzsche versus Wagner." For unlike Schopenhauer, Nietzsche

Clippings from a local Jewish weekly newspaper, with ads and announcements that include or concern the Fackenheim family in Halle. From top to bottom: March 11, 1927, an advertisement of the HTV 04 for training in Jiu-Jitsu. RA Dr. Julius Fackenheim signs as *Turnwart*, Curt Lewin as president. January 23, 1931, an advertisement of a lecture for Jewish women, "The tasks of the present for Jewish women." The lecture is sponsored by four Jewish women's organizations. My grandmother, Flora Schlesinger, was president of the lady's aid society Israelitischer Frauenverein. March 6, 1931, an announcement of the Bar Mitzvah of Wolfgang Fackenheim. May 13,1932, an announcement of an award to RA Dr. Julius Fackenheim in recognition of his merits for the Deutsche Turnerschaft. Clear proof that as late as 1932 not all Germans were Nazis.

was honest, and only through distortion, especially that of his sister, Elizabeth Förster Nietzsche, could the Nazis have heroized both him and Wagner. As for Spengler, I have never read him. But Rosenzweig I have studied.

Despite these private troubles—wartime German, postwar Jewish—how did we children have a happy childhood? We did have happy holidays too. *Simchat Torah* was bedlam, for when the children followed the Torah scrolls with their flags, the men were near them, with my father always carrying a huge bag of candy, enough to create bedlam around him. But the women really caused it, for they were on the balcony upstairs, peppering the kids with candy.

As in America, Hanukkah was a rival to Christmas. The large festive room in our house, normally used only for special occasions, had its big table full of presents, all at once, on the first day of the eight; although the miracle increased gradually with the lights becoming more numerous, our parents gave us (and we greedy hogs wanted) all the presents at once. (When Yossi was young I did the same with him, when returning from abroad: in these as in more serious matters, I have no patience.) Of course, we never had a Christmas tree, but year by year I was invited by the Wenzlau family for Christmas Eve; it was a serious night for them, for the family alone, but because of my friend Jürgen, whom I will mention shortly, I was special.

For the rest we were "under the shadow of the wings" of our elders. Grandma Ozi, a Victorian woman, was modern before her time: when her husband died, she went to work in a three-story household-goods store downtown, with a decent Gentile partner, and we never heard a complaint from her. Many years later, the partner's family remained decent: After the two totalitarian regimes were gone, courts were established for us Schlesingers to petition against the "Aryanizing" Nazi theft and for the Leonhardts (their heirs) to appeal against the "socializing" version of East Germany. The Leonhardt heiress told her lawyer to find a Schlesinger heir, if one was still alive; after both thefts, she wanted it to be a fifty-fifty share as before.

In 1993 the lawyer found me by accident, for I had come to Halle University for a lecture. He had good and bad news: the good news, that the court had decided for us Leonhards and Schlesingers (gladly, I assume, for a friendship between Germans and German Jews that outlasted the Nazi years was not all that common), the bad news, that they had given my share to the Claims Conference (which uses properties of murdered Jews for Jewish communal purposes). I had entrusted myself to the combined efforts of a Tel Aviv charlatan and a Berlin lawyer who was, at best, incompetent. From my father's experience—he had been a lawyer—I should have known that post-Nazi "restitution," for the aged and those reluctant to deal with German *Schererei* (nuisance, bother), attracts incompetent lawyers. It took my own lawyer, Zvi Ehrenberg, supported by Berlin's Sebastian Schütz (whose father had been Germany's first ambassador to Israel) to straighten things out. Although we had to pay the *Schererei* lawyers, I am glad we are now finished with them.

But to stress the positive, the Leonhard granddaughter, herself an old lady, came to Berlin especially to say she remembered me, as a boy, visiting my grandmother.

In her spare time Grandma Ozi was president of the Jewish sisterhood; nobody ever thought of replacing her.

Then there was one-legged Uncle Adolf, my father's legal associate. I knew him well enough, but not his feelings, for he did not speak of them. He never laughed but sometimes smiled and had a dry sense of humor. He was also calm. Later, in Nazi times, the phone rang at our home on a Sunday afternoon; when Aunt Erna picked it up, she heard a drunken Nazi, singing a Nazi song. She gave the receiver to Uncle Adolf. He heard the drunken caller out, then said, "Sie sind ein schwammiges Luder," and hung up. He was not upset and used the polite form of address, *Sie*. I loved him for both, but more for the insult I never forgot. I never heard the expression "spongelike louse" again.

He came to my very first sermon, which I gave in Halle at age nineteen, but criticized my symbolic use of Psalm 115:17: "The dead do not praise the Lord, neither any that go down to silence." The dead, he said, are dead literally.

Uncle Adolf kept his sense of humor even when the Gestapo arrested him one time. When he was released on a Wednesday, he wanted to go back and complain: "I am supposed to get a bath every Thursday."

Then there was Aunt Erna, his wife, who kept the office for her brother and husband, efficiently, cheerfully, always ready for fun with her brother. I recall her with pain. Later, during Kristallnacht, she committed suicide, and when I heard of it when I

Seit 44 Jahren besteht die Fa. Leonhardt & Schlesinger, Halle a. S.

deren Schaufenster in der Gr. Ulrichstraße sowohl die Blicke der Hausfrauen wie der Handwerker, der Landwirte wie der Sportfreunde fesseln. Wer den geräumigen Laden, der sich durch drei Stockwerke hinauf übersichtlich entfaltet, betritt, wird nicht ahnen, daß das Geschäft sich aus den allerbescheidensten Anfängen eines kleinen Eisenwarenladens entwickelt hat. Dieser lag, 1884 gegründet, in der Barfüßerstraße und wagte im nächsten Jahre die Übersiedlung in die Gr. Ulrichstraße, eine Haushaltungsabteilung versuchsweise angliedernd. Beide Zweige entwickelten sich schnell. Und dank dem unverrückbaren Geschäftsgrundsatz **nur Qualitätswaare** zu führen, ist die Entwicklung vom Kleinen zum Großen ohne Unterbrechung vor sich gegangen, und die Firma erfreut sich eines ausgezeichneten Rufes und einer festen Kundschaft. Vor allem sind die Wirtschaftsgegenstände, vom

kleinsten Quirl anfangend, bis zur neusten arbeitserleichternden Maschine dort zu finden. Öfen und Herde aller Heizungsarten folgen, und die modernen Küchen-einrichtungen gipfeln in dem Eschebachschen Muster-schrank, der in gläsernen Innenschubladen Salz, Mehl, Gewürze usw. birgt, ebenso wie Besen, Schüsseln. Töpfe, in bis aufs Letzte durchdachter Zweckmäßigkeit. Gartenmöbel und große Schirme bilden eine Abteilung für sich, ebenso die Lampen neuzeitlichen Geschmacks, die nur ein Teil der vielseitigen elektrischen Artikel aller Art sind. Reichhaltig ist auch das Porzellanlager, besonders in Waschtischgarnituren, aber auch Tafel-service bieten sich in schöner Auswahl, und ihnen reihen sich Geschenktassen, Vasen und Luxusartikel jeder Art an. Metallwaren, Rauchtische und Blumen-krippen.

Doch das alles, andeutungsweise gegeben, ist nur

die eine Hälfte des Geschäfts, die hauptsächlich die Hausfrau interessiert. — Die andere Hälfte aber interessiert den Landwirt und den Handwerker, vor allem den Schlosser. Ketten, Spaten, Hacken, sie füllen die Lagerräume der großen Keller, und wer vermöchte die Nägel, Nieten und Schrauben zu zählen, die in allen Größen und Stärken in Hunderten von Kästen aufgereiht, in langen Gestellen lagern! Und die Schlösser und Schlüssel! Etwa 50000 Schlüssel sind beispielsweise vorrätig. Denn hinter allen Gegenständen, die die der Einzelverkauf im Laden vertreibt, steht die Engros-Belieferung der Unternehmungen und kleinen Geschäfte, die ein Stamm von Vertretern übermittelt. In den großen hellen Büroräumen aber laufen die Fäden zusammen, die vom Erzeuger zum Verbraucher das Wirtschaftsnetz unseres modernen Handels spinnen.

An article in a local newspaper, written most probably in 1928, on the department store established by Emil Schlesinger, my maternal grandfather, and a gentile partner, Leonhardt. My grandfather died before 1916 and from then on my grandmother, Flora Schlesinger, took over his position. Since it is unusual to write such an article at the odd time after forty-four years of a business's existence, my guess is that it was in opposition to Nazi Jew hatred, a condition further emphasized by the fact that the Jewish and the gentile co-owners are not mentioned, but only their reputation for quality and honesty. I knew about this article only on my return to Halle, but, of course, I was in thorough admiration of my grandmother.

got out of Sachsenhausen three months later, I remember feeling: "I must think about this later. Later, for I must get out first." I am thinking about it now.

Then there was our father, Julius, who taught the three of us to have a "stiff upper lip," or its Prussian Jewish equivalent. And there was our mother, Meta, who may have kept from me philosophy, but not from any of us her love of music, languages, and travel. My father, a workaholic, wanted to go year after year to the same place, Binz on the Baltic, and relax for two weeks of the summer's obligatory four-week vacation. (In the first week, he was still working; in the last, already back at work.)[5] But my mother was always studying maps, travelogues, and languages, which is why we once got to Abbazia and Venice. I never forgot Venice and always meant to return. But I doubt I ever will. I am too much like my father. My parents went on vacation by themselves also, for example, once to Saint-Moritz, at which time we children stayed with Grandma Ozi.

Few seem still to understand how it was for German Jews before Hitler. We did not need much protection, what little we needed, we had from our elders, and they had German friends.

Why did my parents flee from Germany only when it was almost too late? But even the thinkers within Judaism, from Mendelssohn to Rosenzweig, Buber and Baeck, thought that the God of Israel had a permanent home in Germany.

2

Halle under Nazism

1933-1935

The date was January 31, 1933. Hitler had come to power the day before. I was walking to school with Jürgen Wenzlau, my best friend. (He remained that to the end, or, as I will show, almost to the end.) On the way he tried to comfort me. "This is the best thing that could have happened. The Nazis know how to rouse the rabble in the streets but not how to run the country. In six weeks they will be through." I paraphrase his words, but the bit about six weeks I remember verbatim. Jürgen remained an anti-Nazi throughout, as did the whole Wenzlau family, friends of my own.

But he was killed on the Russian front fighting the wrong war, or on the wrong side of it. German Jews made a costly mistake in their appraisal of Nazi Germany. But so, on that last day of January in 1933, did the best friend of my youth.

Jürgen was not the only one on my side that day in the *Stadtgymnasium*. But then, for my family and me, my high school was not a strange place, let alone a hostile one. My father had attended it, and some of his teachers were mine also. All three of us boys went to the *Stadtgymnasium:* our parents would not have dreamt of sending us anywhere else.

In schools such as ours, the chief subjects of instruction, approached in importance only by mathematics and German, were Latin and Greek, and these I was predisposed to respect. "The classics" had a revered tradition. It is venerable to me still, for Schelling and Hegel were part of it—the two moderns to whom, decades later, I would look to most for depth in philosophy. (In the late 1950s in Toronto, did I retrieve the influences of my youth? Or had I never turned my back on them?)

The tradition had once been alive, but when we attended the *Stadtgymnasium*, its vitality was nearly gone; the veneration, however, was not. The attitude of the school was that pupils had better swallow the classics as long as they were in attendance, Greek as well as Latin, even if they forgot them the day after they left school. My older brother Alex, poor fellow, did swallow them until he quit school at the first opportunity, at age sixteen. Wolfgang, my younger brother, not one either to be conditioned or to swallow the unpalatable, eyed the newly allowed alternative—once untouchable, a shock to old timers—and bravely, instead of Greek, chose French. If I kept the respect, it was because I was fond of Latin. Once Greek came, however, a couple of years after Latin, I lost my fondness for Rome. It was as if I had already learned from Hegel (whose name I had not yet heard) that the only thing Romans could do was die bravely, and this they shared with criminals condemned to death. Ever since, "Athens" has never ceased to challenge "Jerusalem" for me: Rome never did. Even in high school, few Romans remained heroes, except Caesar. Once in a class debate I sided with him, while most of the others preferred Brutus. I did so because Caesar wanted to end aristocratic privilege, was a friend of the people and thus also of democracy. Most of my classmates did not think much of democracy. Whether Caesar was "good for the Jews," it did not then occur to me to ask. Also, had I known that Schelling knew Hebrew as well as Latin and Greek, it would have meant little or nothing. Later it came to mean a lot. But only now, as I try to recapture something of my eight years at the *Stadtgymnasium*, do I ask: What if the classics venerated by the German humanistic tradition—by the Halle *Stadtgymnasium*—had been three instead of just two, Hebrew as well as Latin and Greek? My mind boggles.

My high school, then, was home, for me and my family. Once the principal called in the fathers of Wolfgang's class because of behavior problems. My father pleaded eloquently, as other attending fathers expected him to, to the effect that boys will be boys. The principal replied that only one class in recent memory had been equally bad, the one of which his other son was a member, meaning me.

Wolfgang and I had the same problem: we were good at school but afraid to be considered teachers' pets, all the more because, most of the time, we were the only Jew in class. So we resorted to what my Greek teacher called *allotria*, finding expression in firecrackers and *Knallerbsen*, small balls that explode with a big noise when dropped. I even invented a method of using them without getting caught. You shoot your *Knallerbse* with a slingshot high into the air; by the time it hits the ground you are somewhere else, looking innocent. No, the *Stadtgymnasium* was no alien place for the Fackenheim family. All the more startling would be my eventual return on February 8, 1993, after sixty years.

After that fateful last day in January 1933, when, as usual, Jürgen and I went to school together—the day on which life-as-usual came to an end.

The school was still home when Jürgen and I arrived. There was no jubilation or pro-Hitler demonstration. This could have been in tactful respect for me, their Jewish classmate. But there was more. In 1933 there were only three democrats in my class, Jürgen, a boy named Schreiber, and me. But there were also just three Nazis. The tone was set by old-style conservatives who wanted a kaiser, the old one, or his son or grandson as the new one. As for what they considered the vulgar Nazi rabble, these conservatives—especially the two von Krosigk brothers and, to a lesser extent, a boy named Jüttner whose father was in the *Reichswehr*—could barely conceal their contempt. And their best-available kaiser substitute, President Paul von Hindenburg, was in the habit of referring to Hitler as "that Bohemian corporal." He did so until he caved in and made Hitler chancellor. For this he was criticized by fellow World War hero Erich Ludendorff. Once a Hitler ally in the 1923 putsch, Ludendorff had not learned much, but at least he had learned something about Hitler and now wrote to Hindenburg: "I solemnly prophecy that this accursed man will cast our Reich into the abyss and bring our nation to inconceivable misery. Future generations will damn you in your grave for what you have done."[1]

Of the three Nazis in my class, a fellow named Most (a recent arrival who never belonged and departed soon after) was a hate-filled fanatic with whom I never exchanged a word. The second, Gustav Hennig (of whom more will be said later), was a friend of mine. The true-blue and indeed führer-type Nazi was Gernot

Ulrich Sporn. I once argued with him about his Weltanschauung, and he had the answer to every question except one: "What will happen when Hitler *nicht mehr ist* (is no more)?" He conceded, "We do not know." Except by way of this circumlocution, Sporn could not bring himself to refer to Hitler's death. But for his "concept of hero," Sporn might have mentioned—as, according to Albert Speer, did Hitler himself—"Napoleon and Old Shatterhand in one sentence."[2]

That the self-confident contempt of the conservatives for the Nazi rabble was misplaced might have dawned on the von Krosigks and Jüttners when, one day, the subject in history class was the Great War. The kaiser had invaded neutral Belgium but had apologized. What was the view of the class, the teacher wanted to know. We democrats argued that the kaiser had been wrong to invade Belgium. The conservatives defended the kaiser, both the military necessity of the invasion and the morality of his apology. But the Nazis won the argument. (This incident may have happened even before 1933; I do not remember.) I cannot recall whether Most was with us at the time, and Hennig would not have joined in this kind of debate. All by himself Sporn could have won, and probably did: The kaiser should have invaded Belgium and blamed it on the Belgians!

People forget, so I will remind them of how Hitler started the Second World War. He had some hapless concentration-camp prisoners dress in Polish uniforms, had them stage an "attack" on a German radio station in Gleiwitz, near the Polish border, and invaded Poland "in self defense." The concentration-camp victims were murdered, of course, lest there be survivors to tell the tale. (Although if one wins, Hitler thought, who asks questions? And if one gambles and loses, all is lost anyway. There was a nihilistic streak in Hitler.)

Why did the kaiser lose the war? Because he had lacked a coherent Weltanschauung, that's why! So Hitler charged and, with the help of a Weltanschauung of his own, coherent as it certainly was, he would win the next one. (Ribbentrop still maintained at the Nuremberg trials that if Hitler, "the greatest war lord of all time," had been in charge in 1914–1918, Germany would have won.)

Thus Hitler in theory in the 1920s, in *Mein Kampf,* and in practice on September 1, 1939, the day he invaded Poland. As for

Gernot Ulrich Sporn, he had absorbed Hitler's Weltanschauung at age sixteen or even earlier. Thus he chided the conservatives: Look at what your *noblesse* got Germany, he told them, a lost war! The Deutsch Nationalen, I heard Sporn say more than once, had *abgewirtschaftet*—were through.

I ponder all this, nearly fifty years after Hitler *nicht mehr ist,* and a wartime promise of Churchill's comes to mind, his vow not to rest until the world was rid of Hitler's shadow. But is the world rid of it yet? Once—it seems long ago—there was a courtly custom among states and nations of declaring war before waging it. The custom had a civilizing effect also, for, with two clearly distinct conditions, one of peace and one of war, treaties had a chance of being kept. Where has that custom gone? And what has happened to treaties? Perhaps—with so many wars in the past half-century, I lose track—the last declaration of war was Hitler's own on the United States. If so, this action of Hitler's is doubly ironical: It was out of character, and it helped spell his doom. One ponders this irony and thinks of Churchill once more, of the saying he was fond of citing—that the mills of God grind slowly, but grind mighty fine. But this is not always the case.

Why have I interrupted with this aside? Perhaps so as to delay a question I would rather not ask but must. On January 31, 1933, the *noblesse* of my conservative classmates was still intact. As far as my experience goes, it was still intact when I left school in 1935; but what became of it during the war, a mere four or five years later? A Jüttner is mentioned in Raul Hilberg's *Destruction of the European Jews,* as a highly placed SS officer: he could have been the father of my classmate. Two other classmates, the von Krosigks, almost certainly became Wehrmacht officers, and not a few of these were implicated in SS crimes. Lutz Schwerin von Krosigk was a war criminal at Nuremberg, but he was perhaps just a distant relative or no relative at all. Was another von Krosigk, this one listed by Hilberg, one of the two brothers? I hope not. I have no wish to find out.

Among our teachers the political constellation in 1933 was much the same. Only one teacher, Sporn's father, was known to be a Nazi, and we never had him for a teacher. Boyke, the English teacher, who had made much of his democratic convictions prior to 1933 but now made much of his Nazi ones, was despised. I could not stand him myself. After *Untersekunda*, at age sixteen, German schools have a beer-drinking party and publish a *Bierzeitung*, with poems about teachers. I wrote a nasty one about Boyke and a nice one, in the style of Voss's German translation of Homer in hexameter, about Lörcher, of whom I will say more later. (Typically, Boyke tried to discover who was the author but nobody told him.)

I remember these poems. The one about Boyke, to the effect that he can curse better than he can speak English, went as follows:

> Herr Boyke ist ein Englishman
> bei dem man Englisch lernen kann.
> auch schimpfen kann er gar nicht kläglich
> Rotzlöffel und Kotze sind ganz alltäglich.

After we had read Nathaniel Hawthorne's *Scarlet Letter* we discussed it. I protested that it was necessary to discuss love but not sex, but Boyke accused me of hypocrisy and of having it *faustdick hinter den Ohren* (to be crafty or sly). The whole class defended me: everyone said I was naive but honest. They all disliked him, with good reason.

The first verse of my poem about Lörcher is as follows:

> Nenne mir, Muse den Mann, den vielfach geprüften
> Welcher wanderte aus dem herrlichen Württemberg
> Zu sehen die Hallesche Salzstadt.
> Lehren wollt' er die Schüler die Sprache des schönen Hellas.
> Mit Undank doch lohnten die Bösen den herrlichen Dulder.

The gist of the verse, which is in hexameters and archaic German, is that Lörcher received no reward for teaching Greek very well. Speaking of beer, on Purim we usually had wieners, potato salad, and beer at Aunt Erna's place, except during the *Bierzeitung* year, when she invited me and my friends—if I remember correctly, the three musical ones—for a strawberry punch; we all got a little bit drunk. And speaking of her, once a year, probably on a holiday, I forget which, my aunt and my uncle invited us to eat goose. Goose was a special, once-a-year dinner. But Uncle Adolf always said, "Last year it was better."

Conditions did not deteriorate much while I was at school. Sometime, in 1934 or 1935, all the students had to write on "Why I am a National Socialist"—all except me, the only Jew. A fellow named Meier, who had never been known for political convictions, now wrote that he had always been a National Socialist, had always hated the Jews, and so on. The teacher, Jürgen's father, gave him a five, the worst mark. Old man Wenzlau was a good democrat, but no great hero: that he needed no courage to flunk Meier was proved by the sequel. The word about that essay got around. Somebody snatched it, took it to the podium, and read it aloud while imitating Hitler in voice and gestures; getting into the fun, the other students kept shouting *"Sieg Heil"* and giving the Hitler salute. While they carried on, the Nazis kept quiet: perhaps even Sporn was embarrassed by Meier's opportunism or, to use the appropriate German word, his *Anscheisserei*. The rest of the students were disgusted. Thus it took no courage for me to walk over to Meier and announce that I was breaking off relations. Meier said that I was different, but I told him I did not want to be.

The way the Hitler salute was introduced is interesting. At first teachers just had to raise an arm, with some being more serious and some, such as Lörcher and Wenzlau, even Henkel, the music teacher, doing it *wegwerfend*, contemptuously, thus producing laughter. Soon the *Machthaber* (rulers) had no choice but to dictate the words.

Another incident of that time stays with me, a competition in *Turnen* among the high schools of Halle. What with the HTV 04 and my father's influence, I was good at high and parallel bars, so when the committee chose two youths to represent the *Stadtgymnasium*, my classmate Rossmann, the best *Turner* in the school, was the obvious first choice, but they chose me as second. At the competition I was so flustered, on the one hand, by the honor of representing the school, on the other, by doing it as a Jew, that I messed up my exercise. People were nice about it, but I was disconsolate, my comfort being that Rossmann did not win either.

Rossmann was a decent fellow. At age eighteen I won the *Sportabzeichen*, a medal for sport and *Turnen*. I looked forward to wearing it if only to impress the girls, but couldn't because it had a swastika; Rossmann was older and had obtained it before the Nazis got around to their swastika, so I asked him to swap medals, for it wouldn't matter to him. But Rossmann said he didn't want the damned thing either.

Die Juden werden in

Deutjchland totgejchlagen

Das ist noch die mildeste Behauptung des Judentums, die es außerhalb Deutschlands im Ausland verbreitet. Diese Greuelpropaganda, in der behauptet wird, daß die Juden zu Tode gemartert und gepeinigt werden, in der von den scheußlichsten Mordtaten und Bestialitäten gesprochen wird, soll im Ausland den Eindruck erreichen, als ob wir Deutschen die Hunnen wären, als die wir während des Krieges schon einmal von der Judenpresse hingestellt worden sind.

Juden, kauft keine deutschen Waren!

Das ist die Forderung, die das Auslandsjudentum in Verbindung mit der Greuelpropaganda erhebt. Das bedeutet, das hiermit das Judentum Deutschland den Krieg erklärt hat, da die Juden wollen, daß durch diese Parole das Arbeitslosenheer noch weiter wachsen soll, denn durch den Boykott der deutschen Waren will man die Absatzmöglichkeit der deutschen Waren im Ausland vernichten.

Der Kampf des Judentums richtet sich gegen jeden Deutschen!

Ganz gleich, in welchem politischen Lager der einzelne deutsche Volksgenosse steht, ganz gleich, wie er in anderen Dingen eingestellt ist, das Judentum will durch den wirtschaftlichen Kampf gegen Deutschland jeden einzelnen deutschen Volksgenossen treffen und muß jeden einzelnen deutschen Volksgenossen treffen! Das Judentum fragt nicht, wer in Deutschland judenfeindlich eingestellt ist, oder nicht, sondern für den Vernichtungskampf ist ihm jeder deutsche schaffende Mensch gleich.

Deutsche Volksgenossen! Schließt Euch zusammen!

Die Antwort auf die jüdische Greuelpropaganda, die Antwort auf die Boykotterklärung der deutschen Waren durch das Judentum kann nur sein, daß es jeder deutsche Volksgenosse unter seiner Würde empfinden und als einen Verrat an den deutschen Schaffenden, an den deutschen Arbeitern der Stirn und der Faust betrachten würde, wenn er in Zukunft noch bei einem Juden kaufen würde.

Es ist endlich Zeit, daß wir daran gehen, den deutschen Mittelstand, die deutschen Gewerbetreibenden, vor den jüdischen Waren und auch vor jedem einzelnen jüdischen Geschäftsmann unbedingt zu schützen, ehe der deutsche Mittelstand restlos vernichtet ist. Wäre der deutsche Mittelstand restlos vernichtet, wie es das Judentum gewollt hat, so wäre der Boykotterklärung des Judentums im Ausland eine Boykotterklärung der Juden in Deutschland gefolgt. Noch an deutsche Volksgenossen Lebensmittel zu verkaufen, um sie auf diese Art und Weise zu vernichten. Aus diesem Grunde ist es unsere Pflicht, dieses Ziel des Judentums zum Scheitern zu bringen.

Darum lautet die Parole für jeden deutschen Arbeiter der Stirn und der Faust:

Deutsche, kauft nicht beim Juden!

A Nazi pamphlet, distributed in Halle by the local branch of the NSDAP, accusing the Jews on the front page of doing what the Nazis, later, would do themselves.

Die Juden wollen Deutschland vernichten. Aus diesem Grunde haben sie Deutschland den wirtschaftlichen Kampf angesagt. Sie fordern den Boykott aller deutschen Waren.

Wir Deutsche wehren uns und fordern deswegen:

Deutsche, kauft nicht beim Juden!
Deutsche, lehnt es ab,
Euer Geld zu jüdischen Rechtsanwälten und Aerzten zu tragen!

Folgende Geschäfte, Rechtsanwälte und Aerzte sind jüdisch:

Rechtsanwälte
Justizrat Aronson, Gr. Steinstr. 33/34.
Sauchwitz, Brüderstr. 10.
Dr. Bieber, Salzgrafenstr. 2.
Dr. Fackenheim u. Goldberg, Große Steinstr. 12.
Dr. Felixbrodt, Gr. Ulrichstr. 33/34.
Hesse, Leipziger Str. 8.
Dr. Marcus, Am Steintor 18.
Meyerstein, Kl. Steinstr. 3.
Dr. Albert Müller, Gr. Steinstr.
Riemann, Leipziger Str. 15.
Pinthus, Martplatz 23.
Jacobowicz, Leipziger Str. 14.

Aerzte
Dr. Bilski, Mozartstr. 18.
Dr. Eltinger, Leipziger Str. 66.
Dr. Kirchfeld, Lindenstr. 48.
Dr. Markus, Gr. Ulrichstr. 29.
Dr. Oppenheimer, Leipziger Str. 70.
Dr. Goldstücker, Magdeburg. Str. 40.
Dr. Cohn, Laudwehrstr. 3.
Dr. Jastrowitz, Händelstr. 26.
Prof. Hauptmann, Jul.-Kühn-Str. 6.
Dr. Schloß, Magdeburger Str. 49.
Dr. Weinberg, Magdeburger Str. 33.

Geschäfte
Grünfeld, Gr. Steinstr. 10.
Grünfeld, Leipziger Str. 27.
Cita, Leipziger Str. 53.
Markstahl, Gr. Ulrichstr.
Löwendahl, Gr. Ulrichstr.
Brumner u. Benjamin, Gr. Ulrichstraße.
Sobel, Gr. Ulrichstr.
Bohlwert, Gr. Ulrichstr.
Sponner, Gr. Ulrichstr.
Haus der Hüte, Gr. Ulrichstr.
Hammerschmidt, Gr. Ulrichstr.
Michel, Kleinschmieden.
Guth, Marktplatz.
Lewin, Marktplatz.
Burghardt u. Becher, Leipziger Str.
Freund u. Co., Leipziger Str.
E. Weiß, Leipziger Str.
Friedrich Oelschläger, nur Leipziger Straße 3.

Tack u. Co., Leipziger Str.
Sobel am Reileck.
Sobel am Steinweg.
Brummer am Rannischen Plug.
Moriz Rosenthal, Leipziger Str.
Siegmund Adler, Bank, Händelstr. 1.
Julius Bacher, Sporthaus, Leipziger Straße.
Jakob Blocher, Landesprodukte, Marstr. 10.
Rud. Mosse, Brüderstr.
Janowitz u. Co., Lofferbau, Universitätsring 8.
Baich, Schmeerstr. 16.
Baich, Geiststr. 18.
Kuno Lehmann, Steinweg 20.
Rautenberg, Gr. Steinstr.
Fleischhacker, Leipziger Str.
Rudolf Leichinsky, Gr. Steinstr.
Glaser, Schillerstr.
Pfifferling, Franckestr.
Schwab, Delitzscher Str.
Frank, Delitzscher Str.
Astoria, Tanzkaffee, Ferry Rosen, Gr. Ulrichstr.
Hans Koch, Inh. Levi, Gr. Steinstr.
Rosenthal, Universitätsring.
Methner, Gardinen, Leipziger Str.
Mettner, Konfektion, Leipziger Str.
Wagner, Kleiderfabr., Leipziger Str.
Feuchtwanger, Druckerei, Fischerplan.
Gebr. Manasse, Magdeburger Str.
Ettinger, Talamstr. 4.
Landau, Eierhandlg., Gr. Klausstr. 4.
H. Frid u. Co., Gr. Steinstr. 76.
Cahn, Gr. Ulrichstr.
Rosenberg, Geiststr. 21.
Bilezki, Clearinstr. 10.
H. Kernel, Rannischestr. 22.
L. Schlesinger, Alter Markt 3.
S. Weinglaß, Beesener Str. 10.
Marklse, Leipziger Str. 5.
Engleitner, Leipziger Str. 66.
Julius Cohn, Bank, Magdeburger Straße 45.
Bata, Deutsche Schuh A. G., Große Ulrichstr. 52.

Krauer, Kaufhaus, Steinweg 36.
Jakob Lichtenstein, Hutgeschäft, Sternstr. 1.
Schuhhaus Roland, Leo Lubliner, Steinweg 19.
Alfred Silberberg, Herrenbekleidung, Gr. Ulrichstr. 29.
Leopold Silberberg u. Sohn, Tuche, Magdeburger Str. 48.
Leo Lipper, Gr. Steinstr. 35.
Salomon Kanner, Reilstr. 18.
Moriz Knauer, Geiststr. 15.
Arthur Simonsohn, Steintor-Buchhandlung, Gr. Steinstr. 54/55.
R. Fuchs, G. m. b. H., Gr. Ulrichstr. 58, Abzahlungsgeschäft.
Eichmann u. Co., Gr. Ulrichstr. 51, Abzahlungsgeschäft.
Karl Klingler, Leipziger Str. 11, Abzahlungsgeschäft.
Paul Sommer, Leipziger Str. 14, Abzahlungsgeschäft.
Bilezki, Landwehrstr. 3, 1.
Adler u. Co., Francostr. 18.
B. J. Baer, Bank, Preußenring 17.
Schwab, Delitzscher Str., Viehhandlg.
Frank, Delitzscher Str., Viehhandlg.
Möbelhaus Hallensia, Merseburger Straße 1.
Weinreb, am Güterbahnhof.
Molkerei Trotha, Hansestr.
Armand Weiß, Uhren, Kleineschmieden.
Sommer, Landwehrstr. 9.
Waschbär, Sternstr. 2.
Israel, Rannischestr., gegenüber Sternstr.
Zuckermann, Rannischestr.
Siegfried Schwarz, Sporthaus, Leipziger Str. 50.
Flora Menecirein, Speisehaus, Sternstraße 14.
Geminder, Bernburger Str. 16.
Neumann, Leipziger Str.
Obersky, Leipziger Str. 103.
Deutscher Hut-Vertrieb, Leipz. Str.
Deutscher Hut Vertrieb, Gr. Ulrichstraße.

Wer weiter zu ihnen geht, und ihnen sein Geld hinträgt, bekämpft und verrät sein Volk und sich selbst!

Nationalsozialistische Deutsche Arbeiterpartei, Kreisleitung Halle-Stadt

Verantwortlich: K. Ließler, Halle. Rotationsdruck: W. Keisten, Halle.

On the back page are listed Jewish lawyers, medical doctors and business stores, among them RA Dr. Julius Fackenheim and RA Adolf Goldberg. Not listed is the store of Flora Schlesinger, who had a gentile partner in her business. I did not see this until 1998 when I was visiting Halle. All we were told by our parents in 1933 was that they are boycotting Jews. Seeing it now, I could make a strong case for the "intentional" school of historians—that with Hitler's Weltanschauung they intended the Holocaust from the start. True, they stopped for a while, largely because of the Olympic Games in 1936, but after "Munich's" betrayal of the Czechs by Britain and France, they thought they could do with Jews what they wanted.

Evidently in my high school of 1933-1935 Jewish students such as I were protected by the remnant of an old-fashioned, conservative, if slightly anti-Semitic decency, and my brother Wolfgang, who graduated a year afterward, found it still to be the case in 1936.

Once I believed a movie could wipe out anti-Semitism. *Ben Hur* was in town, everybody had seen it, and they were discussing it. The discussion soon focused on me and, unlike Lewin, the other Jew in the class at the time, I was good at sports, and even looked a bit like Ben Hur. (One student brought to school a headband like Ben Hur's in the movie and wanted me to try it on.) They were puzzled about the anti-Semitic stereotypes, for Ben Hur and I were so different, until one had a bright idea: is there a Jewish aristocracy like that among Germans? I sheepishly said I was a Levi, and they were satisfied. "Aha, that's the difference!" This must have been before 1933, for after that I would have said what I did to Meier in 1934. Also, of course, Lewin was a Levi as well.

On occasion the outside world intruded into the *Gymnasium*. Once, during recess, we shared the courtyard with a much older class from the nearby commercial school. One of their students came over and baited Schreiber, whose father had been a minister in a Prussian government in Weimar days. The Nazi, half a head taller than Schreiber, kept up his baiting until Schreiber exploded. He pounced on his tormentor like a tiger and, when a teacher intervened, got at him too. Schreiber's father became the first postwar mayor of Berlin. I could have written to him about his son but did not. I regret this now, nearly fifty years too late.

Once I was scared. We all had to sit through the frequent Nazi celebrations held in the auditorium. I must have sat through one with my hands in my pockets, for a Nazi came over, criticized my impiety, and threatened me with expulsion. "We have the might," he said, "and the right." But I soon stopped being scared. I should have been scared longer and more often.

Another time my classmates and I were in the skating rink. The rink was at the edge of town, and it was getting dark. An older Nazi came over and threatened to waylay me next time I came to the rink. I never told my parents, partly because I was ashamed to be scared, partly in order not to worry them. I stopped going skating for a while but soon went again and nothing happened. I should not have been ashamed. Also, I should have told my father, so as to scare him.

The school's protective atmosphere prevailed until my graduation. Right to the end a small musical band kept meeting at our house, for my parents were known for their hospitality. (Or perhaps it was because nobody else had a set of drums.) Jürgen, of course, was one of the band; he played the violin. Herbert Thiess, a decent sort of whose politics, if he had any, I knew nothing, played the trumpet and the French horn. While I could play the piano, I played only the drums in the band, for Gustav Hennig was the best pianist in the school.

Never in my life have I met a more unlikely Nazi than Gustav. An intellectual, absorbed in music and physics but nothing else, and miserable at sports, he was more like the Jew of caricature, although he did not look like the stereotype. (I still have a picture of the band.) Why had he become a Nazi? Richard Wagner, that's why, with a bit of help from Houston Stewart Chamberlain! It was Wagner's music as much as his ideology, and since I too went for Wagner at the time—his music, of course, not his ideology—we kept arguing about it. At matriculation, Gustav would have failed without me. Henkel, the music teacher, had used a great deal of Gustav's time, for his choir as well as for his orchestra. Now he felt obliged to push him through the matriculation, so he made me write the Greek exam for him and surreptitiously pass it on to Hennig.

I left the *Stadtgymnasium* in 1935 with a good feeling, for good reasons. With Greek the number one subject of both the school and myself, I passed the matriculation with first class honors, the only one in the class. Hence the old boys organization should have awarded their prize to me but, the year being 1935, they gave it instead to Jürgen, who had the highest B. Of course, they had no choice, and I knew it. But Hitler or no Hitler, some old boys protested against this discrimination, and a few even threatened to resign. Whether anyone did, I do not know.

My good feeling for the *Stadtgymnasium,* as for most things German, was destroyed by the Kristallnacht of November 9, 1938, and its sequels. My good feeling for Adolph Lörcher was never even threatened. Almost all my teachers were not Nazis and some were even anti-Nazi: Lörcher alone was steadfast, courageous, spelling it out. One day in the first week of July 1934 he stormed into class and verbally attacked Hitler. "What Hitler did on June 30 he may never do again!" He meant that Hitler's actions were criminal and he should be toppled; but if Lörcher had said so explicitly, he would have been silenced, in one way or another, and he knew he must stay at his post.

What had happened in the so-called night of long knives? Without warning, in cold blood, Hitler had let his Black Shirts murder a large but motley group of opponents, and, a few days later, he had the Reichstag retroactively legalize the murders, while at the same time declaring himself supreme judge of Germany: thus in a single week what was left of law or freedom in the country was destroyed. This is not the place to discuss how historians explain the "night of long knives." (Much evidence immediately vanished, but years later during the Holocaust Himmler praised the courage of his own SS at that time.) Suffice it to mention what historian George Mosse once told me: after that week, the regime could no longer be overthrown from within but could only be destroyed from without. Before then, the catastrophe might have been averted by still-existing political parties, churches, universities, especially by *Reichswehr* officers with their famous courage. But they failed to recognize imminent danger, caved in, or shamelessly sold out. Adolph Lörcher, an insignificant high school teacher, recognized what he saw and did what he could. I take that back: He may have been powerless but he was not insignificant.

Lörcher's war on Nazism was no one-time affair but was waged every single week, in religion class. In Germany religion was taught in school, and in Halle this meant Lutheranism. Jews and Catholics were exempt, and my class had one Catholic. The two of us usually stayed away, but when Lörcher taught, I attended voluntarily, for his teaching of Christianity was inseparable from war on Nazism, and he also invoked German patriotism. In years to come I had much cause to become anti-German as well as anti-Christian. But just by himself Adolph Lörcher made both impossible.

Lörcher taught religion, but his chief subject and love was Greek language, literature, and also, it came out toward the end, philosophy. His predecessor, a weary, nearly retired man named Reinecke—why, perversely, do I remember his name when I forget others I want to remember—had announced that he did not care whether we learned, for he got his salary anyway; and the result was that nobody learned. Fortunately Reinecke retired, and next year we got Lörcher. His first announcement was about cleaning the "Augian stable," and he was as good as his word. He loved Homer and Plato, but drilling had to come first. His weeks with Greek irregular verbs taught me a distinction many students never learn, between guessing and knowing. And, with the "Augian stable" cleaned, I learned to read Homer without a dictionary. (I have forgotten all my Greek; sometimes forgetting languages I once knew seems to be the story of my life.)

I have forgotten Greek, but, beside the distinction between guessing and knowing, Homer remains. To this day I regard Greek myths as the profoundest expression of paganism. And in telling my students, only half in jest, that some of my best friends are pagans—not idolaters, of course—I may have in mind contemporaries, but primarily such examples as Ulysses on his visit to Hades and Athena and Ares when they fight each other, the one on behalf of the Greeks, the other on behalf of the Trojans.

Toward the end of my last year in high school, Lörcher tried us on Plato. When we complained that it was abstruse quibbling, he took me aside and said he believed such complaints of others but not of me, and he was soon proved right. For matriculation one had to specialize, and I chose Plato's *Phaedrus*, the work that admits philosophy, the love of wisdom, to be what others say it is, namely, a madness, for this madness, unlike others, is divine.

On leaving the *Stadtgymnasium* I still listed Greek philology, along with Jewish theology, as subjects for college study. Had there been no Hitler, might I have ended up as a classics professor at the Halle/Wittenberg Martin Luther University?

Just one more unanswerable question: When deciding to study Judaism—and with it, the possibility of the rabbinate as a profession—I was bothered by Halle having only one rabbi, and Kahlberg being a long way from retirement. As late as in 1935, was Halle still the *Heimat* I did not want to leave?

With these two questions, both unanswerable, I turn from our German to our Jewish condition in 1933. We already had the HTV 04, but now also got Jewish dance lessons, and, of course, Jewish girlfriends and boyfriends. Wolfgang had a "steady," but I kept wavering between Inge and Eva. I have kept in touch with both. Inge is now a great-grandmother in the United States. Eva, widowed twice, has just died.

With my infatuation with *Tannhäuser*—Heine's and Wagner's—Inge was my Venus, and Eva was my Elisabeth. There was no sex with either, of course, but I wrote a song with poetry for Inge; Eva just listened to me hold forth. Once Inge came to Berlin for her U.S. visa, at the time I was studying there. I recently asked, on the phone, whether she would have waited for me, and her reply was: "You never asked me." I proposed to Eva only *als alle Stricke rissen*—when everything was uncertain: we were interned, didn't know where we would be sent. My proposal was by letter, she accepted me, also by letter, but she was allowed by the military to visit only when we were already in Canada. When I fell in love with Ellen two years later, I broke it off, also by letter.

I saw both again: Eva when Rose was in a nursing-home with Alzheimer's and I was in London, visiting Suzy and Mark; Inge, who was an enterprising travel agent, whenever she and her husband, Joseph, came to Jerusalem.

But these and other social responses paled compared with the need to respond ideologically. I followed my father, already the head of the local RjF, and soon head of the province-wide one: he truly hurled himself into Jewish community activities, for his profession had already come to an end in 1933. This was unusual for, with Hindenburg still alive, if feebly, Jews who either had fought in the war or had been lawyers before 1914 were left alone, and to my father both conditions applied. Yet he was ousted from the courts in 1933 because he had communist clients in the 1920s—that was all I remember, or all he knew or told us—but it was only an excuse, for his communist clients didn't make him one. Only recently did I discover the real reason for his ouster. On April 1, 1933, the Nazis staged a boycott-the-Jews-day, with SA men standing before Jewish stores and medical and law offices. (Although neither we nor the world wanted details then, the Nazi Weltanschauung was already spelled out fully, as evidenced in a 1933 pamphlet that I had not seen before and was given during a 1998 visit to Halle.) My father was to appear that day in court but refused: since the Nazis were boycotting him, he was honor bound to boycott them. So the jurors had to be sent home, and my father was ousted within weeks.

But Uncle Adolf's behavior was even more dramatic, and of this we youngsters were fully informed. With his cane he hobbled up to the two SA men, hardly more than adolescents, and told them to inform their superiors they were boycotting a man who had lost a leg for Germany while they were shitting in their diapers. But these new Weltanschauung Germans knew that *Juden* were Germany's *Unglück* (misfortune), perhaps above all Jews such as Uncle Adolf. This subject I have already mentioned in the preface. I must get back to it seriously and, after a discovery I only recently made, with a bitterness I had not suspected when I started writing these memoirs; I guess the bitterness will continue to grow after I am finished. (And indeed it has.)

If in 1933 I became a Jewish youth leader of the Bund deutsch-jüdischer Jugend (Association of German Jewish youth; BdjJ), it was under my father's influence, even though he liked to run things, and I did not.

Our youth organization was ideologically derivative of the RjF. More than once we went to the Jewish cemetery to remember our dead—of whom my Uncle Willy was one—with my father and his *Kameraden*.[3]

In this day and age, who wants to admit the German Jewish anguish of those early Nazi days? Once I would have been ashamed even to mention it, but now, in my eighties, I want it fully spelled out, both as part of my own self-liberation and, more importantly, as part of an epitaph for German Judaism. There is plenty of need for shame in this story, but none on the part of the victims.[4]

The anguish of 1933 was gone sooner than the confusion. Hitler began rearming Germany in 1935, and as late as that year, I, now a committed Jew studying Judaism in Berlin, still wondered, together with similarly committed colleagues, whether it was honorable for us to volunteer for the *Vaterland* or dishonorable to cave in to Hitler. I remember a colleague, Hans-Georg Hanff, arguing strongly for Jewish pacifism. I had forgotten Hanff, but had cause to remember him, sadly, in 1977. In that year, Rose and I went to the Soviet Union to encourage *refuseniks*, and near Riga we visited a place called Rumbula, where, we were told, Jews from Berlin had been murdered and buried. Back in 1935, however, Hanff had quoted Rosenzweig in support of his pacifism, that the Jewish Ghetto was there, but it was up to us to make it a garden.

To return to the BdjJ, I cannot recall what we read—except perhaps Heinrich Heine's poem about his "sleeplessness" when "thinking about Germany at night"—or talked about in 1933. We went on *Fahrten* (trips) but also had *Heimabende* (home evenings). I was in charge of the group, but what did we *do* on these *Abende*? Seventy years later, can it still be too painful to remember?[5]

We needed an ideology, but it did not exist.

Something sticks in my memory, perhaps because of its content, perhaps because I composed it, a song that became the Halle BdjJ song. I also wrote the words:

> Mitten durch Wald und Weiden
> Quer über Flur und Feld
> Wollen wir mutig schreiten
> Dorthin, wo's uns gefällt.
> Fern von dem ew'gen Streiten
> Und dem Gezänk der Welt . . .
>
> [Across woods and meadows
> Through grassland and field
> We will stride courageously
> Wherever we want.
> Far from the eternal strife
> And the quarrels of the world . . .]

The last two lines I have forgotten.

This song has elements of traditional juvenile ideology. At one time German *Wandervögel* rejected the adult world, its bourgeois complacency, its commercialism, its wars, its hypocrisies; and they would sit at night around campfires, celebrating their youth and its purity. But this ideology did not fit us, for a far worse world—and by no means its adult part only—was rejecting *us*; *gleichgeschaltet* (synchronized) into Hitler Jugend, the youth also rejected us. The words of my song said that we did reject a world that rejected us, while our *Fahrten* would take us where *we* wanted, away from the world and its eternal quarrels and strife.

But what demanded *our* rejection was *not* an "eternal" strife between adults and youth but a *particular* one, and not "the world" in general but *German in particular*. My song, in short, was escapist. Still, it was a protest, genuinely felt by the sixteen-year-old youth who composed it and the twelve- and thirteen-year-old children who sang it.

Within a year we changed our name, not just locally but nationwide, from BdjJ to Ring, and then we read Buber's Hasidic tales.

Not just these but some of the nearly one hundred books of the Schocken Bücherei. This is a long forgotten chapter of Jewish resistance. Someone ought to study these small volumes, once cheap, easily available, and meant for German Jewish *amcha*, study them carefully and ponder why particular texts were chosen. The first volume was Isaiah, chapters 40–53, titled *Die Tröstung Israels*. It was not yet known that there would be no *Tröstung*, no comfort.

My whole life could be summed up by three trips, two by plane and one by train: from Germany to England, in May 1939, to escape the SS; from Toronto to Tel Aviv, in October 1983, to reach Jerusalem; and, in the spring of 1935, from Halle to Berlin, for a commitment to the Jewish people and Judaism.

The trip mentioned last has remained decisive. I didn't know much during my youth in Halle, but I did know that Nazism was an unprecedented assault on Jews and an unprecedented insult to Judaism. I had to have knowledge of Jews and Judaism to know what to think of the assault and the insult and how to respond.

Nobody could then have foreseen the horrors that would follow; that a world war would have to be waged and won to avert a never-before-seen *Unwelt*—a moral desert, with no Jews left and from which saints and honest philosophers would want to flee, if they knew where.

But some of us are still here in the aftermath.

3

"Finish Studies First, Emigrate Later"
Berlin, Spring 1935–November 10, 1938

In the spring of 1935 I moved to Berlin, to study Judaism at the Hochschule für die Wissenschaft des Judentums. The *Hochschule* seemed preferable to the alternative, the Breslau liberal rabbinical seminary, for several reasons, some substantial (of which more later) others mundane. Berlin was just a short train ride from Halle, and my father had a room there, where he stayed except for weekends when he came home. The plan was that I would stay with him while looking for a room with a Jewish family. I was just eighteen years old and would be away from home for the first time; this was Nazi Berlin, and my mother— although she tried not to show it—was worried.

My father was in Berlin on a job. Barred from court since 1933, he could still engage in other legal activities. His current Berlin clients were Jewish armament factory owners whom the regime was trying to expropriate legally. My father's job was to fight the attempt, also legally. As I think of it now, it was the equivalent, in 1935, of slapping the Nazi heckler in 1924.

One night during my first week in Berlin, my father did not come home. I phoned the office and was told the Gestapo had arrested him as well as the two factory owners. I asked the company chauffeur to come with me for moral support and went to Gestapo headquarters. When I asked to see my father and was told to come back the next day, I protested: "You can't keep him overnight!" The Gestapo man gave me a funny look. "You had better leave while the leaving is good," he said, or stronger words to this effect. (It was 1935, before the 1936 Olympics when—to fool German Jews and the world—the Nazis treated Jews gently, and long before 1938 when, after Munich and because of it, they could do with Jews what they wanted.)

The three were kept for six weeks and released only after the factory owners signed their property over to the Reich. In 1933 the criminals had hijacked the law, a fact of Nazism with which my father could not cope. (I still recall his impotent fury later, in Scotland, about Roland Freisler and his despair about the German *Rechtsstaat*. Freisler was Hitler's tutor in legality—but who was the tutor, who the disciple—and also president of the Berlin *Volksgericht* [People's Court], a joke of a *Gericht*, however, *für das Volk*.) By 1935 the Nazis were violating even their own laws, with Jews in particular as victims. Nor was such victimization, strictly speaking, a violation, for Nazi law stipulated that a direct *Führerbefehl* (führer order) superseded it. In the Berlin of 1935, my father had forced the Nazi mountebanks to give up their legal theater. He must have done a good job.

My Berlin studies began with my father's Gestapo arrest in 1935; they ended with my own in 1938. The scheduled *Hochschule* course of studies was for six years, but I never thought I would have that much time: eventually I would complete it in three and a half. I was always in haste, never without urgency. In subsequent years I would sometimes have time for philosophy— hence a "home"—for philosophy in a hurry is a contradiction in terms. But I could never philosophize out of idle curiosity about subjects that are trivial to everyone except idle philosophers, for a sense of urgency has never left me. Patience has never been my virtue, but it has often been a necessity.

The teacher I met first filled me with awe. Leo Baeck was national president of the B'nai B'rith Lodge, and my father was president of the local chapter in Halle, so he knew Baeck slightly and took me to meet him a few weeks before classes. Baeck was also head of the *Reichsvertretung,* representing German Jews to the regime; hence he had weightier things on his mind than meeting a student from high school. Yet meet us he did, with the politeness for which he was famous. "I hope to see you soon in our home," he said to me. "Mrs. Baeck is looking forward to meeting you." I had come to the *Hochschule,* hoping Berlin would be a center of the Jewish world, and now I knew it would be.

I was right, not only about Baeck, but also about the *Hochschule,* for it was a Jewish center for Jewish spirit in radical question and self-questioning, always under stress, never far from the edge. (My mother had distant family in Berlin. My cousin Lisa, then still in Berlin, once asked how I could study at such a time; I replied we were sitting on a powder keg but must be calm enough to smoke cigars on it.) Lisa was a *Berliner, amcha,* of nonacademic Jewish folk; and what was true of the *Hochschule* was true of Jewish Berlin as a whole: until it was destroyed during the Kristallnacht, a Jewish renaissance flourished in Berlin. Jews would flock to synagogues on Shabbat to hear sermons as events of the week, given not only by well-established rabbis, but also by young ones, now rising to meteoric fame: Joachim Prinz, Max Nussbaum, and Manfred Swarsenski. When I met Swarsenski, decades later in America, he referred to that time as "the good old days." Had I heard right? But, on reflection, he was right. Swarsenski was then Hillel rabbi at the University of Wisconsin, but the Jewish needs of his students for a rabbi must have been slight compared to those of Jews in Nazi Berlin. For Swarsenski, his rabbinate could never again be the same.

I was right about Berlin as a center of the Jewish world, but also about Baeck as a teacher. Among the first to recognize that the Nazis would be the end of German Judaism, he had vowed to stay in Berlin as long as there was a minyan, the quorum of ten men required for a religious service; and although, as head of the *Reichsvertretung,* he had to meet the Gestapo perhaps once or twice weekly, he also taught the ten or twenty of us, also twice weekly, as if nothing more important was on his mind. This was not just our impression. It was so in fact.

Baeck taught midrash. One midrash I remember is on Song of Songs 2:7: "Oh daughters of Jerusalem, I adjure you that you not awaken or stir up Love until it pleases."

A secular love song, but for the midrash the love is between God and Israel. Baeck taught this midrash in Berlin and perhaps also in Theresienstadt. Because of an SS oversight he survived Theresienstadt; could he still teach it thereafter, in London and Cincinnati? The pious had waited long for Love to awaken. Too long.

Baeck also taught homiletics, and—other than being scared when it was time for one's *Probepredigt,* one's "trial sermon"— just one of his teachings I remember to this day: a word *never* to put into a sermon is "I," "Ego." In this he may have been extreme, but later, he kept the horror he knew to himself; he took it silently to his grave.

After the war, in 1948, I visited Baeck in London, and he told me how he and another Jew had discussed Plato and Isaiah while pulling a heavy wagon in Theresienstadt. He did not mention Nazi atrocities, and I did not dare to ask. But he did write something in Adler's book about Theresienstadt, in no more than the one-page preface. Theresienstadt was a place for Jewish dying, not for Jewish living; and it was meant to drive or manipulate Jews into crime, in order then, by Nazi "justice," to punish them.

Baeck's favorite theological expression was *das Zwiefache* (the twofold), and its main manifestation in Judaism was *Geheimnis und Gebot* (mystery and commandment). For this concept he depended on neo-Kantian Hermann Cohen and thus on Kant himself, but he did not make "moral autonomy" absolute, alone, by itself. (This widely held view of Kant is, in any case, mistaken.)[1]

For Baeck, beyond "commandment" there is "mystery," a term that—with deliberate obscurity—refers to God. But why *"das Zwiefache"*? There must be a reason, or even an overarching system. Perhaps I was already looking beyond Baeck for Hegel and, after Hegel, for Rosenzweig. Baeck was my main inspiration in Berlin, but for my main teacher I wanted a philosopher.[2]

This teacher was Max Wiener. He supervised my thesis on "The Judgments of S. D. Luzzatto on Maimonides" and taught me three lessons, one of which I learned at once: "Not to shoot with cannons at sparrows," that is, to take on a figure such as Luzzatto, a minor figure in modern conservative Jewish thought, on behalf of such figures as Maimonides and classical Judaism. (With few great exceptions, all modern Judaism is slight.) Wiener's second lesson I have learned only slowly but, I hope, thoroughly: had my thesis been written in English rather than in German, it would have been less obscure. But Wiener's third lesson, for me at least, was most important: how can Judaism, unlike Christianity and Islam, claim revealed truth without missionizing, that is, how can it keep this truth to itself? Wiener asked us to think about this issue for a week. I have done so all my life. The last time I thought about this problem was perhaps the deepest, in my essay titled "Hegel and the Jewish Problem," which I wrote for my eighty-fifth birthday.

The Jewish world knows Moses Mendelssohn, perhaps Hermann Cohen, and certainly Leo Baeck, at least his name. But Max Wiener is forgotten. Yet he wrote a book, itself forgotten, that is not only a description of German Judaism but also a critique of it.[3]

Besides Wiener (who was in Berlin) there were two philosophers elsewhere who were my "teachers." Wiener taught what Maimonides said, but I wanted to know whether it was true, and I had read Leo Strauss's *Philosophie und Gesetz* (Philosophy and law). Is it possible, Strauss asked himself and his readers, that the "unenlightened" medievals are more critical—also more self-critical—than the self-defined "enlightened" moderns? The latter reduce *torah min ha-shamayim,* Torah from heaven, to a fact of merely human experience, that is, they presuppose that it is not from heaven; the former, in contrast, confront the claim of its being from heaven and hence the possibility that reason itself is subject to it. Strauss advised his readers to reopen those "dusty books," not only for history but also in search of truth. I would follow Strauss's advice for many years, until my 1945 Toronto doctoral dissertation. Strauss was a mentor whom I would visit from time to time in America, once I got there.[4]

The other absent thinker, whom I already mentioned, was Martin Buber. If Strauss looked for the word of God in "dusty" old books—in Maimonides, but also in many old books, even in Plato, although in that case one might have to choose between "Athens" and "Jerusalem"—Buber looked for it here and now. "When was the Torah given? Whenever a Jew receives it." Martin Buber supported this Hasidic saying, at least since his *I and Thou* (1923). Even interhuman "dialogues" are not between self-contained, solitary individuals, ships that pass each other at sea; in any genuine dialogue between an "I" and a "Thou" the truth is in *"the between"*; and from dialogue with God—the "infinite Thou"—"a person does not pass, from the moment of supreme meeting, the same as he entered it."[5]

On Christians as well as Jews, *I and Thou* had a great influence. As late as the Jerusalem of 1957, Buber could still write, in an afterword: "The mutuality between God and man is *unbeweisbar*, as 'indemonstrable' as God's existence. But one who, nonetheless, dares speak of it, bears witness to Him, and is calling for bearing witness also to the other he speaks to, present or future."[6]

On German Jewry as a whole, Buber's influence was enormous, but his more technical writings influenced us Berlin students in particular. Doubtless the former was true, because Buber was still in Germany. All the more, because Gentiles—liberals, Christians, philosophers, once thought of as friends—had abandoned us, even Jaspers, to say nothing of Heidegger. Almost all by himself—although he "philosophized only when necessary"— Buber stood the test.

One instance was especially shocking, both because it involved a Protestant theologian, who was well thought of and himself the son of a distinguished Bible scholar, and because of Buber's courageous reaction. Gerhard Kittel sent Buber his *Die Judenfrage* (The Jewish question, 1933) and was tactless enough to ask Buber for a public comment. Kittel had written that if Jews, redefined by the Nazi "revolution" as "guests," behaved as "decent" ones, the time might come when they would be treated as only "relatively inferior," no longer as *"minderwertig"* (absolutely inferior): in short, Kittel was a Nazi.

Buber did reply publicly and in icy tones: his reply remains a classic in content and—Kittel had made it necessary—in diplomacy.[7] Buber had to consider how much he could get away with, and his response to Kittel was courageous.

In a way, a response Buber made in 1939, when he was safe in Palestine, was more courageous, for he revered the man with whom he had to dissent. Jewish friends had asked none other than Gandhi to respond to Kristallnacht, but his response must have made them sorry they had asked. Yet, half a century later, I, unlike others, am glad they asked him, for in response Buber wrote his most militant statement on Zionism. He dealt only briefly with Gandhi's absurdities. ("This cry for a national home affords a colorable justification for your [that is, German Jewish] expulsion": this from a man who was asking not only for India's independence, but also for equal rights for Indians in South Africa.) Buber got to the core already at the beginning: "[Zion] is the prophetic image of a promise to mankind; but it would be a vain metaphor if Mount Zion did not actually exist. This land is called 'Holy'; but this is not the holiness of an idea, it is the holiness of a piece of earth. That which is merely an idea and nothing more cannot become holy; but a piece of earth can become holy just as a mother's womb can become holy." He added that "dispersion" can be "purposeful," but that without union in a center—that "piece of earth"—it is "dismemberment."[8]

Much later, when the "piece of earth" was threatened, this passage was one reason for our aliyah. Of course, this was not the only reason. My wife, Rose, favored it immediately, but I needed reasons.[9] This chapter does not discuss either Hegel or Primo Levi, for I had not yet studied Hegel in depth and I was not yet aware of Primo Levi. Buber is included, of course, but at that point I was not yet critical of Buber himself.

But I had to part company with Buber on another point in his letter to Gandhi; sadly in this case my lingering grievance is not with Gandhi but with Buber himself. Gandhi had compared Jewish suffering in Germany with Indian suffering in South Africa and urged passive resistance on German Jews, if necessary, unto death. Buber replied: "Do you know, Mahatma, what a concentration camp is and what happens in them, its methods of slow and quick murder?" He went on: "In the five years I have lived under the present [Nazi] regime, I have seen many actions of genuine strength of soul by Jews, who would not give up their rights or surrender, and used neither force nor cunning to escape the consequences of their actions. *But these actions had no effect on the other side.*"[10] If so, how can Buber write elsewhere that "one cannot do evil with the whole soul, i.e., one can only do it through holding down forcibly the forces striving against it—they are not to be stifled."[11]

Buber must have been asked many questions, even when he was young. When he was old, I asked him about his recent assertion of an "Eclipse of God" as constituting a "most troubling question."[12] Buber replied as follows: "These last years in a great searching and questioning, seized ever anew by the shudder of the now, I have arrived no further than that I now distinguish a revelation through the hiding of the face, a speaking through the silence. The eclipse of God can be seen with one's eyes, it will be seen. He, however, who today knows nothing other to say than 'See there, it grows lighter!' he leads into error."[13] Also, the following passage should not be ignored: "Genuine faith says: I know nothing about death, but I know that God is Eternity, and also that He is my God."[14]

Even before the Six-Day War, I had to think about radical evil and intelligibility. If evil is truly radical, efforts to understand it are never enough.[15]

The wisdom of Buber's friend Franz Rosenzweig was much less accessible to us in Berlin; his *Star of Redemption* is a difficult and challenging work, and during our crisis, he was no longer there, for he had died in 1929. I remember wrestling for weeks with a single Rosenzweig passage: *Vayered* (he descended) *vayomer* (and spoke). For him the first rendering is literally true, but the second is a human interpretation. My intellectual grappling was necessary, for to interpret *Vayered vayomer* as literally true would be a retreat into premodern, "fundamentalist" orthodoxy; and to give the expression a human interpretation would have lost transcendence. But what exactly is an "incursion" of the Divine into the human world, whose *facticity alone* is *literally* true? Perhaps to address this issue one must plow through the *Star of Redemption* and understand it as Rosenzweig did, that is, as *post-Hegel mortuum*.[16]

Thus in these hectic Berlin years, our primary search was for a divine Presence, directly or indirectly, here and now, even for Jews in Berlin, the Nazi capital.

If, among the teachers at the *Hochschule*, Baeck and Wiener were helpful, with Moshe Sister I had an ongoing fight. It was friendly, for Sister was a warm person, not at all like a professor, let alone a German one, almost one of the boys. But the confrontation was serious because his chief subject—he taught Hebrew also—was *Tanach*, the Jewish Bible. For him such study meant modern *Bibelwissenschaft*, Biblical criticism, a discipline that dissects the Torah into sources—*J* for "Jahvist," *E* for "Elohist," *P* for "Priestly Code," *D* for "Deuternomist," with the critics ever prepared to subdissect these sources still further. The *Hochschule* was supposedly *"für die Wissenschaft des Judentums,"* and this purpose—*Wissenschaft*, objective, critical scholarship—had been one reason for my choosing the *Hochschule* rather than the Breslau seminary. (Did the seminary sermonize Judaism, that is, avoid problems that had to be faced?) But now I had trouble even with *Wissenschaft*, indeed, with the very concept. How could *Wissenschaft* tear the Bible to pieces, when the Bible was also, for faith, *min ha-shamayim*—"from heaven"? Given Sister's approach to *Tanach*, it was natural for conflict to develop between us.

When *Wissenschaft* flourished in nineteenth-century Germany, Jewish scholars founded the *Wissenschaft des Judentums*. Its pioneer, Leopold Zunz, was a formidable scholar. Others hardly less formidable were Moritz Steinschneider and Abraham Geiger, the latter the founder of the *Hochschule* in 1872. (As in the past because of anti-Semitism, in 1934 its name was reduced to *Lehranstalt* [educational establishment], but I will not use the Nazi-imposed name.) The *Hochschule* was supposed to train *Wissenschaft* scholars, but inevitably it trained liberal rabbis also, for how many positions were there for professors of Jewish studies at German universities? Zunz once launched an appeal to the Prussian minister of education for the establishment of just one chair of Jewish studies. His request was turned down.

The *Hochschule* itself, then, not I alone, had a problem with its very concept. Geiger, who believed in a future, liberal, *wissenschaftlich*-oriented Judaism, also supported the training of rabbis. But Steinschneider was a scholar's scholar. Once asked why he devoted such painstaking labors to deciphering Jewish manuscripts, he replied that Judaism was dead but that he was giving it a decent funeral. The "decency" of the "funeral" was removing lies about Judaism. Or else the "decency" was *Wissenschaft* for its own sake. But I wanted a Judaism that was alive.

Consequently, I had trouble even with Wiener, for I wanted to know, not what Maimonides had said, but whether it was true. My difficulties with *Wissenschaft* climaxed, however, with Sister, for whereas philosophy is only the "word of man," the Torah— so Jews have believed through the generations—is *min ha-shamayim*, "from heaven," the Word of God.

In 1935 the great figures of the *Wissenschaft des Judentums* had already left for the Hebrew University of Jerusalem—Julius Guttmann, the philosopher, Chaim Albeck, the Talmudist, and Harry Torczyner, the Biblical critic. Moshe Sister was Torczyner's replacement, and, if not the greatest representative of the *Wissenschaft des Judentums*, he surely was its most passionate, for his *Wissenschaft* was intertwined with his life. Like other Jews before him, but none after him, he had fled from the "darkness" of the "medieval" Polish ghetto to the "light" of the "modern" German academy, but at a time when, with a worse darkness of its own, the academy would shut him out. The *Hochschule* was thus his sole refuge, home, and place for self-fulfillment, but his time there was tragically brief. His level-headed wife had remained in Poland, refusing to join him in Nazi Germany, while he led a bachelor-like existence in a rented room in Berlin. The couple was at length reunited in Israel, but, with academic posts in Israel scarce at the time, Sister ended up a Tel Aviv high school principal. His *Hochschule* career was cut short suddenly, cruelly, in the fall of 1938—with momentous consequences, not only for him, but also for three of his students, of whom I was one.

The relation between Sister and myself was absurd yet typical for the time. For just as he, a Biblical critic with passion—reinforced by Marxism—was an Eastern Jew storming westward, bursting into our lives to debunk what he saw as our bourgeois pieties, we Western Jews were looking eastward, groping for a more profound, more vital, all-encompassing Jewish existence to replace our much too thin, much too merely cerebral liberal Judaism. In this eastward view we had much inspiration, in Buber's writings on Hasidism and, to a lesser extent, in Franz Rosenzweig and even in the very German and very Kantian Hermann Cohen. Doubtless romanticism played a role in our attitude toward Polish Judaism, and this would have driven a lesser and weaker man than Sister out of his mind. But Sister was not a lesser man, and he was not weak.

I was not yet skilled in "post-Hegelian" "new thinking" when I once got into a ferocious argument with Sister about a text, with him arguing for its corruptness and me defending its integrity. At last Sister hollered: "Use your reason, and you'll see the text is corrupt!" I replied: "Maybe my reason is corrupt." I still had to find better ways to defend *Torah min ha-shamayim*. This bit of obscurantism left Sister speechless.

I have talked about some of the teachers at the *Hochschule*, but who were the students? Of the hundred or so enrolled in 1935–1938, one group was the "boring" old-timers; enrolled before 1933, they wanted, in our harsh judgment, a prestigious job but not one that was difficult, such as a doctor's or a lawyer's. (Heinz Warschauer, later my friend, came and left in that period; he found it depressing.) The second group was depressing by any standard: men and a few women waiting for Nazism to go away, or just waiting. The third group was ours, "existentially" minded after 1933 and because of it. We had heard of Heidegger and some of us had read him, and we all had read Karl Jaspers's *Die geistige Situation der Zeit* (The intellectual situation of the age).

We were unsure *they* were "existential" but sure *we* were, for they were "situated" merely in the world in general, whereas we, as Jews, were situated in Nazi Germany in particular. They were *entschlossen* (decisive) without *Entschluss* (decision), whereas we were *entschlossen* to go where our Jewish existence required. We would not leave Germany as Nazi Germany wanted us to, following the maxim *rette sich wer kann*, helter-skelter "save your skin." *Sein und Zeit* treats time as "authentic," but space as "inauthentic": this flight from space—space *in general*, not post–World War I *Germany in particular*—is the core of Heidegger's later inauthenticity.

By 1938 political developments made us come closer to decisions in two ways, both of which involved Günther Friedländer, a student like us, except that he was a *Macher*, an "operator," a national "Ring leader" with connections.[17] He had managed to get group visas for Argentina: his group, a remnant of the Ring, did not wish to flee helter-skelter but intended to leave as conscious, knowledgeable Jews.

Normally, I would go home to Halle during vacation. But during the summer of 1938, I stayed in Berlin with Günther, preparing the group for a Jewish future. Hanns Harf also stayed, for he planned to go with them as their rabbi. I am still in touch with Hanns, long a retired rabbi in Buenos Aires. Once a visitor to Toronto from Buenos Aires paid him a big compliment: "Harf would let them cut off his arm rather than give up his rabbinate."

They had discussions about why they had chosen Argentina, but at the time I thought that, unlike these sophisticated Berliners, I was from Halle, too dumb to understand. The United States was "late" capitalism, hence it also would have its crisis, whereas Argentina was "early" capitalism? Of course, such thinking was, in fact, just primitive Marx, retrospective proof that we all were confused and bewildered by what had happened in Germany and when, how, and where we should leave: why should hatred of Jews be part of even "late" capitalism?

Another plan of Günther's was just as "existential" but came to nothing: we would not leave Germany without articulating in a collection of essays our Jewish Weltanschauung, that is, what

Jewishness and Judaism meant to us. Harf would write an essay on congregational life, Heinz Fischel on the Bible, Manfred Bräude on the spiritual situation, Friedländer on theology, I on Halakhah, the religious commandments for non-Orthodox Jews. Günther already had a publisher. But it was too late for this plan; perhaps my essay was the only one ever written, and it was published only thirty years later.[18]

But 1938 was threatening; hence we had an "existential" bull session. Fischel, Bräude, and I participated. Harf was a friend of Fischel's, and Karl Rautenberg a friend of mine, but these two would be rabbis, destined elsewhere. But what were our "non-rabbi" Jewish choices? We were in a situation of Jewish crisis, hence only two choices were "authentic," that is, genuine responses: we could go to Palestine, join a kibbutz, build the country, and rebuild the Jewish people. The alternative was heading West to rejuvenate Jewish thought, and this we chose. (Our decision was not as "authentic" — "existentially" earnest — as we may then have thought, for Zionism, alien at the time but looming large later, did not yet seriously count.)

But all this was still in the "study now, emigrate later" spirit of our Berlin existence: we were serious about *Entschlossenheit* but not yet about an *Entschluss*. We talked as if we could go wherever we wanted, but the British kept the number of immigrants into Palestine low, and the United States had a waiting list.

All this would end suddenly, abruptly — and, as it turned out, absurdly, but also, at least for three of us, Manfred Bräude, Fischel, and myself, luckily — a few weeks before Kristallnacht. The Nazis were rounding up Jews with Polish passports to deport them to Poland; the Poles didn't want them either so they would be in no-man's-land misery until relief was found. (This brutal action led to the assassination of Freiherr vom Rath in Paris by seventeen-year-old Herschel Grynspan. The Nazis had deported Grynspan's parents and, blind with rage, Grynspan had shot the first German he could find. Vom Rath at the German Embassy in Paris was not even a Nazi, but this did not stop Goebbels, with Hitler's secret consent, from launching Kristallnacht.)

Moshe Sister had a Polish passport, and the Nazis arrested him but wouldn't let him even take a suitcase. His landlady phoned one of us students. Fischel and I packed a suitcase and found him at a Berlin railway station.

Our shock at this sight—those forlorn Jews at the railway station, and Sister one of them—was such that, at last waking up, Bräude, Fischel, and I came together for an *Entschluss:* we must do *something* to get out of Germany. But what? Visas anywhere were hard to get, almost impossible, and one action seemed as good as another, one as useless as another. But in keeping with our earlier bull session, we went through the motions, composed a letter, had it translated and copied, and sent ten copies to U.S. universities. We asked for scholarships in the United States and visitors' visas to get there.

I mailed the last copies two or three days before Kristallnacht.

‡

But I don't want to end this chapter with storm troopers and burning synagogues, for despite the despairs of Jews in the Nazi capital, it was also, not only for us "existential" students, but also for *amcha* as a whole, a Jewish renaissance, a story of courage, faith, or the quest for both when one is near the edge.

Of our teachers, Baeck was inspiring and distant, Sister just one of the boys, and Wiener couldn't remember anybody's name.

Ismar Elbogen, the head of the *Hochschule,* was also its heart and soul. There wasn't one of the hundred-odd students he didn't know by name and personally. He knew both our fears and our hopes, and when there was no hope, the courage.

I didn't appreciate Elbogen as a teacher of history, for I wanted Jewish history from an "eagle" perspective—great ideals, deep meaning—but Elbogen taught it from a "frog" perspective: how Jews made a living when persecuted, how they survived.

Elbogen liked me from the start when I registered and showed him my *Abitur* certificate, not for my A in Greek and mathematics (which he seemed to take for granted), but for the A in gymnastics and *Rassenkunde* (study of races). (I explained to him that our teacher had sabotaged Nazism and taught anthropology.)

But now in view of what happened afterward—so soon afterward—perhaps, among my *Hochschule* teachers, I owe Ismar Elbogen the greatest debt.

4

Last Chance in Halle

Spring 1937–November 10, 1938

In 1935 I had left Halle for the Berlin *Hochschule*. In 1937 I returned, as if giving the city a last chance. This period ended on November 10, 1938, the day after Kristallnacht. Why did I return?

The *Hochschule* expected its rabbinical students to obtain a doctorate in addition to ordination, for a German rabbi who was not also *Herr Doktor* was unthinkable. Only the Orthodox were exempt, but even they at times were drawn in: Joseph Soloveitchik had a Berlin doctorate.

But today's reader should not be overawed by these German rabbinic doctorates. A good many of them were from Würzburg, and legend had it that the stationmaster would announce: "Doctoral candidates from Berlin, *bitte aussteigen* (alight if you please). Train will return to Berlin tomorrow." (Or was it Erlangen? I forget.)

In 1957–1958, when I was in New York on a Guggenheim fellowship and working on Kant, I once took a day off to look at the Columbia library's German Ph.D. dissertations on Kant. Surely German philosophy students must know their Kant! I found that many Toronto master's theses were better.

But the Berlin University doctorate was serious. Leo Baeck, writing on Spinoza, obtained it as early as 1895; Soloveitchik, writing on Hermann Cohen, as late as 1931. As far as I know, from 1933 on only a few Jewish students were admitted, and by 1935 it was hopeless. I had applied but was rejected. This distressed me, for I wanted what was left of the once great German university education.

My distress was not deep, however, for while the regime was forcing Jews into ghettoes, the *Hochschule* refused to be ghettoized: the regime was expelling Jewish professors, but the *Hochschule* tried to get the best, bringing them into its physically (but not otherwise) narrow walls.

Not a great page in the history of Jewish resistance to Nazism, but for me it was important and, in one instance, crucial. Of the professors brought to the *Hochschule*—a philosopher, several historians, a sociologist, a psychologist, an Arabist, others— two were important for me. Eugen Täubler had been a full professor at Heidelberg, rare for a Jew, let alone a forthright one, and Täubler had been forthright on Judaism and Zionism and, most recently, in resigning in protest before being dismissed. (His students pleaded for his reinstatement, needless to say, in vain.) Täubler was a breath of fresh air in the *Hochschule*, a builder of morale.

Täubler was great for our morale, but not for his own. I have never met a German Jewish scholar so deep in despair. He knew what Heidelberg once was and also what it had become. Once Fischel and I visited him at Cincinnati's Hebrew Union College, where he had found an unhappy refuge. The three of us met several of his colleagues, and he couldn't decide which was the greatest swindler. (They did not meet the standards that had once been Heidelberg's.) But the core of his despair was Heidelberg now. I tried to comfort him: "*Aber Herr Professor, es gibt immer noch Wissenschaft!*" (But Herr Professor, there's always scholarship/science). He replied that *Wissenschaft* was the greatest swindle of all. Not an incorrect judgment at the time.

If Täubler was important, Arnold Metzger was more so, and thus I had better describe a notable evening with him. He had been an assistant to Husserl but did not teach long in the *Hochschule*, for he had no patience with the unphilosophical. However, he invited those who cared about philosophy into his home.

One Saturday night he began solemnly. "In one way or another," he declared, holding a bottle, "by the time this night is over, this liqueur must also be gone." After this came the text, the preface to Hegel's *Phenomenology of the Spirit*. By the time the bottle was empty and we left, it must have been four in the morning;

and I came away thinking, I must understand that work, if ever I am to know philosophy.

Metzger himself had much to do with my feeling, for I have never had a teacher who taught so thrillingly—and was himself so thrilled—about "Philosophy and the Present Age": everything seemed to depend, that night, on how "the Absolute" was present in—or absent from—Nazi Berlin.[1]

In 1935 I had been rejected by Berlin University, but in 1937 I thought, if not Berlin, why not Halle? I applied, was accepted, and did not know—when in 1993 I first sketched this chapter—whether it was in protest against regulations or in conformity with them. If there still was a *numerus clausus* for Jews—one reason why I may not have gotten into Berlin University in 1935—I was well within it now, for, so far as I knew, I was the only Jew left in Halle University. (In 1998 I found out: to its credit, the university had defied Nazi regulations by accepting me, for "non-Aryans" were to be excluded; but to its discredit, it cancelled my acceptance on November 2, 1938, one week before Kristallnacht.) For three semesters I commuted between Halle and Berlin, a train ride of a hundred miles, spending two days a week in Halle.

In these two years much had changed. In Berlin we were in a ghetto, comprised of our rented room, the *Hochschule,* and the Jewish restaurant around the corner. Now even the train ride was a venture into the "Aryan" world. Normally, I would sit in a compartment, in the always-crowded train, trying to look inconspicuous. On one trip a Dane entered my compartment, a world traveler to judge by his luggage labels and the amount of it. His effort to find room for his luggage caused mutterings among the Germans, who seemed never to have seen a foreign world traveler and didn't want to see this one now. But well-prepared, the Dane pulled out a newspaper article by Goebbels and read it aloud, saying that foreigners were welcome in the new Germany. The face of a woman opposite me, red already, got redder: she didn't have to tolerate being lectured to by foreigners in her own country! She said so to the Dane. The silence, already frozen when the Dane came in, could now have been cut with a knife. Just then, foolishly, I was carried away by the Dane's behavior and said, loud enough for everyone to hear, that I had seen his Tel Aviv label: how had he liked it there? He lavishly praised Tel

The Martin Luther University Halle/Wittenberg defied laws when they accepted me on March 30, 1937. But not when they expelled me on November 2, 1938, one week before Kristallnacht. When in 1935 I enrolled at the *Hochschule* in Berlin I also tried to enroll at the university in Berlin but was rejected. Two years later I enrolled in Halle and spent two days there every week. I stayed overnight with my parents.

XVII. Jahrgang, Nr. 1, 7. Januar 1938*

KAMERADSCHAFT!
Ein Mahnwort von Kam. Dr. F a c k e n h e i m, Halle a. S.
Ortsgruppenvorsitzender und Landessportleiter Mitteldeutschland im Sportbund
"Schild"

Die häufigen Berichte im "Schild" über unsere Kriegsopferveranstaltungen im
ganzen Reiche sind ein Anlaß zu rechter Freude: Ein reges Leben ist es, das da
in diesen Ortsgruppen erblüht. Es ist hier wie mit dem Gedenken an unsere
gefallenen Kameraden: das Ende des Großen Krieges jährt sich bald zum 20.
Male, und statt daß die Erinnerung an sie nach so langer Zeit zu verblassen
beginnt, vertieft und verinnerlicht sie sich von Jahr zu Jahr. - So ist es mit dem
Kameradschaftsgedanken in den Kriegsopfergruppen des Bundes: Gemeinsames,
unvergeßliches Erleben d a m a l s draußen, und der Ernst der Zeit und
gleiches Erleben j e t z t binden uns Kameraden immer fester aneinander!
So ist es, und so soll es sein!
Der Frontbund ist kein "Geselligkeitsverein", zu dem man gehen oder von dem
man wegbleiben kann, wie es einem beliebt! Die Kameraden gehören zusammen, und
der wäre kein rechter Kamerad, der glaubt, seiner Pflicht genügt zu haben, wenn
er seinen Beitrag zahlt: ein Kamerad, der nicht zahlt, weil er nicht zahlen
kann, aber zu uns kommt und Anteil an unserer Arbeit nimmt, ist wertvoller als
ein solcher, der zwar zahlt, aber beharrlich fernbleibt und dadurch seinen
Mangel an Interesse bekundet.
Und "obere Zehntausend", eine "haute volée", gesellschaftliche Unterschiede
irgendwelcher Art hat es bei uns im Frontbund nie gegeben: E i n   j e d e r   i
s t   K a m e r a d, mag er nun Kaufmann, Handwerker, "Studierter" oder - gar
nichts sein. Wohlverstandene Kameradschaft läßt alle Kameraden im Bunde gleich
gelten, ebenso wie draußen der Dienst alle gleich machte und es nur darauf
ankam, ob unter dem Waffenrock ein gutes Kameradenherz schlug.
Der Bundesvorsitzende führt den Bund, jeder Landesverbandsvorsitzende seinen
Landesverband, jeder Ortsgruppenvorsitzende seine Ortsgruppe aus reinem
Idealismus, aus s e l b s t l o s e m
P f l i c h t - u n d   K a m e r a d e n g e f ü h l. Die einfachste
Kameradschaftserwägung lehrt, daß dagegen die ganze Kameradschaft in treuer
Anhänglichkeit g e s c h l o s s e n   h i n t e r   i h n gehört, insbesondere
Anteil an seiner Kriegsopferarbeit nimmt und d a   i s t, wenn er ruft. Daheim
hinter dem warmen Ofen zu sitzen, ist für jeden bequemer - auch für den
Ortsgruppenvorsitzenden!

Dafür ist ein rechter Ortsgruppenvorsitzender für seine Kameraden und
Kriegsopfer s t e t s   d a mit warmem Herzen und gutem kameradschaftlichem Rat
in allen Angelegenheiten des täglichen Lebens - vier Augen sehen mehr als zwei,
und in freundschaftlicher Aussprache kommt Licht in Dunkel und manches schwere
Los trägt sich leichter. Der Ortsgruppenvorsitzende als getreuer Eckart seiner
Kameraden - das ist die Idealfigur eines Ortsgruppenvorsitzenden!

Ohne alle Überheblichkeit darf gesagt werden, daß dem Frontbund im Judentum
sich nichts an die Seite stellen kann, weil sonst keine Vereinigung über eine
solche, durch gleiches, einzigartiges Erleben geschmiedete Gemeinschaft
verfügt, die in schöner Selbstlosigkeit nichts weiter erstrebt als

> das Andenken der gefallenen Kameraden
> zu pflegen, unsere Kriegsopfer nach besten
> Kräften zu betreuen und ein Bund von
> Kameraden in des Wortes bester Bedeutung
> zu sein.

Das   i s t   er, und das soll er   b l e i b e n !

An article published on January 7, 1938, in *Schild,* the organ of the Jewish ex-
soldiers, which, amazingly, Heydrich had still permitted. It is my father's last
appeal to Jewish ex-service men to remain faithful to the memory of their fallen
and to each other. I did not know about this document until my visit to Halle in
1983. My father died in 1970. This is a crucial document, even for scholars. I do
not think scholars can find out any more about Heydrich. See also page 209.

Aviv and what the Jews were doing and invited me to Denmark. The silence was now more frozen than ever, and I, belatedly scared, found myself wishing the brief Berlin-Halle train ride were not so long.

The Martin Luther University Halle/Wittenberg had been distinguished in the past and had invited Kant to the university; although Halle/Wittenberg was superior to Königsberg, Kant had been too set in his ways and had declined. When my father attended the university, it had still been significant. How would it be now? As the sole Jewish student, I found it novel but disconcerting to seem to be the only one, trusted by others, to hear their whispered criticisms, as was true of two confessional church students I became friendly with and of my Arabic teacher, Hans Wehr.

The university departments were a mixed story, with some members supporting the "new order," others mildly or strongly opposed. Thus in Old Testament, I attended Kurt Galling only once, for, although a well-known scholar, his assertion that Deuteronomy's social order resembled that of National Socialism was too much. But Otto Eissfeld was different. He had a Ras Shamra seminar for which he invited the three or four students to his home, although having me in his home was a risk. He also had predicted in print in 1934 that the Hebrew Bible would soon have another creative period, a prediction of Israel, it seems to me now, for without the Bible, the Jewish state would not exist. When he taught Isaiah's "daughter of Zion" as a "hut" in the "cucumber field" (Isa. 1:8)—it barely stands, but threatens to fall—he seemed to be speaking directly to me, the only Jew among about seventy others.

With philosophy it was similar. I attended Paul Menzer's seminar on Kant's *Critique of Judgment*. No deep Kant scholar but of outstanding Kantian character, Menzer lost no chance to attack Nazism in the name of Goethe, Schiller, and Kant himself. He even urged students to denounce him, and some may have done so. But the Gestapo must have thought it wiser to leave the old man alone; he was already near retirement. Menzer lived until the age of ninety in Halle but never saw another day of freedom.

Menzer was in philosophy, but so were Stammler and Reiner. Gerhard Stammler, a competent philosopher and son of a distinguished one, once declared in his class that today he was proud to be a German. The previous day the Germans had bombed defenseless Guernica. Then he gave his lecture on ethics.

Hans Reiner came to class in an SA uniform, to a seminar on Schelling. He had only three students, two the confessional church students already mentioned and I the third. (What Nazi was interested in Schelling?) Reiner promised to show that Schelling had anticipated National Socialism, but the three of us fought him, and within a few weeks Reiner "proved" that Schelling had renewed the Old and New Testament, the latter, we supposed, for my two fellow students, the former for me.

In post-Nazi West Germany, philosophers had two fig leaves with which to cover their opportunistic nakedness, Christianity and Kant. Reiner had become a Christian Kantian.

5

Six Months of Collapse
November 11, 1938–May 12, 1939

On November 10, 1938, Karl Rautenberg and I went to the *Hochschule* as usual. We arrived at the building in Artilleriestrasse, but the door was locked. That was strange. It had never happened before. Something must be up. We waited, but after a while walked away.

In the next block we saw a piano in the street, with some bystanders. One walked to the instrument and touched a key. He laughed briefly. "The Jew can still play." This was our first evidence of Kristallnacht.

Knowing now that something was happening, we decided we must see for ourselves and walked over much of Berlin, at length reaching Kurfürstendamm, Berlin's Fifth Avenue, there to see the worst sight I ever beheld. Sachsenhausen, after all, was run by the SS and kapos, but here, in this most famous of Berlin's fashionable streets, well-dressed men and women, presumably otherwise law abiding, stepped over all that broken glass into Jewish stores, there to help themselves to coats, shoes, gloves, and whatever else struck their fancy. In 1935 the regime had passed the Nuremberg laws that made Jews *vogelfrei*. (To a *vogelfrei* person one can do whatever one likes.) Three years later, in a country once priding itself on being a *Rechtsstaat*, these laws had done their work: law-abiding citizens had become common thieves.[1]

Later that day it occurred to us that what happened in Berlin might have happened throughout Germany, so I got together with my brother Alex. (He too was in Berlin. My father made him learn typing, since it might be useful *im Ausland* [abroad].) I phoned home. My mother answered in hysterics: they had taken my father. I said that one of us would come and hung up.

There was no choice regarding who should go. Alex was no man of action, and, if only compared to him, I was. I took the train, avoided the Halle streetcar and walked home, did not even turn on the hall light in our house. I would lie low at home, for the safest place was where the Gestapo had already been. But next morning, at ten o'clock, the doorbell rang. They had tapped my phone call.

The two Gestapo men walked me through town to head-quarters and jail. One spoke. "You seem to be a nice fellow," he said, or words to that effect. "Why didn't you realize you are not wanted and leave Germany in time?" I told him at first we did not wish to leave home, and when later we wanted to, there were few opportunities. The other Gestapo man, not liking this friendly chitchat, cut in and hissed: "Why didn't you go to Russia?" I said that one distant relative had done so but had not been heard from since.

They kept us in jail for two days, some twenty in a cell for six. (Our group was the leftover; the bulk had been taken the day before.) Since our community was not large, most of us knew each other, if only slightly. There was a depressed silence in that cell.

Then an older man spoke. "Fackenheim, you have studied Judaism. We haven't. What does Judaism say to us now?"

I said nothing. They were honest enough citizens and decent enough Jews. I would not say we were punished for our sins, or suffered vicariously for the sins of others, or even that it had some purpose, known only to God.

Half a century later, I tried to answer that man's question, to a new generation, in *What Is Judaism?*

Much of Sachsenhausen, after all these years, is dim in memory, but I remember our arrival quite exactly, even how I had felt. (I even re-feel the feeling.) There had been rumors about concentration camps for years: how does it feel to be in one? Stark terror? A numb sense "this cannot be true, a nightmarish mistake"? Just one feeling is utterly out of place: exhilaration, a macho confidence, the feeling that, whatever they would do, we could take it, would beat it. Yet this is, absurdly, how I felt.

There was a primitive cause. For well over two hours we had sat in trucks. There were two of them, one covered, one open. It was November; the night was cold and—naturally, they were Nazis—they had filled the open one, only putting the overflow in the other. Sitting in the open truck, I was frozen, so that when they ordered us to get out and run, the sheer pleasure of it made me feel as I did. Matter over mind, alas! A grim lesson, but proper for Sachsenhausen.

We had arrived at night, and they made us run and walk all night. It was hard on the older ones, and I heard an old man cry, insanely, that they had taken his cow, but that night I paid little attention to the old, for I was still in that macho mood, and twenty-two years old.

Next morning they lined us up in six rows for an "interrogation." An SS officer came, in leisurely fashion, stopped in front of someone, and asked him, quietly, about his profession. The answer—"a doctor"—produced an explosion of abuse and beating. "You *Judenschwein*," he screamed, "you have seduced Aryan women." He subsided, but the same happened again and again. "A lawyer" and "a businessman" produced the same explosion, with blows and insults: "You have perverted German law" and "You have cheated Aryan customers."

Then he came to a man who said he was a bricklayer; one look showed that he was. But the SS officer, more apoplectic than ever, screamed, "You liar, you are a banker," and the man was too simple to understand that, had he said, "Sorry, I lied," the beating might have stopped.

That first day we were heroes, for tomorrow could be our last, and we were not ashamed of our professions. But later we discovered that the questions were always asked but answers never checked, so we lied. On that first day I had said "rabbinical student" and got blows, but later when I said "public schoolteacher" I got by. We thought we were smart and beat the system. But *the system was beating us,* for in lying about honest professions we lost self-respect.

Other attempts to demoralize us were too obvious for the Nazis to disguise. We were shocked to see the *Arbeitsscheuen* (those too lazy to work) among our fellow prisoners, Gypsies (*arbeitsscheu* by definition) and the unemployed, who were viewed as unemployable. Nazi Germany had three ways to fight unemployment:

rearmament, the SA (later the SS), and the concentration camp. These *Arbeitsscheuen*, already undernourished before their arrival in the KZ (concentration camp), looked literally starved, and, when they asked for bread, we gave them some. But a loudspeaker announced that Jewish rations were cut in half, for the Jews were giving it away. Damaging intergroup solidarity.

Life in camp consisted of work, most of which was at the *Klinkerwerke*, several miles away from the camp, carrying hundred pound bags, shoveling sand into a boat, pushing lorries. In this place much depended on the kapo. Often we were lucky, for we had Karl. He was a petty thief, who, he boasted, had stolen from the rich but never from the poor. At the end of each day, a kapo was supposed to point out the nonworkers under him. Karl never did, and in punishment he would have to stand at attention for an hour or two in the cold and the snow.

We were not supposed to eat while working, and the hours until the lunch break were long. Once Karl caught me. "Don't you know you must not eat while working?" "I am not working," I said, and in mock anger, Karl replied, "I have never seen such a *Frechheit* (an impudence)." "Such chutzpah," he would have said, had he known the word.

But kapos were a matter of luck, and once we had an anti-Semitic communist, out to torment us, but luckily Karl was nearby. We were helpless vis-à-vis a kapo, but kapos could fight each other. Karl came over, asked our kapo to stop it, and, when he refused, Karl beat him up. We watched and enjoyed.

But Karl was not always nearby. Once we had a kapo who was a murderer and well-known sadist. Our job was hard anyway, for the four of us had to push a full lorry up a hill and then, on the double, down to have it refilled. But the ball bearings of our lorry were broken, and finally, whatever our lot from the kapo might be, we gave up. We could not do it and just sat down. He got ten others to try, but even they couldn't move it any more. That was one of my longest days in Sachsenhausen. But there were others.

This was work with a purpose, and sometimes we could boost our morale through petty sabotage. A bag dropped and broken, sand shoveled into the river instead of the boat. But other work was designed to destroy our morale and had no other purpose. A pile of sand was at one place and we had to carry it to another, but not in wheelbarrows. We had to take off our jackets, put them on again the wrong way, and carry the sand by the corners of our jackets. Next day we would carry the sand back to the old place. This was meaningless labor, meant to destroy our morale, but we knew it and, knowing so, we could fight back.

But did we *always* know? Could we always fight? In 1975 I published an article, "Sachsenhausen 1938: Groundwork for Auschwitz." I had come upon an article by Dr. Ball-Kaduri, who was in Sachsenhausen when I was but was older and more perceptive. The daily march to and from the *Klinkerwerke* had not been orderly, he argued, but deliberately chaotic, with those behind always running into the ones in front and with the SS hitting stragglers with rifle butts, a cruel perversion of Prussian order, in which yet—this was Ball-Kaduri's point—the "fiction" was maintained that *Ordnung Muss Sein* (there must be order).

In the march to and from the *Klinkerwerke*, this fiction was extended even to songs, not Nazi but German songs, probably harking back to army days, among them a sentimental tune about an old mother whose son has been killed in war and a romantic one about a girl, black brown like a hazelnut, black brown as her lover. Not knowing what Ball-Kaduri wrote, if only thereafter, we prisoners sang the song. I make no apology for our being taken in: many others were. In concentration camps—later murder camps—they used German traditions, not to cheer their soldiers, but to destroy their victims. Count Stauffenberg, the hero who had tried to kill Hitler, alas, was wrong to shout "long live holy Germany" before they killed him. If ever there was a time for "holy Germany" it was much too late: *Ordnung Muss Sein* at Sachsenhausen had become the groundwork for *Arbeit Macht Frei* (work makes one free) at Auschwitz.

But a still more basic characteristic even Ball-Kaduri—we all—failed to recognize. Everybody was in Sachsenhausen for *something he had done*, designated by a red triangle for politics, a green one for crime, a brown one for *arbeitsscheu*, and so on. We, however, had *two* triangles, arranged by SS thought into a Star of David; while the red one was for *what we had done*, the yellow one was for what, *as Jews, we were*. Naturally, we thought a lot about the last category, the yellow triangle, but not about the red one; we used to laugh to ourselves when they made us say *im Sprechchor* (in chorus) that we had plotted the murder of Freiherr vom

Rath, for that I or the Jew next to me had anything to do with it was ridiculous. But we should not have laughed, for *not we* but *they* were meant to believe it or, more precisely, were to *act* as if they believed it: our Star of David was a synthesis—*at once diabolical and Nazi-style humorous*—that being a *Jew* (yellow) was ipso facto being *political* (red). Soon they forgot about the "red" and made the *whole* star yellow. We understood a lot at Sachsenhausen, that is, that the timing of Kristallnacht was only accidentally related to the Paris killing, that Britain and France, who at Munich had done nothing for the Czechs, would do nothing for German, Austrian, and Sudeten Jews.

But one fact, a much more significant one, we did not understand: it was about the two triangles—soon to be one, a Star of David all yellow: from now on "the Jews" had started *the last war*, had started *every war*, were the enemies *of Germany*, were the enemies *of the world*, were parasites, a tuberculosis needing Hitler as discoverer; Jewish guilt was in the *Jewish blood*, so that even babies, if Jewish, were criminals to be not only *"exterminated"* but also *tortured*.[2] Witness: "The Jew Grynspan was the representative of Jewry. The German vom Rath was the representative of the German people. Thus Jewry has fired on the German people. The German government will answer legally but harshly" (Goebbels in the *Völkischer Beobachter*, November 12, 1938).

To cite an even better—because later—authority: Heinrich Himmler maintained that Jews were not a *Weltanschauungsfrage*, but a *Reinlichkeitsangelegenheit* (a matter of cleanliness), so that one must get rid of them as of vermin. But since one does not torture vermin, Himmler wavered between this and an even better definition. Unlike other *Völker*, Jews are *Träger einer zu einem Scheinvolk zusammengeschlossenen Erbkriminalität* (bearers of hereditary criminality, synthesized into a pseudo people): just to get rid of them is not enough.[3]

What we did not know was that Kristallnacht was the beginning of the Holocaust. There still is an argument between "intentionalist" and "functionalist" scholars about whether Hitler planned the Holocaust from the start or whether "it happened" gradually. Whatever the answer—scholars may never reach an agreement—Kristallnacht, in any case, was when it happened.

This is a hindsight view, of course. Now it is a common thought among historians that the Great War has shaped the twentieth century, that is, that without World War I, there would have been no World War II, no Hitler.

But within this consensus, there exists a sharp dissent. Gerhard L. Weinberg (who has discovered and deeply reflected on Hitler's "second book," kept secret because it clearly states his aims) stresses *the difference* between the two wars, that Hitler was a *Raumpolitiker* (politician of space) scornful of all World War I *Grenzpolitiker* (politicians of borders), the Germans included; and that World War II "was about who would live . . . and which people would disappear entirely because they were believed to be inferior or undesirable by the aggressor."[4] (Some historians ignore Hitler's second book, or think it should not be taken seriously.)

In contrast, Jay Winter and Blaine Baggett assert a *continuity* between the two wars, thus trivializing the difference. Hence— after many examples, complete with photographs—they find themselves able to write: "*Arbeit Macht Frei* . . . is the message that greeted the millions of people brought to the gates of Auschwitz. Höss knew what prison meant: boredom, fear, despair. He did not use this phrase cynically, but as a symbol of the religion of obedience he clung to throughout his life."[5] "Höss was an anti-Semite, dedicated to the elimination of 'Jewish supremacy.' But he found the more vulgar forms of Nazi propaganda distasteful. Hatred was no part of his nature or his task, but systematic killing was."[6]

Winter and Baggett's most general—as it were, "philosophical"—statement about the two wars is: "Millions of men had served in the German Army in both wars without committing crimes against humanity. What the 1914–18 war did was to make these crimes possible. The war opened the doorway to brutality through which men like Höss willingly passed." Made the crimes *possible*? (Why not among English, Americans, even Russians?) Passed *willingly*? Höss's dedication to duty was *ironclad*? These "as it were, philosophical" assertions call for genuine philosophy, not only, with great shock, regarding Winter and Baggett, but also, with less, regarding Weinberg, who, although expressing opposition, is himself among the school of historians whom he criticizes for not giving Hitler's role in exterminating Jews "the attention it deserves."[7]

From historians of Nazism a question arises for philosophy: is to *explain* radical evil ipso facto to *trivialize* it, make it less than radical? (What is explanation in history, anyway?) We must return to these questions, if fragmentarily, in chapter 13 and the epilogue of this book.

But these questions, although philosophical, have now been answered by a historical study that supersedes the ones mentioned earlier: the work of Ian Kershaw, two thousand pages, two volumes, titled *Hitler, 1889–1936: Hubris* and *Hitler, 1936–1945: Nemesis,* respectively. Kershaw shows in volume one that the Nazi Weltanschauung, not just Hitler's private experience, was the cause of the Holocaust, and in chapters 3 and 10 of volume two describes the terrible way in which the Weltanschauung was carried out. Thus he supersedes Joachim Fest's *Hitler,* the best book before his, which had wrongly attributed to Hitler a remnant of "bourgeois morality" that made Fest unable to face the implications of the Holocaust.

‡

How was our morale in Sachsenhausen? Of course, we had gallows humor. Fischel had been arrested in Berlin, as had Harf and Rautenberg. Karl in any case had a "nebbish philosophy," well suited for the KZ. But Fischel was good at this humor too. Once he said we were okay in Sachsenhausen but would be in trouble when we got out.

What, exactly, is a nebbish? (The way the Nazis got Rautenberg shows what a nebbish is: the SS tried to get him, but not finding him at home, took his father instead; when, to get his father released, Rautenberg turned himself in, the SS kept them both.) A nebbish is close to a schlamazel (who attracts bad luck) but is sharply distinct from a schlemiel (who has two left feet). When the schlemiel spills his coffee, it lands on the trousers of the schlamazel.

Others had gallows humor too. Once I stood in front of the medical hut with Rabbi Swarsenski, for we had sore legs. An SS "doctor" came out and kicked us: "Run, Jews!" As we were running, Swarsenski turned to me and said: "Bist Du noch krank?" (Still sick?)

But there was one form of resistance by humor we did not think of, and would not have dared to act on, had we thought of it. Luitpold Wallach, an older friend, already had a congregation.

During Kristallnacht the Nazis wanted a list of its members, but Luitpold said he had lost it. They took him to Dachau; there an SS officer told the Jews that the Nazis would take Warsaw, Paris, London, other cities, then asked whether he had forgotten any. Luitpold said he had forgotten *Misse Meshine,* and the SS man then said they would also take *Misse Meshine.* (The term means "ugly death" in Yiddish.) Luitpold could not resist even a dangerous joke, much less one that was merely rude. He was my successor as rabbi for the Hamilton congregation, a position for which I, with poor judgment, had recommended him. He lasted only one year.

Jokes were a morale builder, but true morale existed only in one hope, nonexistent for some: release. Every morning at roll call, they announced lists of those to be released, one day fifty, another thirty, and we believed we would all eventually get out. But gradually the numbers got smaller, releases rarer. In February 1939, of the original 6,000 prisoners, only 280 were left.

On February 8, 1939, two things happened. At night I heard someone vomit and in the morning found my jacket on the floor with vomit on it: this was serious, for I had to clean the jacket and risk pneumonia. Already depressed, I became even more so by allowing a thought that I had previously not admitted to enter my mind. What if a remnant would *never* be released?

Nobody will believe this, every reader will think I am dramatizing, and there are no more witnesses: that morning they called out three names, and one was mine.

I left behind Erich Kohlhagen, my best pal after Fischel was gone: he belonged to that remnant. Erich survived until the end of the war, until the Americans came. So did his morale. (His sister told me when I got to Dayton much later. Erich had already died.)

Would I have survived? Would my morale have survived? I do not know.

They returned my clothes, ordered me to report to the Halle Gestapo, and let me go.

But I stopped first at the *Hochschule* to warn the other students. In Berlin, unlike in Halle, one could lie low, and I assumed they had done so. I went to the library, on the third floor in the Artilleriestrasse building, and there they were, studying.

I told them it was too late, that the time for "study now, emigrate later" was past; that they must do what they could to get out. But I do not know whether I failed to convince them or whether they tried and did not succeed.

Then I went to the Halle Gestapo. They gave me a choice: six weeks to leave or back to Sachsenhausen.

Then, home at last, I was overwhelmed with news. My father had long been released, Wolfgang was already in England, and there were emigration hopes for my parents and Alexander.

Then the bad news: my father's sister, Aunt Erna, had committed suicide during Kristallnacht. She had anti-Nazi material in her purse, and when the Nazis demanded it, she had taken the poison she always carried and collapsed in Grosse Steinstrasse, true to her life, always with fun but also always in protest, here then in a final one. Of course, this made no difference, any more than had the protest of her husband, in the same street, more than five years earlier. On her stone Uncle Adolf had engraved "To my brave comrade." I did not know this until I saw it in 1999.

And my six weeks deadline? Of our ten letters to U.S. universities, only one had earned a reply, from Harry Wolfson at Harvard. Wolfson got me a librarian's contract at New York's Jewish Institute of Religion, so I went to the U.S. consulate in Berlin, only to learn that ministers and professors, but not librarians and certainly not students, were entitled to nonquota visas: the document that got me out of Sachsenhausen would not get me out of Germany. I recalled Fischel's joke in Sachsenhausen: We were okay in the KZ but not when we got out.

The six weeks were ticking away. Other possibilities—a ticket to Shanghai, a promised visa for a South American country, I forget which one—would end my hope, by now an obsession, for an academic life with a Jewish purpose.

Harvard had already helped by offering the library contract, Wolfson wrote that there were no visitor's visas to the U.S., but that they had written to the Swiss International Student Service. The ISS, in turn, had written to Scotland for three scholarships, for Bräude and Fischel in Edinburgh, for me in Aberdeen. Did I already have Professor Kennedy's letter, inviting me to Aberdeen? Or did it come later? I was too flustered at the time to remember now.

The weeks were still ticking away, for now I was waiting for my Aberdeen visa. Meanwhile I got a visa to the Kitchener camp in England, for refugees without other connections, so I was safe.

I probably could have gone to the Kitchener camp and from there to Aberdeen. But by then I was so skeptical about the chances of getting out of a concentration camp once a person was in one and so thrilled about the "Aberdeen redemption" that— for the first time in six months of being an SS object—I acted as a subject, in charge of my life. I went to the Gestapo, showed my papers, and asked for an extension. I needed it, I told them, because Kitchener camp refugees went in groups. (I had just made that up and gambled on their not checking.) I got the extension, soon afterward the visa, and as soon as possible was off.

In these last weeks I saw Jewish friends, packed, and even did my *Hochschule* ordination exams. But I did not phone Jürgen, my last German friend, for a Jewish contact had become dangerous for him, and he didn't phone me.

But Adolph Lörcher phoned: he would never forgive me, he said, if I did not see him, so, of course, I did. Lörcher had two copies of Martin Buber's *Königtum Gottes* (Kingship of God), both inscribed *dyoin tateron*, "one of two," a custom among "classical" friends when they part. Then he said, "I have always told you not to leave, that the Nazi disease must pass. Now you must leave; but you must promise me to come back, Germany will be destroyed"—by the Nazis, he meant, not by the English, Americans, Russians—"and we shall need you to rebuild it." I replied, "Dr. Lörcher, I have never contradicted you, but now I must. Two or three years ago, I might still have said 'I'll come back,' but now I know that Judaism and the Jewish people will need me more. Germany will have to be rebuilt, but by someone else."

In 1999, after an honorary doctorate at Martin Luther University Halle/Wittenberg, I asked the *Stadtgymnasium* for Lörcher's picture. They got me an article by him written long ago, but no picture; his name was no longer known in Halle.[8]

There was a nasty experience even at the Hamburg airport. My plane was waiting, but I had to fill out a form, and the official said he couldn't read it. I filled it out a second time, in block letters, but he said he still couldn't read it and held on to my passport. Then he threw it at me, and I literally ran from my *Vaterland*, to sit down on what felt like a very soft chair in the plane. I remember that but not whether the plane was Dutch or Danish. But it was not German.

Halle, 1. November 1938.

Zeugnis.

Herr Stud. Emil Fackenheim aus Halle war in den drei obersten Klassen des Gymnasiums bis zum Abitur mein Schüler. Auf Grund eingehender Kenntnis stelle ich seiner Begabung, Leistung und Haltung das beste Zeugnis aus. Seine Leistungen standen in allen Fächern, auch in Turnen und Sport, weit über dem Durchschnitt; in Haltung und Wesen zeigte er sich fest und zuverlässig. Ich bin davon überzeugt, daß er, wo man ihn hinstellt, seinen Mann stehen und etwas Tüchtiges leisten wird.

Dr. A. Lörcher, Studienrat

A letter from Dr. A. Lörcher, written on November 1, 1938, on my last visit to Halle before Kristallnacht and my subsequent arrest while returning from Berlin to Halle to assist my mother. I had kept in touch with Lörcher after I passed the matriculation and left the *Stadtgymnasium,* and I called him up on this occasion with the request for a testimonial. The next day I most probably went back to Berlin; I had no knowledge of the fact that the Martin Luther University Halle/Wittenberg had already expelled me as a student. At the time, I got all sorts of documents, many of which I got because I did not know what I would need. But this is the only one I got from a high school teacher. Many teachers were not Nazis, but Lörcher was the only forthright one, making it impossible for me to become either anti-German or anti-Christian. He was the most outstanding German I knew personally.

When I first wrote these lines, I wrote them abruptly, for the end had itself been abrupt for me personally, the end of the *Hochschule,* of Berlin, of Germany, not to speak of my family. But later I remembered, remorsefully, that it had not been the end of the ordeal for German Jewry, among them Leo Baeck. His Berlin struggle had begun before I had arrived, for on Kol Nidre, the evening of Yom Kippur 1935, he had a prayer read in Berlin synagogues. (It was composed by him personally and is a clear sign of his fidelity in catastrophe, indeed of his character.) The prayer begins: "In this hour all Israel stands before God, the God of righteousness and mercy. Before him we want to test our way fully, to test what we have done and what we have failed to do." Then the focus of the prayer shifted: "We pronounce our abhorrence and see trampled beneath our feet the lies that are turned against us, the slander turned against our religion and its character." The prayer concluded: "We stand before our God. . . . We bow to Him and we stand upright and erect before man."[9] For this prayer, Baeck had been jailed.

After I fled, he kept on teaching at the *Hochschule.* (For reasons never explained, the institution remained open until June 30, 1942.) "I never saw Leo Baeck appear desperate except once," said one of the handful of students at the final class. "That was when he learned that the *Hochschule* would close."

Baeck was the last Jewish scholar in Germany to witness, after a hundred years, the end of German Jewish scholarship.

For him, moreover, the *Hochschule* was all of German Jewry. He also headed the Reichsvertretung deutscher Juden (Reich Representation of German Jews), in 1939 renamed Reichsvereinigung der Juden in Deutschland (Reich Association of Jews in Germany). The Nazi Weltanschauung was fully spelled out. Auschwitz and Treblinka, however, their very existence, these, whether planned by the *Machthaber* then or later, were kept from the victims.

Baeck stayed in Berlin, but he was not alone; with him were Julius Seligson, Hannah Karminski, Cora Berliner, and Dr. Otto Hirsch, the last named the *Reichsvereinigung*'s chief administrator. Why stay? To help other trapped Jews: the infirm, the sick, the old, also the clueless and luckless, all—except for such as these five—abandoned by God and by Man.

Baeck survived Theresienstadt thanks to a Gestapo accident; his name, if not much else, is widely remembered. Not remembered are the others. Those who knew Otto Hirsch think of him as a last worthy representative of German Judaism, to quote Baeck, "erect and upright before man." The Nazis took him to Mauthausen; in June 1941 he was murdered.[10]

Interlude

6

Scottish Interlude
May 12, 1939–June 1940

I arrived in London with clothing, not many books, and a pair of Shabbat candlesticks, the last my only memento from home. (I still have them.) Other mementos I left behind—a picture of Beethoven, gramophone records, even family photographs. Why? Maybe my flight had been precipitous; maybe I thought Scotland would be just an interlude. Or maybe for deeper reasons I will not analyze.

Why only a few books? I sent the bulk to New York for a distant cousin to keep. My future would be more likely in America than in Britain. I arrived, armed with a passport, a valid visa, a one-way London-Aberdeen train ticket, a gigantic salami, and fourteen shillings.

Before traveling to Aberdeen I wrote to Professor Kennedy, not from Germany (where the Gestapo could have intercepted my letter) but, safely, from England, and asked whether I should come. My U.S. librarian contract had made me suspicious, for although it had gotten me out of Sachsenhausen and was meant to get me into the United States, I had learned through the grapevine it was not a job. If Kennedy's response was the same, I would stay in London and sell the ticket.

Needing a place to stay, I went to the local ISS representative, who phoned a hotel and gave me a pound, enough to cover one night's stay minus food. I was glad I had brought the salami.

Since I could not possibly hear from Kennedy within a day, I had to go back to the ISS man, who gave me another pound, with reluctance, I thought, so I never went to him again. Although Wolfgang had arrived just a few weeks earlier, he found me a place for twenty-five shillings a week, four daily meals included. This was my first experience of professionals handling refugees worse than amateurs did. Or another proof that Wolfgang was no amateur.

Before the week Professor Kennedy replied, puzzled. Of course they wanted me to come, he wrote, why else would they have invited me? I went at once.

I knew what Harvard and the Swiss ISS had done, but the real work must have been in Aberdeen. An undergraduate, Norman McIver, had first asked Professor Kennedy to sponsor me with the government, without financial or other responsibilities; then he asked the university to exempt me from fees, then for half a dozen parents of fellow students to take in a refugee for a month or two. So easy had it been to save a refugee, a career, even a life. There was luck, of course, and the world does not have many McIvers. At that time or at any time. A socialist hoping for the end of British imperialism, Norman was the first Aberdeen student to volunteer in the war and the first to get killed.

He had even lined up a holiday in the Scottish Highlands; but I had said no. "There isn't time," I told him, "not for a holiday." There wasn't. My Scottish interlude lasted for just a year.

That there was no time I also told the university authorities. Their master's program required four years of study; because of my rabbinic diploma they would let me do it in three. But I protested that even this was impossible, for there wasn't time. Then these good people ruled my rabbinic diploma the equivalent of their master's degree and let me go on to a Ph.D. This must have been a first—probably remains a first—in Scottish academic history.

I have never been in a kinder, more humane place than legendarily humane Aberdeen, gown and town. If I thought so at the time, it was doubtless by way of contrast. But even now, sixty years later, I couldn't have done better than to urge my parents, when they emigrated, to live in Aberdeen. There they lived and died, my mother in 1954, my father in 1970. After a few years Principal Fyfe made him a professor of comparative law. My father had not studied so hard since his student days. The position did not pay much, and he had only a few students; but it did wonders for his morale.

THE UNIVERSITY OF WISCONSIN PRESS

1930 Monroe Street, 3rd floor, Madison, Wisconsin 53711-2059

FOR IMMEDIATE RELEASE
Contact: Chris Caldwell, Publicity Manager
Ph (608) 263-0734, Fax (608) 263-1132
Email: publicity@uwpress.wisc.edu
http://www.wisc.edu/wisconsinpress/

Publication Date: December 15, 2007
ISBN: 978-0-299-17590-0
Cloth, $39.95
368 pages

"An illuminating and affecting memoir by a seminal Jewish thinker of the twentieth century." —Raul Hilberg, author of *The Destruction of the European Jews*

AN EPITAPH FOR GERMAN JUDAISM
From Halle to Jerusalem

by Emil Fackenheim
Foreword by Michael Morgan

"Fackenheim's influence on present-day Jewish thought has been profound, and these memoirs show why." —Yehuda Bauer, Hebrew University, Jerusalem

Translated by Barbara E. Galli

Foreword by Michael Oppenheim, Introduction by Elliot R. Wolfson

For more information please contact Chris Caldwell, Publicity Manager at 608/263-0734 Ph; 608/263-1132 Fax; or publicity@uwpress.wisc.edu.

We would appreciate receiving a copy of any notice that may appear. Please send tear sheets, noting name and location of publication and date of issue, to the Publicity Department at the University of Wisconsin Press people, Judaism, and an humanity. In this memoir, to which he was making final revisions at the time of his death, Fackenheim looks back on his life, at the profound and painful circumstances that shaped him as a philosopher and a committed Jewish thinker.

Interned for three months in the Sachsenhausen concentration camp after Kristallnacht, Fackenheim was released and escaped to Scotland and then to Canada, where he lived in a refugee internment camp before eventually becoming a congregational rabbi and then, for thirty-five years, a professor of philosophy. He recalls here what it meant to be a German Jew in North America, the desperate need to respond to the crisis in Europe and to cope with its overwhelming implications for Jewish identity and community. His second great turning point came in 1967, as he saw Jews threatened with another Holocaust, this time in Israel. This crisis led him on a pilgrimage to Jerusalem and ultimately back to Germany, where he continued to grapple with the question, How can the Jewish faith—and the Christian faith—exist after the Holocaust?

Emil Fackenheim (1916–2003) was a rabbi and professor of philosophy at the University of Toronto and the Hebrew University, Jerusalem. His many books include *The Religious Dimension in Hegel's Thought*, *God's Presence in History*, *To Mend the World*, and *What Is Judaism?*

This book was published with generous support from the Lucius N. Littauer Foundation and the children of Emil Fackenheim

For more information please contact Chris Caldwell, Publicity Manager at 608/263-0734 Ph; 608/263-1132 Fax; or publicity@uwpress.wisc.edu.

We would appreciate receiving a copy of any notice that may appear. Please send tear sheets, noting name and location of publication and date of issue, to the Publicity Department at the University of Wisconsin Press

But if Aberdeen offered legendary kindness, one of the university's two philosophy professors seemed bent on refuting it. A. S. Ferguson, in Greek philosophy, gave me a private Plato seminar, a reminder of Lörcher. John Laird in modern philosophy said he had no time, but told me to call on him if I had problems. I was studying Descartes at the time and called on him with a problem. Descartes "decides" to doubt but—I was thinking more of Kierkegaard than of Descartes—is doubt a matter of deciding? Laird responded: "What's your problem? Either you doubt or you don't. Next question!" I frantically searched my mind for a problem and found a good one, worth discussing, I thought, for half an hour. "Descartes has a *res extensa* and a *res cogitans.* "But surely"—I was thinking more of Kant, even of Fichte—"the self is not a *res*, a substance." Laird looked at me straight and asked, "Are you a substance?" And when I began with "that depends," he objected to all this shilly-shallying: "Either you are a substance or you are not." I said thank you very much, left, and never saw him again. Laird was not the most effective professor I ever met in getting rid of a student, but he was the bluntest.

Meanwhile war was approaching, and I got a phone call from my father. When I had fled from Halle, their coming had been uncertain, and for a long time my father had thought that the young must go but the old can only stay. But then came hope: a cousin, Fröhlich (I forgot his first name), who had fled from Germany to Spain and then from Spain to Scotland, had persuaded a wealthy Glasgow family to vouch for my parents with the government. So now my father had paid all his taxes. The rest of his property, perhaps 6 percent of it, mostly carpets, was in a cargo box in Hamburg and would have to stay there for six weeks to clear it of any tax obligations, this although taxes had already been paid. Did he have six weeks? I would find out and phone back. I went to Lloyds in Aberdeen: would they insure a lift in Hamburg, Germany? When they said they wouldn't touch it with a ten-foot pole, I phoned my parents back. "Come right away," and they came.

But my father had phoned me earlier, and it pains me to recall it even now. The Gestapo was threatening my parents, and they needed their visas fast. I had met Principal Fyfe of Aberdeen University, phoned and told him the problem, and through his MP he got the visa. Feeling persecuted even in a decent country, I, for the first time in my life, wished I had been a Polish Jew. If I had lied about it, nobody would have been the wiser. My parents were in Halle, threatened by the Gestapo, but Alex was in Berlin, at the time unthreatened. Had I lied to Fyfe that all three were in danger, no one would have known the difference. So when my parents arrived four days before the war began, they came without Alex.

I had made Irish friends who offered a refuge for Alex in neutral Ireland: the problem was how to get him there. When I wrote to a shipping company about boats from Germany to Ireland, the police came after me, and Professor Kennedy had to vouch for me.

The war came, and because I held a German passport, I was suspect. The committee to examine us in Aberdeen consisted of one man, the local professor of law, who asked why I was in the country. Then I said: "I am a refugee from Nazi oppression," he stamped my paper, and when I left him, I was worried how Britain would survive.

I was worried about this at other times too. One month I stayed with a family named Campbell, with three sons I became fond of. Once I joked with one who thought of going into law, maybe into politics, and I said the wrong thing. "Maybe you'll be prime minister, and a better one than Chamberlain." There was silence in the room. "You are welcome in this house," the lady of the house said, "but not if you criticize our leaders."[1]

My parents were in Aberdeen now, but my clock was still ticking, and I ask myself why, for—other than the Ferguson seminar—I was on my own. But the urgency of Berlin was with me still. Under Strauss's influence, I was drawn to medieval philosophy, Muslim rather than Jewish, with this question: What happens to Aristotle in the commentaries of Averroës (his name among the Latins, in the Islamic world he is Ibn Rushd), the most orthodox Aristotelian of the Muslim philosophers? Averroës is credited with saying that "Aristotle was given to us by divine Grace, in order that we may know what is knowable." No wonder he wrote mostly "slavish" commentaries on Aristotle! But what, if anything, remains, remained even then, of Muslim revelation, the word of God? It was still urgent for me to seek it, even if indirectly in the past and in Islam rather than in Judaism. However, by then I had also trained myself to spend a daily hour on Hegel.

But there was no supervisor for me in Aberdeen, and the main lesson I learned in that year is why a thesis needs one: less to tell a candidate what to do than what not to do. This thesis was unmanageable.

But while my clock was ticking, another one also was. Hitler invaded the Netherlands, Belgium, France. Winston Churchill replaced Chamberlain.

Thus I was glad, and not surprised, when two policemen came to see me. They were apologetic, polite, and even called me "sir." "I am sorry, sir," one of them said, "but you have to come with us." They gave me a few minutes to pack, and I packed some forty books, mostly borrowed from the university library. "You won't need all these," one said. "It's only for a few days." I replied: "You know your business, and I know mine."

Internment was for a year and a half. When the Gestapo had taken me, I must have somehow said good-bye to my mother. This time I was living in a different place, so there was no good-bye. It would be eight years before I saw her again.

7

Leaving the "Old World" for a New

June–July 1940

The destination, of course, was internment. With the *Sitzkrieg* now replaced by Hitler's new *Blitzkrieg*, Winston Churchill was at last in power, and among the things he had to deal with, one— a minor one—was us. Informed of what had been done, or rather *not* done, he decreed "collar them all," meaning males age sixteen and over. He could not have done anything else.

On the part of those doing the "collaring," and of us, the "collared," the result was chaos: nothing had been prepared.

This led to one immediate difference between British internment camps and German concentration camps. Our first, in Northern Scotland, was an army camp, and the soldiers, now our guards, had food, but in their haste the army had brought none for us, and our guards shared theirs with us; in Sachsenhausen any kind of sharing between the SS and prisoners was out of the question.

The British were also worried that some prisoners might commit suicide, so shaving was only under supervision, and I decided that if I couldn't shave alone, I wouldn't shave at all. I even formed a small school of nonshavers; although being unshaved was against military regulations, the officer inspecting us, while confessing that those beards "worried" him, did nothing.

The next camp was Huyton near Liverpool. I had already been united with my father in the Scottish camp, and now Fischel and

84

Bräude were also with me. I had seen them from time to time in Edinburgh, but now we were together, with Bräude for half a year, with Fischel for an amazing seven years. I have since lost touch with Bräude, who went back to England, but Fischel is still a friend, and we are regularly in touch.

The chaos was not yet over in Huyton, the main effect being hunger. In Sachsenhausen, Fischel and I had discovered a weapon against boredom. We would imagine a benefactor donating, say, fifty books, if we could name author, title, and publisher, and by the time we had thought up the list, an hour of boring labor was gone. Now we summoned this benefactor again, except that this time he would provide a good meal if we could describe it in fancy detail. But the game did not work this time; to think of steaks and chops only made us hungrier.

Then came the Isle of Man, a camp used for prisoners of war in the Great War; so the chaos was over. But now we learned that we would leave Europe, for where we didn't know. (Wolfgang, I learned later, was sent to Australia.) An Orthodox Jew I knew slightly asked an officer whether we could eat kosher where we were going. The officer said yes, but warned that we might have to sleep in tents. This possibility did not worry that Jew. "Abraham slept in a tent, and what was good enough for him is good enough for me." This was not the first or last time I was cheered by an Orthodox Jew.

The British policy of who could stay and who must go showed consideration: only the young must go; they would be presumably without wives and children and also were considered more likely to pose a threat. A further consideration affected me personally: since the authorities would not split families, and I was with my father, I would have the choice of staying or going.

This led to a discussion with my father, the "text" of which was that, with Hitler in France and all Europe in danger, one family member should get away from the Continent. But there was also a "subtext." Everything else was crumbling, and by then I did not just remember our 1938 bull session but clung to the decision with which it had ended; I saw no hope for it except in America. Hence my father and I parted, my comfort being that he would soon be released to rejoin my mother.

Of the trip to Canada on the HMS *Ettrick*, the less said the better. There was a storm at first, and we were all seasick, and while still ill on Shabbat, I arranged for a service with "Konni" Sawady, who was a teacher but also our cantor. He conducted the service and I spoke. When the seasickness had passed, we were still uneasy for the rest of the trip. Our sister ship, the HMS *Arandora,* like the HMS *Ettrick,* carrying refugees, had been torpedoed; we were berthed on the lowest deck of the ship—German prisoners of war were on top—and knew we would not have a chance if the same fate befell the *Ettrick.* And there was anxiety about Hitler and Europe.

Many years later I ran into someone who had been on the *Ettrick.* He said he had never forgotten what I had said at that Shabbat service. I asked him to remind me. "You said that wherever we were going, God would be with us."

Part 2

Canada

8

"His Majesty's Guests" in Canada

July 1940–December 14, 1941

"Most of you are Jews, aren't you?" the fat major from Ottawa asked. We murmured assent. "Nevertheless you have to keep clean." Having got this off his chest but still on the same subject, he stressed that toilets, too, must be clean. But the purpose of his speech was to make one thing clear: if we played ball with the authorities, they, in turn, would play ball with us. (Some of us did not know much English: "What is he talking about?") We nicknamed him Major Balls.

This speech was our first welcome to Canada, or so it has always seemed, for nothing important had happened before it. We had arrived in Quebec City and had been placed in an army camp temporarily and were arguing about the only thing important to us, that we were not Nazi enemies but bona fide refugees. The authorities said this was understood and would be symbolized by the absence of barbed wire in the permanent camp. "You will like it," said a Jewish official, brought for the occasion.

But there it was, in our Sherbrooke camp, the barbed wire! During our whole time there—for me a year and a half, for others longer—it was never removed. They had lied to us, to get us to go nicely on the train. So we went on a hunger strike, and since the military could not handle it, they had brought in Major Balls.

Later that day a soldier came looking for Heinz Fischel and me. "The major wants to see you." We went. Major Balls was sitting on a chair behind a table and made us stand in front. "I hear you are Jewish clergymen; maybe you have some sense. Hunger strike? Stuff and nonsense, I have never heard of such a thing." We explained that we had been enemies of the Nazis before Canada was, and that some of us had been in concentration camps. He reacted. "You have been in a camp before? Then you know how to behave! Kindly stand at attention."

Obviously, a "wartime blunder" had occurred somewhere, and it seemed clear that while, to help the mother country, Canada wanted prisoners of war, she did not want refugees. Refugees wanted to stay, and Canada's poor record on immigration, of Jews in particular, was well known. Much later I read our full story in Eric Koch's *Deemed Suspect: A Wartime Blunder.*[1] He writes of a camp commandant who blundered worse than Major Balls. He wanted to separate, not Nazis from refugees, but Jews from Gentiles, thus introducing Nazi "Aryan" laws into Canada.

For Heinz and myself, the *novum* in Canada's internment was that, regardless of "Kierkegaardian" doubts, we were now rabbis. In Britain, we had preached the odd sermon in internment but had left being a rabbi to Lemle. An older man, Rabbi Lemle had stayed behind, and now there was no one but us.

I had to be a "clergyman" once before, in the Quebec City camp. The authorities had not yet separated refugees from Nazis, and one of the latter, a German clergyman suspected of Nazi sympathies, had volunteered to the commandant to be head of education, because, so he said, otherwise the communists might take over. A man reported this, a Nazi clergyman in charge of education of mostly Jewish refugees, and I agreed it was scandalous. He suggested that I volunteer also, that for the commandant one "clergyman" would be as good as another, and we could thus keep the suspected Nazi out. I saw the commandant, my offer was accepted, and I was now the camp's "university president." This position was more serious than it sounds, for later our students wrote McGill exams and passed. But keeping the suspected Nazi out was all I had wanted to do.

A few days later someone reported to me that he had enrolled in a class on mathematics and found himself being taught Marx. I had been hornswoggled by communists! I could not denounce them, on the one hand, nor keep on covering for them, on the other. I had a few sleepless nights. Fortunately, soon afterward we moved to Sherbrooke. I was again asked whether I wanted to be president, but I said, "*Ohne mich*" (never again).

Heinz and I had been ordained in Berlin, and now, like it or not, we had a congregation. But it was no normal congregation, defined by shared beliefs or practices, but rather one forced together by events between January 30, 1933, and September 3, 1939. It included Jews whose beliefs ranged from orthodoxy to reform, even including—a challenge—Jews who had been alienated but now wanted to return. Heinz and I thought of ourselves as doing pretty well with *amcha*, until our belief was refuted. Our *amcha*, after all, were "Yekkes," German Jews, and those who came after a while were also *amcha*, but *Ostjuden*, Jews from Eastern Europe. They didn't like our Yekke services. They also didn't like us Yekke rabbis: They know hardly any Talmud! They can't even speak Yiddish! Later we understood, but then we didn't. Since they hadn't brought a rabbi but just a dubious *hazan*, or cantor, named Mühlstock, we tried to assert our rabbinic authority. Because there was no room to separate, we were a divided house, with us Yekkes conducting the services one Shabbat and they the other. (We also had to be policemen but were no good at this either. At Pesach we got matzah and honey for the observant, but had to watch for who was entitled. I once caught a fellow who had bacon with his matzah.) We Yekkes and the Eastern Jews just tolerated each other and sometimes got into absurd quarrels. Mühlstock had a Viennese lawyer named Orgel support him; Heinz and I were single, of course, and Orgel argued that according to some Austrian law rabbis had to be married. Orgel used a law now defunct because of the *Anschluss* to fight us when, while in Canada, we were, legally, His Majesty's British guests.

Sometimes our quarrels were the camp's laughingstock, and Konni Sawady, our Yekke cantor but also the camp's favorite humorist, once got a laugh when he told the *Ostjuden* they might as well accept our Yekke authority, for it was "of-Fischel."

Our Yekke-Polish quarrels were sometimes funny, but not those between us and the communists. They, at least, took the quarrels seriously. The camp had two main halls, one for eating, the other for sleeping. We needed the former for the major services and for the whole day just once a year, on Yom Kippur; the small Christian congregation agreed to eat that day in the sleeping hall. But for the communists the revolution seemed to hinge on this concession; they finally agreed to the arrangement but vowed to play football just outside during our prayers, as their way to observe the day.

If being rabbis was one Sherbrooke *novum* for us, belonging to two worlds was another. On the one hand, as rabbis we belonged to the Jews, committed to Judaism or in search of it; on the other, as scholars, we were outsiders. There was a closely knit group of Cambridge students, and they viewed those committed to Judaism as "narrowly Jewish" or "parochial," while the committed Jews looked on the "Cambridge boys" as "universalist," if not "escapist." But Heinz and I could not help belonging to both groups. I forget what Heinz did, but I studied with Tom Rosenmeyer, then of the Cambridge group but, decades later, a well-known classical scholar in the United States, with him teaching me Greek and me teaching him Arabic.

But both these groups were Yekkes, and this played a role in our choice of a camp spokesman. A grandson of the kaiser, Count Lingen was one of the Cambridge group, and we voted for him as our spokesman, unanimously, if I remember correctly. Nor did we ever regret it. It must have been the one time in history that a Hohenzollern walked through the camp on Friday afternoons, announcing the time for Shabbat services.

During my time in Sherbrooke I got a letter from an old aunt, Martha Fröhlich, left behind in Berlin. My brother Alex had collapsed in the bathroom, of undetected diabetes, and died in the hospital without regaining consciousness. My father was back in Aberdeen, long released from internment, so at least my mother was not alone, and I could write to both. But to this day I do not know how Alex died. That aunt's daughter, my cousin Lisa, by then in New York, wrote that her mother had given me a comforting lie, that in fact Alexander had taken an overdose of sleeping pills and drowned himself in the bathtub. But at least I know this much: Alex escaped the SS and Treblinka.

Years afterwards some of us had a meeting, trying to assess the Sherbrooke experience. At the time a year or two of even halfway decent internment had been a waste. But in retrospect one tries to find meaning in it. (Harry Rasky did a CBC movie about *The Spies Who Never Were*.) I said at that meeting that at Sherbrooke I learned something about being a rabbi and a lot about dealing with communists.

Of my friends I was the first to get out, but within a few weeks I was back in Sherbrooke. I had come to conduct a wedding and visited Fischel and Warschauer. (We had become friends with Warschauer; more on him later.) There was a grayness about the camp, metaphorical but also literal, and without noticing it, they were part of it, as I had been shortly before. But soon they would be out, they would all be out.

Years later Warschauer and I once drove to Quebec. We looked for our camp in Sherbrooke. But we could not find it.

9

University of Toronto

"Second-First" Welcome to Canada, December 15, 1941–Spring 1943

"I am sorry I am late," I said to the dean. "The academic year is half over. I cannot expect credit for the year."

I had arrived in Toronto on December 15, 1941, at 9 a.m. By noon I was at the university, for an appointment with Dean G. S. Brett. Brett was head of the Philosophy Department and also, lucky for me, dean of the Graduate School.

"Never mind that," the dean replied, or words to that effect. (Unlike some exchanges of long ago, I do not remember this one verbatim, but I can vouch for its overall accuracy). "You can show what you can do."

"There is a further problem," I went on. "I have no academic degree, only ordination as a rabbi, but on the strength of that, Aberdeen University accepted me for the Ph.D. program."

"What was good enough for Aberdeen," was Brett's response, "is good enough for us." *These* words I remember verbatim. And then, as if impatient with all this, he changed the subject to Aristotle, making me feel as if I had never left home.

If Major Balls's had been our collective "first welcome" to Canada, Dean Brett's, for me personally, was the second. More precisely, it was "second-first," for if one is held behind barbed wire in a country, and was brought to it for that purpose, in what sense is one really *in* it?

In the decades to follow, this "second-first" welcome to Canada has loomed much larger than the first; but there have been reminders of the "first," and I should not neglect them.

After that interview, I went back to 20 South Drive to get acquainted with my hostess. In the morning I had been too flustered to realize that Mrs. Simon was speaking German and I English. The departure from camp, the bright lights of Montreal, the arrival in Toronto, the meeting with my hostess, and the impending interview, all this after a year and a half of gray sameness, had been too much at once, too sudden, too intense. But now, with the interview over and me so full of joy, I relaxed.

The word "joy," I believe, appears in these memoirs only a few times, only two of them crucial.

Not until 1948, when I was invited to join the staff, would the University of Toronto become the place I had no wish to leave. But Dean Brett's welcome in mid–December 1941 already made it home, or as close to home as was possible after 1933.[1]

The Simons had come from Vienna, luckily long before the *Anschluss*. Mrs. Simon, a widow who seemed of somewhat Victorian bent, made it easy for me, easier because of her graciousness, and because her background and mine were nearly the same— "nearly," for there *is* a difference between Austria and Germany, between cosmopolitan Vienna and middletown semi-Prussian Halle. (Once part of Saxony, the city had long been Prussian.) But there was also a much greater difference: the Simons had left before Hitler, and I, after six years in his *Reich*. Mrs. Simon had her sister living with her, a refugee from Munich where she had moved from Vienna. Once the newspapers reported a murder, prompting Mrs. Ullmann to say that Canada was a "wild country." I thought that nobody who had lived under Hitler could think of Canada as wild. For Mrs. Simon, I thought, but also for her sister, Vienna was still theater and music.

But recently, after all these years, I have checked with Ellen, the younger Simon daughter, and realized that I had it wrong: the Simon family had left long before the *Anschluss*, but the atmosphere had already been poisonous; her father had died while trying to save friends and even total strangers; and Ellen's mother, while a "private person," had invited me into their home in his memory.

I fell in love with Ellen Simon. My love was deep and lasted for years. Ellen, an artist, has lived in New York for decades, but she annually returns to Toronto. Now, after six decades, I view us as driven apart by events into opposite directions, both equally vital. Consider these returns: in 1998 Ellen, still living in New York, returned to Toronto again, after sixty years of "bearing witness" against war, for humanity, both emphasized in her most characteristic art work, "The Earth Mother, with Her Children, Black, Yellow, and White."

I knew she was friends with Barker Fairley, famous for his book on Goethe, but I did not know Fairley had also written on Heine. Ellen and I have one shared product in the dining hall of the University of Toronto's Trinity College: mine is David in her stained-glass window, hers is his dropping his weapon and reaching for his musical instrument. This joint product also marks our difference, for to me it is too soon to drop weapons and will remain so for a long time. Jerusalem still is embattled, but it is not, as critics charge, Sparta nor, as woolly friends wish, Athens.

And I, having moved to Jerusalem, returned to Halle on May 12, 1999, the sixtieth anniversary of my flight, exactly to the day, there to accept an honorary doctorate from my one-time *Heimat-universität* (home university), and hear my work described as a *Höllenfahrt der Selbsterkenntnis* (descent into hell of the self-knowledge). For many, the Holocaust, the Third Reich, the Second World War happened so long ago they are no longer true, and all who died—the Holocaust victims, the Allies fighting Hitler, and those who, like Jürgen Wenzlau, were manipulated into fighting for him—are almost forgotten. Hope, however, is needed, but it comes only with memory, at best from those who—as former *Heimatstadt* philosopher, much too young Rainer Enskat did—"visit the hell" of *Selbsterkenntnis*—"who would I be, had I lived then: a perpetrator; a bystander; an ordinary *Third Reich Krieger*, who didn't know and didn't want to; a victim?"[2]

Only through this "visit-in-hell" can there be "destructive recovery."[3]

Compared to my friends—Manfred had gone back to England but Heinz Warschauer had also come to Canada—I was lucky, not only with the university, but also with my hostess. Their respective hosts viewed the two "Heinzes" as temporary. (Henceforth I shall call Fischel "Henry," both because he changed his name and to avoid confusion.) But I was a member of the Simon family.

Other than the Simons, my friends were Heinz and Henry but soon also the Sauers. They had fled from Germany to Italy and then fled once more to Canada as farmers. As far as immigrants were concerned, Canada viewed only farmers with favor; the Sauers promised to farm, kept their promise, loved farming, but while he farmed, Hermann also had political thoughts; once we talked about neo-Nazis in Canada, and he said, the great thing about a farm was that, if someone was offensive, he could throw him out. Though much younger, Hermann Sauer was much like my father.

With the Simons I shared summer holidays and also their synagogue. My relation to Holy Blossom Temple abides to this day, largely because of the attitude shown there from the start.

This attitude was not the rule in Jewish Toronto. As ordained liberal rabbis, Henry and I thought Toronto must have a place for us, but there seemed to be no positions except for teaching the *aleph beth* to small children. Once, after constantly seeing pictures drawn by children, in proof of both their creativity and the progressiveness of the school, Henry said he felt like an iconoclast. Another incident was more serious. Principal W. R. Taylor of University College told us the university wanted Jewish Studies, and we seemed suitable teachers, so why didn't we go to the Canadian Jewish Congress in search of funding for this effort. This seemed odd, for beneficiaries to ask a charitable organization for money, in effect, for themselves. Still, if a principal had suggested it, it must be how things are done in Canada, so we went to the congress. The person we saw agreed that the organization wanted Jewish studies, but someone of the stature of Einstein; as for the two of us, there was a war on, so why didn't we work on a farm. I ran into this expert on Judaica some five years later. "I hear you got an appointment at the university," he said. "Do you know what I enjoy about it most?" I replied. "That I got it without your help." He looked at me blankly. I had not forgotten this early insult, but to him, insulting insecure refugees had meant nothing.

But based on my subsequent experience, the principal's advice reflects poorly on him too. At the time, the university was held together by compromise; as a graduate school, it encompassed all the colleges and the Pontifical Institute of Medieval Studies: everyone could teach Greek philosophy, Catholics only medieval, non-Catholics only modern philosophy.

But for undergraduates the compromise was between the university and the arts colleges, Saint Michael's (Catholic), Trinity (Anglican), Victoria (United Church), and University College (nondenominational). In philosophy, ethics belonged to the colleges, the rest of the discipline to the university. Principal Taylor of University College lectured on ancient Judaism, not, of course, from a Christian perspective, but from what was then called an "academic" point of view, with Jewish "particularism" superseded by Christian "universalism." (If this was supposed to be Hegel, it was a trivial version, almost a caricature.) Some Jews took the course, but not happily. Nobody then thought of having a professor for Jewish studies, and when Taylor did, he picked us two young ones and sent us to the Jewish community, expecting it to pay. He was actually a kind person, even my teacher in Arabic; Jews were simply inferior, in his supposed worldview.

I do not mention these incidents, because of how we felt—as refugees wanting no charity, gladly though it was given—but mainly for contrast with Holy Blossom. Henry taught there for a while and I for over a year, until my move to nearby Hamilton; and I resumed the relationship with that congregation when, five years later, I returned to Toronto as a member of the university faculty.

Indeed, to this day I belong to CCAR, the Central Conference of American Rabbis, not just out of habit, but mainly because of Holy Blossom, its friendship from the beginning and lasting still.

To jump way ahead, on my eightieth birthday, the temple had a party for me, attended by about a hundred Toronto friends. Among them were my closest, the Goulds and the Wintrobs.

Whenever I would travel—I am still jumping ahead way after our marriage in 1957—Rose almost always went with me; we would leave the children and our cat with Merle and Allan Gould. Merle learned to love cats. (One year we were in Chicago four times, for my speeches.) Allan writes books, one of which expressed a lasting concern of his: *What Did They Think of the Jews*.[4] (In a blurb, I ask why so many Gentiles have either hated or loved Jews, have not treated them like ordinary people; my answer: the Bible.) Allan is also a compulsive humorist; in his speech at the birthday party, he recalled my going to a fancy store for a suit and being told "the cheap ones are over there." Merle puts up with him, with both his seriousness and his compulsive humor.

Ralph Wintrob, long ago, was my student, in a course in medieval ethics at University College. Though the college was nondenominational, it wanted the course, but who could teach it? Neither Catholics nor Protestants still was the rule, lest it be partisan. And since my late colleague David Savan was Jewish, but secularist, a specialist on Spinoza and Peirce, the job fell to me. When Ralph once asked whether he should write on Augustine or Aquinas, I suggested Yehuda Halevi. Since then he has left Holy Blossom, joined the Orthodox congregation Sha'arei Shomayim and has become observant. (I could call him my convert, but since conversion was not part of my purpose, I think of him as a convert of Yehuda Halevi.) Whenever Rose and I would return to Toronto from Jerusalem, we stayed with Ralph and Kitty. Their daughter has been the best friend of our daughter, and Suzy and Suzanne are still in contact.

But my membership in the CCAR has always been troubling. Although originating in the nineteenth century, American Reform Judaism seems wedded to the Age of Enlightenment, incapable of a divorce even when one is needed. A religious movement is judged best by its prayer books, and since by 1975 much had happened in the world—and in the Jewish world!—the CCAR commissioned *The New Union Prayer Book*, to replace the *Union Prayer Book*, long in use. The new prayer book has a service for Israel, for, after all, the state *is* new, and also one for *Yom ha Shoah*, this latter, however, so fused with the Ninth of Av as virtually to wipe out the difference between one catastrophe Judaism has lived with—has long come to terms with—and one that still ought to haunt us. But most characteristic of that inability to divorce is a text in the old prayer book that the new just cannot abandon.

In the old *Union Prayer Book*, the Hanukkah hymn ends as follows:

> Children of the martyr race
> Whether free or fettered
> Wake the echoes of the songs
> Where you may be scattered
> Yours the message cheering
> That the time is nearing

Which will see
All men free
Tyrants disappearing.

What, other than the always offensive "martyr race," has changed? ("Always offensive" when sung by well-fed North Americans, the phrase is doubly so after Auschwitz. The harmless new words are "children of the Maccabees.") What else has changed? Nothing.

The worst war in history required the united forces of Stalin, Churchill, and Roosevelt (and after Roosevelt's death, Harry Truman, who destroyed the hopes of Hitler and Goebbels for another *grossen Friedrich* after the death of the czarina) to be won. Jews have suffered a catastrophe from which they have yet to recover and—unless Israel survives, has no enemies left, flourishes—may not. But the prayer still affirms progress, toward a time "near" at hand, when tyrants need not be fought any more but will "disappear."

When, as a small child, our daughter Suzy attended Holy Blossom, a teacher telephoned about Hanukkah and told my wife Reform Jews do not believe in miracles. "Then do we celebrate a victory?" Rose asked. The teacher told her to ask her husband. I said what she knew anyway, that Jews celebrate both the miracle and the victory—if they still can.

It must have been shortly after the pre–Six-Day War anxiety that I was part of a Holy Blossom dialogue with Albert Vorspan, my dialogue partner, then head of the CCAR Washington Social Action Committee. The subject was "The Ethics of Jewish Survival." After the two of us had done our part, someone got up to say he could not worry about his neighbor's toothache when his house was on fire. Vorspan replied: "But my house is on fire; it is the United States." The Judaism of the Social Action Committee has been called "the left wing of the U.S. Democratic Party, when on holiday."

After our marriage Rose did not feel happy with Holy Blossom: its services were too similar to what she was used to. We joined Orthodox Sha'arei Shomayim, which then had, luckily for us, Rabbi Emanuel Forman. The Formans were too restless with Toronto and moved to Israel about when we did. Before then, we once celebrated Passover Seder with them, also with the

Wintrobs, who now were in their congregation. I remember our reading in the Haggadah how Rabbis Eliezer, Joshua, Elazar ben Azarya, Akiba, and Tarfon spent the entire night recalling the Exodus, with us wondering, whether they had plotted a revolt against Rome: before our aliyah, we already were, in spirit, in Israel. There the Formans founded a congregation in Netanya, composed mostly of retirees from England; but they remained restless, even there. Once they spent a year in Hong Kong, then eight months in Bombay, after that two years in Montreal, always with a congregation in trouble, but always returning to Israel. A Toronto friend once asked Emanuel whether he was happy in Israel. Replying that his friend had never asked him that in Toronto, Emanuel offered to visit him on the Ninth of Av, there to mourn with him the ancient destruction of Jerusalem.

‡

Frankly, I have leapt ahead in my narrative to be done with the CCAR: I had not liked their "tyrants' disappearing" in the old version of the *Union Prayer Book;* and in 2000 they had a convention in Pittsburgh, of all places, where they invoked, without a tremor, Jews as "divinely singled out": as if their European brethren had not just been singled out for death. Pittsburgh was the place in 1885, where the "Pittsburgh Platform" had said "goodbye" to the Jews of Europe.

In Toronto, in the spring of 1942, my "second-first" welcome to Canada was less to Toronto Jewry than to the University of Toronto, and here, despite Brett's grandiose opening, tests would be in classes.

Since I had missed the discussion of pragmatism in a course that also covered logical positivism and Whitehead, my first test was unfortunate. At the mere age of twenty-four, A. J. Ayer had written *Language, Truth and Logic,* which had solved all philosophical problems and disposed of humanity's deepest convictions. That only two kinds of statement, logical and empirical, can be proved true or false is standard empiricism. But Ayer went further: nonempirical statements not only cannot be proved true or false; they cannot *be* true or false. "Murder is wrong" and "God exists" are pseudostatements, that is, disguised expressions of emotion; thus "murder is wrong" should be translated into "I 'dislike' or 'disapprove of' murder" and "God exists" into some such formula as "three cheers for the world."

I chuckle at the recollection of my first "contribution" to the seminar, for I have forgotten what I said, remembering only the heat with which I said it, and wonder now whether my heat had produced any light. The professor was the late Tom Goudge, subsequently a valued colleague, at the time a polite and gentle junior professor. What must he have thought of my storm and stress?

Did my 1942 heat have justification? I looked at Ayer's book again recently and found the following: "It is because argument fails us when we come to deal with pure questions of value, as distinct from questions of fact, that we finally resort to mere abuse."[5] In 1936, the year the book appeared, the Oxford Union had voted against fighting for King and Country. Three years later they rescinded their vote, not with a show of hands, but with their lives. And the "abuse" Winston Churchill hurled against Hitler was not caused by an inability to tell right from wrong.

Ayer's book was reprinted in 1946. The passage I have quoted was unchanged.

As little changed as another passage: "Those philosophers who fill their books with assertions that they intuitively 'know' this or that moral or religious truth are merely providing material for the psychoanalyst."[6]

I have never been able to think of Dietrich Bonhoeffer as providing material for the psychoanalyst. Or of Franz Rosenzweig doing so.

Years later, I found I had one thing in common with A. J. Ayer after all. He had been invited to Toronto to speak, and by then I was on the staff. I was coming back on a late plane from Ottawa, and so, presumably from a lecture like me, was he. He was the only passenger on the plane. Would I offend him if I sat somewhere else or be a bother if I sat next to him? I decided to sit next to him, and from his stiffening knew I had done the wrong thing. After an awkward few minutes I made another decision, and this time it was right. "On the plane," I said, "I always read a detective story." Ayer beamed and said, "So do I." He pulled out his detective story and I mine.

I have always had trouble with empiricists but have thought of them mostly as "insular," unconcerned with what went on outside Britain, even outside Oxford or Cambridge.[7]

After Ayer, in my first course A. N. Whitehead was a relief, if only because he was a metaphysician. But such enthusiasm as I had did not last long. After Kant, I could not take seriously philosophies that ignore him and are thus able to proceed from physics to metaphysics. Perhaps *Process and Reality* was a colossus, but it had feet of clay.

Kant was not ignored by Jacques Maritain, Etienne Gilson, and Gerald B. Phelan, all teachers of mine the next year at Toronto's Pontifical Institute for Medieval Studies, and all distinguished neo-Thomists. Phelan, no less distinguished, less well known only because he published little, was the institute's president. He was my teacher and met with me privately and regularly.

Whitehead ignores Kant. The three Thomists—in particular Maritain—confront him. In Kant's view the eye "sees," but the mind does not: "intellectual intuition" is but a philosopher's mistake. Continuing in the Platonic-Aristotelian tradition, neo-Thomists rediscover, on the contrary, that the mind does see. Indeed, quite apart from the *philosophia perennis,* they do some "seeing" of their own. "There are philosophers who see and philosophers who do not," writes Maritain boldly, alluding to, among the nonseeing, none other than Kant.

The private seminar given by Father Phelan was on Thomas Aquinas's *De Ente et Essentia.* The philosopher strips away empirical particularity, say, from a stone or a tree, radically, until none is left. Is *anything* left? For the Thomist there is. He is ready to "see" that "Being is."

Once, years later, an argument started between Gilson and myself, in the midst of a Ph.D. dissertation examination in which we were both examiners: it was about Athens and Jerusalem. In the Bible "the people will ask me," Moses says to God, "who has sent me," and *"sum qui sum"* (I am who I am) is the divine reply (Exod. 3:14). Gilson was famous for taking this text as a Jewish "correction" of Greek metaphysics. But our student quoted me, or Martin Buber through me, that *sum qui sum* mistranslates *ehye asher ehyeh;* that "I shall be who I shall be" means "listen to the future and my word in it." But good philosophy has often come from bad translations; the case "Athens and Jerusalem" is alive to this day.

Once I came into Father Phelan's office and saw a pamphlet on "Saint Thomas and the Jews," written by a French Canadian Catholic. I wanted it, but he didn't want to give it to me, yet finally did. The pamphlet had collected Thomistic passages rejecting Jewish emancipation. Phelan and I never discussed that pamphlet or the subject, for we then thought that, in waging war on the evils of our time, what mattered was defense of the True, the Good, the Beautiful; all the rest was derivative.

My view at the time is not mine anymore.[8] Then, after all the crisis philosophy in "old world" Europe, it was exhilarating to come, in the "New World," upon philosophies reaffirming the *philosophia perennis* and its verities. But although exhilarating, it did not remain convincing. Leo Strauss's retrieval, after Heidegger, of Plato and Maimonides has remained. Maritain, Gilson, and Phelan have not.[9]

But these neo-Thomists were not indifferent to what was happening. Phelan gave me a speech by Judah Magnes, in which the Hebrew University president quotes Psalm 44:23: "for Thy sake we are killed every day." And Jacques Maritain (whose wife was Jewish) coined a sentence, the full meaning of which must still be expressed by the Vatican: "The people of Christ have become the Christ of the peoples."

After Brett's death, F. H. Anderson became head of the department. He once told me that he staked his reputation on the department's quality, and with this judgment I fully agreed.

Anderson was a Bacon and Locke scholar and was rumored to be a Platonist, but no one could have guessed it from the conduct of his seminar "Relations between Metaphysics and Epistemology." This seminar was famous, but many considered it notorious. John Laird was a butcher, Anderson once said to me, and on this I could bear him out. But many considered Anderson a butcher also, and like Laird, he looked formidable and acted formidable in class. But Anderson was no butcher; his acting formidable was a teaching style he had devised for a purpose itself formidable, strenuous philosophical thought. For his seminar one did not wade through many books or search for esoteric references nor even struggle with a difficult text. Such efforts might have served the evasion of sheer, relentless thought. "For next week"—to give an example—"I want you to write an essay about the mind: the logical mind, the psychological mind, the epistemological mind, the metaphysical mind." One was not to quote this or that philosopher, and the essay was to be no longer than five pages—short enough for close grilling. One such paper of five pages was often harder to write and defend than would have been a thirty-page paper. And preparing for Anderson's seminar often meant neglecting one's other work.

I have had three great teachers in philosophy: Arnold Metzger, Leo Strauss, and Fulton Henry Anderson. Metzger inspired by making philosophy seem momentous: nothing less than the presence—or absence—of "the Absolute" in Nazi Berlin was in question. Strauss never taught me, but as a mentor made me take texts seriously. Torturing my mind with philosophical problems, Anderson taught me to torture my mind myself.

I did not complete my thesis until 1945, but the end of the Anderson seminar in 1943 also was the end of my university attendance, with the Ph.D. comprehensive exams, written and oral.

Of the orals I remember the last question, Anderson's. "What is metaphysics?" he asked, sounding as formidable as ever. "It is the human attempt to achieve self-transcendence," I replied. I was an existentialist of sorts then and maybe still am. "That's just a psychological definition," Anderson shot back. "It is an attempt," I corrected, transforming a psychological into an epistemological statement, "that sometimes succeeds." Anderson laughed, and with his laugh my time with the University of Toronto, for the time being, was over.

10

Second Rabbinate, Hamilton
1943–1948

"We all know what is happening. Why twist the knife? Why don't you stop it?" Jack Mandell, president of Congregation Anshe Shalom in Hamilton, Canada, posed this question. This position was my first congregation but, after Sherbrooke, my second rabbinate. After the congregation in Hamilton, there has been no other.

I came to Hamilton when the Holocaust was at its worst, and while we did not know nearly everything, even approximately, we knew enough. I introduced a prayer for Shabbat services, in memory of Jews murdered during that week. We were impotent, but the least we could do was remember the victims in prayer. But when Jack, a Jew from Eastern Europe with relatives there, asked me to stop, I stopped. I still don't know whether I did the right thing.

That incident comes to my mind now: I was not aware of its full significance then. Despite what had happened in the eight years since that train ride to Berlin, my outlook was still what it had been in 1935, because of a religious commitment I had already made: the true Jewish response to Nazism was renewal of Judaism. Thus when Leo Barnett, a wealthy member of my new congregation, wanted to spend some money on me, I asked him to print and distribute among Hamilton Jewry an essay I had written for that purpose. I called it "The Jewish Problem: Judaism."

This may be a better way to begin my memories of Hamilton: I learned that my Men's Club sponsored lectures, so I offered a year-long course, not on esoteric philosophy or theology, but on plain, down-to-earth history. But the club at once reduced my lecture time to three evenings, one each for ancient, medieval, and modern: I had not been down-to-earth enough. That even this reduction did not suffice I found out after my first lecture. The chairman suggested a change: he knew a detective and could get him to talk about investigating. My lecture must have been pretty bad, but perhaps not as bad as that of the proverbial clergyman, straight from theological school: "Dear friends! You must often have wondered whether the ontological argument for the existence of God is really valid."

But this is not the right beginning either, for it makes me sound like a snob, and if I had not learned to appreciate *amcha* in the Halle Turnverein, I learned it in Sachsenhausen. The Men's Club was composed of ordinary fellows, getting together twice a month for cigars, cards, but also, after a day's long hours, for some—not too much—education.

The true beginning of the Hamilton story is different still. The congregation that employed me was small, just over fifty families, almost a club, and my duties were light. Friday night services, Sunday morning school, twice weekly Hebrew lessons, twice monthly the Men's Club, and the few weddings and funerals that there were during the year. I rarely had a minyan even for Shabbat morning services.

Once only an old codger named Goldberg showed up, and while we vainly waited for others, he explained why he had come and how he was urging others to come as well. "When your store is full, you feel pretty good," so he reported the argument he was giving to others, then asked me whether he was right or wrong. "And you feel bad when your store is empty," he continued, still anxious to get my assurance that he was right rather than wrong. "And why is this so? Because the store is your racket! So come to the synagogue, for this is the rabbi's racket." I vaguely recall that, fortunately, this time he forgot to ask whether he was right or wrong.

My paid duties to my congregation, then, were light, but my unpaid ones, largely of my own conscience, were heavy, for Hamilton had a Jewish population of three thousand. I belonged to the ministerial association, was chairman of committees, head of public relations, and there never seemed to be an evening when some of us were not together in a committee.

Perhaps I should say *huddled* together, for the meetings rarely had more than a trivial purpose and more than trifling results. For about the big purpose—rescuing Jews—we could do nothing, and our impotence was not often far from our minds and rarely from mine.

Once I spoke to the Hamilton ministerial association about Sachsenhausen. The association consisted of Protestant ministers and the Reform rabbi. (My predecessor, Rabbi Feldman, had helped found it.) This being war time, my speech was popular, and many churches wanted me to repeat it. But I kept being dismayed by one response from Christians, so it seemed, mostly from women: "Isn't there a Hitler in all of us?" I failed to convey the unique horror that Canadian soldiers, even then, were fighting. Or the temptation Christians in Germany had to resist but, for the most part, did not.

Once the *Hamilton Spectator* published a story or editorial, I forget which, to the effect that too many Jews were communists, and that in this they were playing with fire. A Hamilton professor, Watson Kirkconnell, had taken the trouble to study the ethnic press in Canada and found that in all cases except the Jewish, the papers were divided into communist and anticommunist. We couldn't explain to Kirkconnell that, with the Nazis murdering all Jews, we couldn't afford these internecine quarrels.

This did not mean that the communists did not exploit the tolerance of the Jewish community. For a while one of them, a man by the name of Paikin, was president of the Hamilton Jewish community, for the simple reason that no one else wanted the job that much; Paikin also ran the small paper the community published from time to time.

One raw deal of Paikin's still sticks in my memory. He once suggested three editorials for a Passover issue, one by my Orthodox colleague, one by me, a third by himself. To keep Paikin out, I said that one was enough, and that my Orthodox colleague should write it. Paikin made himself ridiculous by arguing that as a Reform rabbi, I could not agree with orthodoxy, yet the one editorial was decided on, to be written by the Orthodox rabbi. This was on a Sunday. On Tuesday he called an emergency meeting, attended only by his two or three stooges. What was the emergency? The rabbi had invoked miracles, and these could not be community opinion! So the three or four of them decided to reject the Orthodox story and published Paikin's Marxist interpretation of Passover; for this I demanded and got Paikin's resignation.

Compared to what was at stake for the world—for Jews!— these and other Hamilton fights I could relate were tempests in a teapot. But I already knew from Sherbrooke that, for communists, there are no teapot tempests.

Since I was in charge of public relations, I had many trivial experiences, but only one that was dramatic and important. The war was over, Ernest Bevin was British foreign secretary, and survivors had organized Brichah, trying to get into Palestine whether Bevin liked it or not. United Nations Relief and Rehabilitation Administration (UNNRA) representative Frederick Morgan, although reportedly a warm human being, was cajoled by reporters into talking like Bevin, that these Brichah refugees had "pockets bulging with money."[1] I called a meeting, of course, and while all I could think of was yet another letter to the paper, a member of my committee who was the head of a radio station had a reporter phone a well-known friend of refugees; the next day his interview was all over Canada. I remember station CHML, but have forgotten the name of its enterprising head and also the name of the friend of refugees.

In this difficult postwar situation, two lecturers came to the Hamilton Jewish community, one a problem for me, the public relations chairman, the other, a wonderful solution. (Must all Jewish "public relations" be negative, i.e., against anti-Semitism? Can some of it not be positive?) Ludwig Lewinsohn, an American Jewish writer famous at the time, made a speech declaring war on the British Empire, which was widely reported. But not only did the empire-loving *Hamilton Spectator* dislike it, but Jews, too, thought it was ill advised. Despite Bevin, I myself had to remember that the present troubles of the British Empire were attributable to Winston Churchill's courage in 1940; Jewish leaders in Palestine had opposed the prewar White Paper, virtually ending Jewish immigration, yet, with few exceptions, their slogan supported—had to support—Britain in the war effort.

The other speaker to the Jewish community was Ruth Gruber, then unknown, drawing no reporters, but giving so impassioned a speech on Jewish refugees as to have us all in tears, making us better Jews, more caring human beings. As for me, never before did I love a lecture so much as love the lecturer.

Ruth Gruber's picture was recently in the papers, at eighty-eight, still beautiful, still working. The reporter asked her how she does it. Her answer: never, never, never retire.

One incident I remember because I looked on it in one way at the time, but in quite another some thirty-five years later. Jewish immigration to Canada had begun later than to the United States, so Hamilton had four Orthodox congregations, all East European, and just one assimilated and Reform, mine. As chairman of public relations, I once was phoned by one of the Orthodox congregations: an emergency, come down at once! I jumped on the bus. What had happened? Some kids had thrown stones at synagogue windows and broken them! I explained they might have thrown them at a church also and went home thinking some Jews still fear an anti-Semite behind every bush.

I spoke of this incident differently in one of the lectures in the Harry S. Crowe Memorial series at Toronto's York University in 1982. Crowe had been a professor at York University who had headed an annual University of Toronto symposium in the huge convocation hall. Rather than address the merits and drawbacks of Zionism, the symposium was straight Zionist; the critics of Zionism, protesting with signs and posters outside, Crowe had felt, could have their own meeting at some other time. The lecture series was in honor of Crowe's memory.

On this occasion I said that these Jewish newcomers from Europe, of thirty-five or so years ago, had every right to fear the worst, for in Europe virulent anti-Semitism was rampant. And while Canadian soldiers were then fighting Hitler, they did not like to think of themselves as fighting for Jews and never were told to. Even so, these old, unassimilated Jews had had enough trust in Canada to want me to write letters to papers all over the country.

What, in those five years, did I do for Anshe Shalom, my own congregation? Perhaps just one of my actions had lasting impact. As I have said, the congregation was like a club, and the school was as if for the club's children. Of the fifty or so members, quite a few were aged, and of the four or five classes, there were two or three kids in each. My action was to open the school to all Hamilton Jews, and as a result many formerly unaffiliated Jews became members.

My action ran afoul of the synagogue's club mentality, as had happened once before. Some nonmembers had wanted to get married at Anshe Shalom, and the then-president, J. J. Morris, had said the bylaws forbade it, and he was their guardian. I actually found some bylaws—they must have been old—that said nonmembers could get married in the synagogue for two dollars. Feeling like Perry Mason, I waved these bylaws at Morris during a stormy meeting.

The club mentality reared its head again when I argued about the school, even though as a consequence the synagogue grew, and some of the unaffiliated became members.

However, the congregation would pay only for its children, not for all these others. In response, I formed an anticlub committee. I organized an annual concert, with a program containing ads, which the half-dozen committee members would get people to sponsor.

The other committee members got a few customers. But for Lou Rosing, collecting the lion's share seemed to become the meaning of his life. We often had lunch, with him always telling the waitress "no bread," but nonetheless losing his fight against becoming overweight. He would ask me what I knew, "What do you know?" and I said "nothing" and then asked him the same, "What do you know?" and he said "not much"; there was not a great deal of brilliance by way of luncheon talk. But I never forgot Lou Rosing.

Lou must long be gone, and we don't know much about the world to come. But Lou Rosing must still be buttonholing people for an ad, crossing the street to catch someone trying to avoid him, for even in the world to come Jewish children must have a Jewish education.

‡

As I said in the introduction, I wrote an addition to this chapter in 2001: When I first wrote the chapter, I must have been affected by Jack Mandell in the beginning, Lou Rosing at the end, in between especially by committees huddling together in evenings, solving trivial problems, impotent regarding the big one, saving Jews: the time was the Holocaust at its worst. But I forgot to write about what I did most mornings. Now, I must add something I originally omitted, lest my development as a Jewish philosopher be incomplete.

As far back as in Berlin, Leo Strauss, never my teacher but subsequently my mentor, had made me think about medieval Arabic philosophy, its dependence on the Greek, and it influence on the Jewish. I was determined to become a Jewish philosopher, not, however, a parochial one. Back in Aberdeen I had used my time, short as I knew it would be, to begin a thesis on Ibn Rushd, known in Latin as Averroës. He is supposed to have said that all truth available is in Aristotle: no wonder most of his books are commentaries on the Stagirite! Even so, what remained for him of Islam?

I did better in Toronto than in Aberdeen, although none of my supervisors was a specialist either. Still, I had Father Gerald B. Phelan in Medieval Latin philosophy, W. R. Taylor on Arabic, and, of course, F. H. Anderson. I finished the thesis in 1945: "Substance and Perseity in Medieval Arabic Philosophy, with Introductory Chapters on Aristotle, Plotinus, and Proclus." It may sound formidable, but it had become manageable, because I could show the interplay between Aristotle, neo-Platonism, and the several Muslim philosophers, of whom Ibn Rushd was only the last. The main Muslim contribution was a concept of *perseitas*, an ontological distinction between God and everything else.

And what of my remaining Hamilton years? 1947 saw the publication of my first essay on Maimonides and the *falasifa*, Muslim philosophers: I would be a Jewish philosopher, but not a parochial one.

My whole family together, before catastrophe. Taken on a Sunday afternoon's *Kaffeeklatsch* around 1933, maybe grandmother's seventieth birthday, at my family's home. The picture was taken on the rare occasion of a visit to Halle by Aunt Martha Fröhlich from Berlin and Aunt Trude Fackenheim from Kassel. From left to right: my brother, Wolfgang; my brother, Alexander; my aunt, Trude Fackenheim (standing); my aunt, Erna Goldberg; my mother, Meta Fackenheim; my grandmother, Flora Schlesinger; my great-aunt, Martha Fröhlich; me; my uncle, RA Adolf Goldberg. My father, Julius Fackenheim, took the picture.

Grandmother Ozi, with nurse, in the backyard of the Fackenheim home in Halle, 1934 or 1935. My grandmother was a Victorian woman before her time, when her husband died, after whom I am named, she took his place in the three-story hardware store, which was co-owned by a gentile. I loved her and when she had a stroke at about age seventy I was greatly aggrieved, even though, with the help of the nurse in the picture, she still tried to look as strong as possible.

Me, age sixteen in 1933 or 1934, at a meeting of the BdjJ, of which I was the local leader. This is the only picture I still have of myself as local leader of a German Jewish group when German Jewry still seemed to have a chance. By 1935 we had changed our minds. But even in 1935 I would not have thought I would become a Zionist and, going further, actually practice it by moving to Jerusalem. To my left is Inge Burckhardt, an unidentified girl, and Eva Cohn.

Dancing lessons, a Jewish group with a gentile teacher in 1933 or 1934. It shows a time when as Jews we still thought it possible to somehow survive the Nazi regime, hoping of course for a speedy end. I am sitting at the far left of the front row.

HTV 04, in Halle, 1933 or 1934. The Jewish sports club was still playing with the local gentile sports club in Halle in 1933 until the Nazis expelled us from the *Deutsche Turnerschaft*. Thereafter, we could play only with other Jewish clubs, thus visiting Dresden once and the Dresden sports club coming in return to Halle. On this occasion RA Fackenheim had to fight for a field for the groups to play on. In the background a fairly large crowd is looking on. After the expulsion from the *Deutsche Turnerschaft* the sports club

played once again, on the initiative of RA Fackenheim, *Faustball* with a gentile group. I am next to Erich Kohlhagen, who later in Sachsenhausen became my friend after all the others had left and who survived the whole war in concentration camp. When I visited his family in Dayton, Ohio, he had already died. Back row, from left to right: Erich Kohlhagen, me, one of the Bluth twins, unknown, the other of the Bluth twins, unknown, unknown, Alexander Fackenheim; front row: all unknown.

Alexander Fackenheim, me, Wolf-gang Fackenheim. These pictures were taken after 1935, but before Kris-tallnacht in 1938. When the family was still together, the enormity of the Nazi assault was not yet known, could not have been.

Meta Fackenheim, RA Dr. Julius Fackenheim, Trude Fackenheim. These pictures were taken in Germany at about
the same time as the pictures of the
three brothers, perhaps for an identifi-
cation card or passport, which might
have been true also for our pictures.
After years of Nazism my mother already looks sad but my father's *Haltung* (attitude) still remains intact. I
remember Aunt Trude very fondly.
She married a war-blinded man and
lived to ninety-six. She and her husband survived Theresienstadt and he,
helpless because he was blind, saved
her life three times. In Theresienstadt
they wanted to deport her, but when
he said he would go if she went, they
left them alone. This at least is what I
guessed.

My brother Wolfgang and my aunt Erna in 1937 or 1938, before, in Kristall-nacht, she committed suicide.

The picture, *top left*, was taken on the occasion of the quartet's performance at my family's home in Halle, probably in 1934. This picture is important for two reasons: first, the band came to the our home, for only there were there drums; second, the whole Wenzlau family attended, including our teacher—they were all anti-Nazis. Front row, left to right: our quartet, Jürgen Wenzlau, me, Gustav Hennig, Herbert Thiess; second row, Alexander Fackenheim, Trude Fackenheim, Jürgen Wenzlau's older brother; third row, Meta Fackenheim, Jürgen Wenzlau's father (our teacher at the Halle *Stadtgymnasium*), Jürgen Wenzlau's mother, Wolfgang Fackenheim; back row, the two sisters of Jürgen Wenzlau.

Three Campbell boys I was friendly with in Aberdeen and in whose house I stayed for two months. Once I was joking with one of them who said he might get involved with politics and I said, "Maybe you will be a prime minister but better than Chamberlain." There was stunned silence. Mrs. Campbell said, "You are welcome here, but not if you criticize our government." Thirty years later I knew she was right. Chamberlain declared war on Hitler because Hitler had broken his promise. Arafat has broken more promises than I can count, but what has been the response?

The *Hochschule* in 1937, while the whole group still was there. After the Kristallnacht of November 9, 1938, everything collapsed. But Leo Baeck still taught until the *Hochschule* was closed in 1942. Baeck sits on the very right; Ismar Elbogen stands next to Baeck; Moshe Sister stands in the aisle between Elbogen and Baeck; Mrs. Elbogen sits next to Elbogen; then there are two unidentified women and an unidentified man; Max Wiener, standing with folded hands; cantor Heiser stands behind Wiener; in the middle is Rautenberg and next to him is Harff; and Alexander Guttman, standing with crossed arms. I am in the back row in front of the left side of the middle shelf, with glasses.

Leo Baeck with Martin Buber, in London on the occasion of Buber's visit in 1947. Two of the greatest Jewish leaders at the final collapse. One, Buber, whose thought I followed as much as possible, the other, Baeck, my teacher, in the most terrible period of German Judaism. Both survived and went on teaching.

Georg Wilhelm Friedrich Hegel. When I first taught a graduate course it was on the British Hegelian F. H. Bradley's *Appearance and Reality,* called by a wit the *Disappearance of Reality.* Unlike Bradley, Hegel himself was first to take history seriously, but unlike Heidegger, honestly, for he was also deeply puzzled by the survival of Jews and the continued relevance of Jewish monotheism. Not without reason did I spend ten years of my life on a book on Hegel, not to mention teaching a course on him until my retirement. This image hangs in a frame on the wall of my study in Jerusalem.

Franz Rosenzweig is uniquely tragic—perhaps in all philosophy, certainly Jewish—because for me he was the greatest Jewish philosopher in modernity, who died less than four years before the Hitler *Machtergreifung.* His one hundredth birthday in 1986 was commemorated in Kassel, the city of his birth. The two volumes on him edited by Wolfdietrich Schmied-Kowarzik were both heroic and quixotic; but because of the honesty of the editor I came back to Kassel for three months in 1996.

Friedrich Wilhelm Joseph von Schelling. There is a painting of Schelling in his late twenties, already famous then, which differs greatly from this image. Here, in his sixties, Schelling has perceived evil. His thought was that all previous philosophy, not only Hegel's but also is own, had only been of "essence"; now a "leap" was necessary to existence—not only the existence of God, but *all* of it.

Meta and Julius Fackenheim. This picture, taken some time around 1948, is grievous, even though my parents had escaped to Scotland, for the Gestapo had forced them to flee and they had to leave my older brother Alex behind. I tried to arrange for him to escape to friends in neutral Ireland, but could not do it, for the war had already begun. My parents express these circumstances; my father took a strong *Haltung* to whatever happened, but my mother shows more. She simply could not do it.

Me with Michael, three months after his birth in summer 1961. Rose and I were very happy with our first child. Only more than two years later did we discover it is bad when a child does not cry and makes no fuss. Michael is autistic, but we were lucky when Dr. Havlikova told us the truth. We rejected it, of course, but had to accept it in the end.

William Alan Frazer (Wolfgang Amadeus Fackenheim) and Suzy in 1985 on the occasion of his only visit to Israel with his wife Edith. I did not mind my brother changing his name. Unlike in Canada, it was almost necessary in England—he never would have been honored by the Queen of England without the change. While in Israel he insisted on climbing Masada. He died six weeks later of cancer.

Suzy preparing lunch for Yossi in the kitchen of our home in Jerusalem in 1987. When Rose and I told Suzy and David that we were having another child Suzy named him Yossi. Most times when we climbed Mount Sinai she had a crush on the guide called Yossi. Yossi, of course, is short for Joseph.

Bob Miller, retired and living on Vancouver Island, after 1992. Bob was the greatest Christian preacher I ever heard, but after he faced the Holocaust he never preached again. I included a section on Christianity in my *To Mend the World* hoping that he could preach again. Thereafter Bob opened the Bob Miller Book Room which, to my knowledge, is still in existence and where my wife Rose worked for years. Also, the book room was a place where Jews and Christians could engage in dialogue.

Rose and me in 1992. We had already moved to Israel, but Rose had not yet shown symptoms of Alzheimer's.

While teaching at Kassel University in 1996, I went on a visit to London on the occasion of my grandson's circumcision. I visited Ilse Strauss, the daughter of Curt and Hannah Lewin, and we talked about old times, especially about Reinhard Heydrich, who had been their neighbor. When my father was in Buchenwald, I in Sachsenhausen, and Wolfgang imprisoned in Stuttgart, my mother was alone in the house and Hannah Lewin invited her to move in with them. So far as I knew, Curt was the only male in Halle left alone. Heydrich had protected him. After Heydrich was assassinated there was no one to protect Ilse's parents, and they were murdered in the Holocaust.

In front of the former Fackenheim home in Wettiner Strasse 17, Halle/Saale, Germany, in 1993. On my first visit to Halle fifty-four years after fleeing, and only because Halle was no longer communist, I went to see our house. It was one of the few houses in the street whose windows were not smashed when the bourgeoisie fled from the communists at the end of World War II. The people my father had sold the house to in 1939 were still there in 1993. It was this house, since Bar Mitzvah days, that I had been brought up. I looked at the name of the owners, but even though they buzzed I would not go in.

When I was a student the *Stephanskirche* was opposite our house, with a swastika flag hanging outside, at least from 1935 on. But even before the Nazis, "Jewish-Christian dialogue" was impossible in Germany, as Eberhard Bethge has testified. Even between Leo Baeck and Dietrich Bonhoeffer, both in Berlin, it was unthinkable.

Visiting the former *Stadtgymnasium*, where I had been a student for nine years. It is still a school. I talked to the students, of course, and found them receptive. But it was the teachers who shocked me. One mentioned that Bruno Heydrich had been music director, but none of them seemed to know that Reinhard Heydrich was his son: communist education, including neglecting the Holocaust, must have been thorough.

Standing on the stairs in front of the entrance of the destroyed Halle synagogue with Guenther Helbig, the president of the community, who lived in Berlin. In Halle there were only a handful of Jews, of them only a few survivors. Unlike synagogues in Berlin this one was in a back alley; even so the Nazis had burned it. This is enough reason for me never to go back to Germany to live: the Jewish-Christian dialogue, necessary after the Holocaust, has not even started. Already during communist times the architectural remnant of the synagogue was turned into a monument.

Veranstaltungskalender des Leopold-Zunz-Zentrum zur Erforschung des Europäischen Judentums/ Stiftung LEUCOREA in Wittenberg/ Seminar für Jüdische Studien Martin Luther-Universität Halle/Wittenberg/ Sommersemester 1998, on the cover a picture of Leopold Zunz, taken in Berlin, 1869, by Julius Löwensohn. In 1823 Zunz got his Ph.D. at Halle. After German reunification, they established a Zunz-Institute for the study of Jews in Europe.

A statue of Georg Friedrich Händel, born in Halle in 1685, on the Halle *Marktplatz*. I got this picture especially for this purpose from the Oberbürgermeisterin of Halle, Frau Ingrid Häussler, who showed a remarkable interest in Jewish philosophy. Händel lived most of his life in England, of course, but Halle never forgot him. The Nazis would doubtless have destroyed the statue had they had their thousand years, even though twelve years were enough for them to make Germany *judenrein*. Luckily for Germany and the world, they had only twelve. (G. Hensling, Stadt Halle [Saale], Presseamt/ Bildstelle, D-06 100 Halle [Saale])

Attended by Oberbuergermeister, a.D. der Stadt Halle, Dr. Klaus Rauen, I entered my name in the *Goldenes Buch* of the city Halle during a reception in the city hall's festive rooms in May 1999. I knew right away I had to accept when my *Heimatstadt Universität* offered me an honorary doctorate, simply because it was so long ago and one cannot hold the grandchildren responsible for what their elders did. Moreover, when Rector Kreckel publicly apologized for Halle University's theft of my father's doctorate—which he had honestly got—and Dean Schenkluhn said a veritable *Graben*, "abyss," separates the university now from the university then, I was happy I had come.

Receiving an honorary doctorate from Martin Luther-Universitaet Halle/Wittenberg and lecturing on the occasion of my visit to my *Heimatstadt*, May 12, 1999. The following quotation was publicized: "If you want to honor me, you have to listen to me."

Bernburg used to be a *Heil-und Pflegeanstalt*, an institute for healing and comfort. In Nazi times they were still healing and comforting the fit, while in one room in one of the basements they murdered the "insane," among them my uncle Adolf.

When I visited Bernburg for the first time in July 2002, I placed a plate commemorating my uncle in one of the rooms used for murder.

The house in which the Heydrichs and the Lewins lived. The Lewin family lived on the first floor (not the ground floor), the Heydrich family on the second floor.

This picture was taken in July 2002. The occasion was a stone consecration for my older brother, Ernst Alexander Fackenheim, who was stuck in Germany and died on April 22, 1941. I was at the Weissensee cemetery, at one time Europe's largest Jewish cemetery, once before with Professor Peter von der Osten-Sacken. Only after I decided there was room in Germany not only for Jews but also the Jewish religion did I feel up to erecting the stone.

A May 2001 family reunion in special celebration of three events at once: my eighty-fifth birthday, the engagement of my son Yossi, and the birth of my youngest grandchild Gideon. The greatest thing for me was that all the family was together including not only those in Jerusalem, but also Suzy, Mark and their children from London. This was the end; the beginning had been the 1924 picture, and it is a complete refutation of Hitler's Weltanschauung. When I married Rose, a Protestant of Hungarian extraction, she, at twenty-five, persuaded me, at forty-one, that I was not too old for children. She converted to Judaism only when we were in Jerusalem, for only then was it "for real." Also, Mark is not Jewish, hence Benjy is 25 percent non-Aryan but looks like a super-Aryan. To refute the Nazi Weltanschaung was, of course, not my intention; but I still fail to understand that the people that once had a "golden age" of philosophers embraced this so-called "Rausch" of an Aryan–non-Aryan dichotomy. Front row, left to right: Adam and Dan Aryeh, Daniella and Benjy Goodwin; sitting: me; back row: Iris and Yossi, David and Wendy Aryeh with Gideon, Suzy and Mark Goodwin.

11

"At Home in Toronto," or "Wearing Two Hats"
1948–1967

The reader will recall that I began these memoirs in 1993, when my wife, Rose, a victim of Alzheimer's, was no longer at home. I also wrote that this epitaph is about German Judaism, that everything merely personal will interest only family and friends. But as I continued writing I found this distinction too rigid: After all, merely personal events and experiences about German Jews, too, are about German Judaism. But where to include them? Perhaps best in this chapter about "being at home," just when Rose could no longer be at home. Sad, even absurd, but appropriate.

Rose died on June 21, 1998, after not recognizing anyone anymore. I owe it to her memory to complete these memoirs, which I did in 2000. But I also owe it to her to write about personal matters. The reader will therefore have to be patient until I get to the proper subject of this chapter, "two hats" in Toronto.

One personal fact I should say at once: Rose was a Christian who, precisely because she was serious about Christianity, could not understand how Christians could have committed the Holocaust; she converted to Judaism, but only after we moved to Israel.

"Why not at marriage? Why now?" her orthodox *bet din* in New York asked. "Because now it is for real," Rose replied.

My friend, the late Rabbi Walter Wuerzburger, then of Sha'arei Shamayim of Toronto, since then of New York, vouched for us when the Orthodox *bet din* converted Suzy and David as children, later also he vouched for Rose herself.

Intermarriage was not easy for either of us, but in retrospect it was easier because Rose took Christianity seriously. (This seriousness also motivated her master's thesis on Orwell and Koestler for the English Department. She also took a course on the Bible at Victoria College with famous English scholar Northrop Frye; she took issue with him for not taking Christianity seriously.)

We were always in harmony on crucial issues: having children, Jewish children, moving to Israel; once she taught David a poem he still remembers, about not feeling sorry for oneself in adversity.

Yet there were personal problems, of course: her parents were recent immigrants from Hungary and—of their two children, brother Mikey was sure to marry an "English" girl—they were hoping for a Hungarian son-in-law. As I will mention more fully in context—in a religious, even theological one—before we ever met, she and her friend Shirley Dorin had gone to Europe for a year, to discover how even nominal Christians could have carried out the Holocaust, even passively let it happen; but when she came back, she still had no answer. Despite limited education, or perhaps because of it, her father, now dead, had been a thoughtful person, including about religion. Much to her credit, her mother tried her best to relate to Rose's Alzheimer's, when we visited her twice in Calgary.

I must not give the impression that her parents did not feel at home in Calgary. In the "Old Shatterhand" days of my youth, I would have loved the Calgary Stampede. But when I got there I said the wrong thing for everybody, Hungarians included: "If you have seen one horse, you have seen them all." I even met a friend of Herman Dorin, a famous Stampede rider, but my attempts at "dialogue" had no response; even when I talked about the weather, he said only, "Yup."

After moving to Israel we could visit only rarely. But we had visited regularly from Toronto and often had steak or hamburgers in the bush. Rose's dad liked his whiskey, always brought it along. Once a bear sat down next to the bottle. He had a hard time chasing it away.

Even after Rose's death, I regret that we had eloped. Only Gene and Estelle Borowitz and two witnesses were present at the wedding, all four there for me. Nobody was there for her: we should have invited her parents. But at the time, in 1957, I was still preoccupied with my problem of marrying a Christian and gave too little thought to her problem of marrying a Jew.

At her funeral I stressed two blessings she had left behind. She had persuaded me that, at forty-one, I was not too old for children, and her persuasion lasted: at Yossi's birth in 1979, she was forty-seven and I sixty-three. Michael had been the first; unhappily he was autistic since birth and institutionalized in Canada. (It is a long story, but we could not bring him to Israel, and this delayed our aliyah.) Suzy and her husband, Mark, are in London; David and his wife, Wendy, here in Jerusalem; and Yossi mostly with me. I have five grandchildren: Daniella and Benjy in London; Dan and Adam in Jerusalem; and—an important event in 2001—David and Wendy just had Gideon.

Years after our immigration, at eighty-four, I walk better with a cane, and when I carry it they are polite at the bank. David left polite-enough Canada at sixteen and has sometimes asked to borrow my cane; his "polite if with cane" has become a family joke, extending even to the Filipino woman now with me. (She told it at the Interior Ministry, where she once lined up for hours for a visa that was not yet there, telling them that if it was not there again, she would bring my cane; but it was there that time, and they laughed.) David has been in the army for three years, and neither there nor elsewhere are Israelis known for their politeness. There are many jokes, one I learned from the mayor of Tel Aviv. A reporter asked four people the same question: "Excuse me, but what is your opinion of the price of meat?" The Russian asked, "What is opinion?" The Pole asked, "What is meat?" The American asked, "What is price?" And the Israeli asked, "What is excuse me?"

Suzy is "with me" through her presents; she gave me *Finest Hour*, the BBC documentary on Britain in 1940, inspired by Churchill and Martin Gilbert. I once visited Gilbert in London: he had a room for every book he was writing; I told him that he was enough to lift the morale of British Jewry, not only in hard times but also in easy ones.

Yossi, born in 1979, is twenty-one years old, will be in the army for another year, and tells me he gets along better with Palestinians than with Jews, even visiting ones but especially the native-born.

I have mentioned that the story of our oldest son, Michael, is a long one, but, since I began this book, I have changed my mind and will say something about it, for, although grievous, good people and good events were in it. As a baby, Michael never cried, which we mistakenly thought was sweet and lovable. But when he was two and a half years old, Dr. Havilkova told us he was autistic, that nobody understood autism, that it was incurable. Shocked, we rejected her diagnosis, of course, with me arguing, "If you don't know what it is, how do you know it is incurable?" She just said, sadly, "Experience."

For a while we tried everything. A place in Toronto attempted to get him to talk: he would get a cookie if he said the word; finally he said it, got the cookie, but threw it down on the floor.

We were lucky, in one respect, in having a doctor tell us the truth. One psychiatrist presupposed it was the mother's fault. An institution would not allow us in to inspect the place, on the same assumption. I will not bore the readers with hopeful "experts" we chased after but get to the end this story at once. When Suzy was born, Dr. Havilkova told us soon afterward that we must send Michael away. Suzy had tried to crawl up to him, and he screamed: did we want a neurotic or psychotic daughter? After much effort, we found Reverend Toombs, who had been a missionary in India but was then running a home for autistic children. With an autistic child of their own, he and Mrs. Toombs had returned to Canada; finding no adequate place for such a child, they decided God wanted them to set up one themselves. ("With God all things are possible," said a sign on their wall.) Michael stayed with them for several years. When we first came to visit, I was used to sitting on the edge of a chair. Mr. Toombs told me to relax: "Michael will not run away." The gate to their place was always open, the serenity was such that no child ever ran away. A friend of Rose's, who had had the same experience, had made a worldwide search and informed us of its result: "You want a place nearby, safe and kind."

When Reverend and Mrs. Toombs got old and had to sell their place, Michael, though to this day unable to say a word, was upset by the sergeant-major people who followed. The year was 1970, when we were scheduled to travel to Bergen-Belsen and then to Israel, where I would deliver my speech "From Bergen-Belsen to Jerusalem." Although this would not be my first speech in Israel, it was my first at the President's House in Jerusalem.

We took Michael to a government institution in Orillia, Ontario—with grave doubts, because of their reputation. There we were told they had a waiting list, so it appeared that we would have to cancel our trip to Jerusalem. The staff of the institution, however, would not hear of it and took Michael at once. (He is still there.)

Thus, we could go on our pilgrimage, which took us first to Bergen-Belsen, then to Jerusalem. In Jerusalem, I made a Hegel-inspired statement: "Only three epoch-making events have happened to the Jewish people since the fall of the Second Temple, and two of them have occurred in this generation, the Emancipation, the Holocaust, and the State of Israel."

I am unsure about either Gershom Scholem or Shneur Shazar on Emancipation, for at least Scholem thought it never took place, but both would have agreed about the other two events, the State of Israel if only because both men had made aliyah.

I wish I had known that President Shazar was the former Zalman Rubaschoff, who had published in 1918 *Erstlinge der Entjudung* (Firstlings of dejudaization), which concerns seven Jews meeting in Berlin in 1819 to consider how one could both remain a Jew and be modern.

More on Rubaschoff: Those who got together in 1819 included Leopold Zunz, Heinrich Heine, and Eduard Gans. They vowed not to convert (which was an escape) but also thought that if they truly wanted to be *both* modern and Jewish, it must be *possible*. But only one of them, Leopold Zunz, both kept his promise not to convert and, by his understanding of it, embraced modernity: he founded the *Wissenschaft des Judentums* (modern Jewish scholarship). The other two, Heine and Gans, broke their vow and converted. Gans became a well-known Hegelian, although Heinrich Graetz, another famous scholar, called Gans's talk "Hegelian gibberish." But Heinrich Heine, who also converted, said, nearly twenty years after Hegel's death, that he had not returned to Judaism, because he had never left it.

Rubaschoff, too, may have thought Gans was talking gibberish, but he could not dismiss its outcome: Heine and Gans had become great only after being lost to the Jewish people; and now he was President Shneur Shazar, presiding in Jerusalem over a "Study Circle of Diaspora Jewry."[1] (Diaspora Jews attending my lecture included Arthur Morse, Piotre Rawicz, Manes Sperber, and Alfred Kazin.)

I wrote the preceding paragraph before rereading my 1970 address. Having done so, two thoughts now surprise me: first, my lecture was more emotional than usual, surely under the impact of my experience at Bergen-Belsen, and second, there is no mention of Hegel. I do not even use his name; only the Hegel-inspired concept "epoch-making events" is present: one case of several when thought had yet to go to school with life.

In 1970 in Jerusalem, everyone made important comments, but Shazar shook me: in August 1914 he was preparing to take the train back from Germany to Russia, but at the last moment he gave his ticket to a friend. Reflecting on my own escape, I asked whether I should thank the SS for expelling me from Germany, before Heydrich corrected his "mistake" that expelling Jews was not enough, killing them was necessary? I once asked this question of Peter von der Osten-Sacken. Shaking him too.

To get back to Michael—it is a bit hard to return—thirty years later he is still at Orillia. Subsequent experience has shown that sometimes governments deserve their reputation. Once the Ontario government sent a supervisor to Orillia with the "modern" theory that children would be better off in normal homes. But the parents were suspicious: The Orillia building is beautiful, close to a lake; most parents thought the government wanted to sell it, hence get rid of the residents, so we held a protest meeting in Toronto's Queen's Park. I still remember hearing one parent complain that her son thought he could drive a car; the government expert smiled and asked: "How do you know he can't?" This was the one time I remember getting mad in public. I stood up and told him he should be ashamed, for he was talking to aggrieved parents. Our protest was successful, of course not because of my protest, but the government sent the supervisor back to Toronto's Queen's Park (where, someone said, he still is, sharpening pencils). They stopped the plan, but I am still suspicious.

But this suspicion does not apply to the people who work in Orillia. We would visit every Sunday and could only wonder at men and women who thought a year well spent if they had taught a resident how to use a spoon. We often thought of this itself as a response to the Third Reich, at least that part of it that murdered cripples as "useless eaters."

Let me return to Rose and the rest of the family.

Mark is not Jewish, but our family has a good history with

mixed marriages. It goes back to Germany and has been tested ever since 1933. This is a good place to mention it.

Both my father's brothers had Gentile wives. (Neither had children.) During Kristallnacht, "non-Aryans" were arrested in *Grossdeutschland*, that is, Germany, Austria, and the Sudetenland; in cases of intermarriages the Nazis tried to break up "non-Aryan" and "Aryan" couples, the males in KZ through threats or worse, the females, outside, through blackmail and propaganda, that is, the Nazi Weltanschauung. When an older pal of mine was released from Sachsenhausen, everything was gone, his wife, his house, his money. It was part of the Kristallnacht assault, too sudden, too comprehensive, for many "Aryan" partners irresistible.

As rabbi in Hamilton I had to perform mixed marriages, for at that time Ontario had no civil marriage, and I could not leave couples without a Jewish alternative. But I never failed to mention my Sachsenhausen pal; that for Gentiles to resist *that* disloyalty was as serious as heeding Mount Sinai. But on those occasions I was often reminded of my church audiences, also in Hamilton: I tried to get my point across, but rarely did.

But neither of my uncles' wives was tested this way. Harry and his wife left for Brazil before Kristallnacht. If her going to Brazil was impressive, the actions of Willy's Lenchen were spectacular. The two did not leave Germany, but Willy was never arrested; this was not uncommon, but the Gentile partner had to have *stamina*. My Orthodox grandparents had tried to dissuade Lenchen from the marriage, but she said Willy was all she wanted; and since 1933 she proved it. After the war I saw Uncle Willy's picture in a Hannover paper, surrounded by cats and dogs. The mayor of Hannover—just about ten miles from Bergen-Belsen— had honored him for looking after stray animals. My uncle must have had it with human beings.

As I mentioned, Rose left behind two blessings at her death. Besides children (and grandchildren), her insistence was, at first stronger than mine, that we must move to Israel. Not until we were there did she convert to Judaism; she told her Orthodox New York *bet din*—"Why not at marriage? Why now?"—that not until we were in Israel was she sure that her conversion was real.

A third blessing Rose left behind I did not mention at her funeral: I became more human. I had not seen Wolfgang for years, out of neglect, not from alienation. True, we had reacted differently to the consequences of Kristallnacht. The change of his name from "Wolfgang Amadeus" to "William Alan Fraser" tells the difference: if Jewish existence could provoke *that*, he wanted no more part of it. Wolf, as I kept calling him, became an Englishman, honored by the Queen because—so I gathered—he was an able organizer, who, whenever two companies merged, emerged on top. But the difference between us was not vast. He never became hostile to either Judaism or Israel, and the one time he visited us in Israel, in 1986, he insisted on climbing Masada. Six weeks later he was dead of cancer.

Also, as I remembered only after his death, he once told me about reading Werfel's *Forty Days of Musa Dagh*; he must have thought hard about what happened to the Armenians.

‡

Since my marriage with Rose was in 1957, and "At Home in Toronto" had begun in 1948, I must define the period differently, as "Wearing Two Hats"—philosophical scholarship and Judaism. I kept the two "hats" apart until, in or about 1970, I could no longer do so: what had happened was catching up with me.

This "at home" might never have happened, for after a 1950 theological conference in Cincinnati, Nelson Glueck hinted that Hebrew Union College might invite me to join the faculty; in the same year I got the same hint from Louis Finkelstein of New York's Jewish Theological Seminary. Had either invitation come, I would have felt duty bound to accept. But I learned through the grapevine that Glueck had heard I was a "card-carrying existentialist." As for Finkelstein—so I gathered from my friend Moshe Davis, years later—he had judged, correctly, that, for years to come, I would be involved in general more than in Jewish philosophy.

In retrospect I am grateful neither invitation ever came. One studies what one teaches, and either position might have made me a "one-hat thinker"; and in Jewish philosophy—the medieval, more especially, the modern—no truly significant figure, Spinoza, Hermann Cohen, Franz Rosenzweig, and my mentor Leo Strauss, was ever that. Not even great medieval philosophers such as Yehuda Halevi and Maimonides were.

The 1950 conference was also important in another respect, for I discovered that I was not theologically alone. With such scholars as Eugene Borowitz, Lou Silberman, and Steven Schwarzschild, I shared theological convictions, forming ties that lasted for years, but most amazing was my rediscovery of Herman Schaalman. Back in 1935, three months in Berlin had been enough to create a solid friendship, after which he went to the United States. (Thus I did not mention him earlier, for he was already gone.) And then, fifteen years later—what years!—our friendship was restored as though nothing had happened. Borowitz and I turned in different directions when our family moved to Israel, although not for that reason alone, but while he would not officiate at our mixed marriage, I shall not forget we were married in the Borowitz home.

For my "two-hat" goals the University of Toronto was ideal; until the call of Jerusalem became irresistible, I never seriously thought of leaving. The idea behind its graduate department was: "great philosophers are timeless, that is, contemporary, and a professor's study of them ought to be just as timeless, that is, until retirement." My friend and colleague Bob McRae got fed up with British empiricism, switched to Descartes, Spinoza, and Leibniz, and never got tired again. For the two of us, not to talk philosophy was almost a policy, so each would feel free to do his own thing. My best friend was John Hunter; we often had lunch together; he was into Wittgenstein and I into Hegel, but we never talked about either. Now John is gone; he died in 1998.

I should mention two offers I investigated, for declining them was significant. In one case, it was easy, but I am doubtful still about the other.

I had four reasons to decline New York University. I visited a professor of English who had moved there, in an office with forty desks, with a chair in front of each. He told me his home was miles away, so he worked in the public library: like Jerusalem— although for different, if not opposite, reasons—New York was no place for philosophy. When I gave an address on Martin Buber to the New York University philosophy club, this became clearer still with regard to Jewish philosophy: the chairman squashed the discussion with the comment that Feuerbach had said the same; that the latter's "I-Thou relation" eliminated God whereas Buber's reaffirmed it did not seem to matter. The third reason was the chairman himself, Sidney Hook: he asked me to find a Kant reference, thanks to great dictionaries a task easily done for scholars using libraries, but Hook viewed me as a great scholar and not a philosopher. I did not think much of his Hegel book either, for to him Hegel was a reactionary, because he attacked H. J. Friess, in Hook's view a democrat; but Friess's view of democracy was hating the French, hating the Jews, and supporting assassination, when it was of enemies of the German *Volk*. (Friess did this at the infamous 1817 Wartburg festival, in poor praise of Martin Luther at his worst, including his hatred of Jews.) Hegel was afraid of German nationalism such as Friess's and stressed what he thought right about Luther: such, in my view, was Hegel's loyalty, if any, to Prussia. Herbert Marcuse, on the other hand, knew Hegel; when teaching Hegel, I used Marcuse's *Reason and Revolution: Hegel and the Rise of Social Theory*.[2] But, when Marcuse abandoned Hegel for Freud, and became famous in post-Hitler Germany, for a while even in America, he kept my interest only in his break with Heidegger, who had once been his teacher. When Heidegger wrote that what Germans did to Jews was no worse than what Russians did to Germans, Marcuse did not reply.

My fourth reason for being dubious about NYU was Heschel's suggestion that I should demand a promotion before accepting, for afterward I would have trouble getting one. When later, in 1970, I gave the first of my three lectures at NYU on "God's Presence in History," Hook, who introduced me for the first lecture, still did not understand why I had turned him down.

Turning down an offer from the University of Chicago was different. There, too, we would have had to live far outside the city, and Rose did not want to live in either New York or Chicago, for the children's sake. (Herman Schaalman would have loved me there.) But in the position I was offered, I would teach only if I had something new and significant to say, in which case I might have become famous. But I was afraid to move, even though Leo Strauss was there to stimulate thought, on both Judaism and philosophy, and Allan Bloom on speaking out. I still remember Bloom with us at a Seder in Toronto: he talked incessantly while carving the turkey, more expertly than I knew how.

But, whatever the reason, I was not ready for instant creativity, because Louis Finkelstein had been right: I was not even sure I would be primarily invested in general or in Jewish philosophy; if Jewish, in the past it had been in relation to Plato (hence also Aristotle) or in relation to Hegel (hence also Kant). But I was not even sure whether the catastrophes of the present—Hitler, Kristallnacht, the devastating Second World War—did not require wholly new possibilities, after Buber-Rosenzweig, Kierkegaard-Heidegger. In short, Hitler was gone but not yet his shadow, and Strauss's final option had been for Plato, not without thoughts, however, on the Jewish Bible. (See his *Studies in Platonic Political Philosophy*, which I once recommended for publication.) But when I received the offer from Chicago I had been into Hegel already for five years and would need five more for *The Religious Dimension in Hegel's Thought;* hence I stayed in Toronto and did not complete the book until 1967.

But Judaism and Jewish philosophy were never far from my thoughts, and Michael Morgan must have had me in mind when he did his doctorate on Plato.

I had begun teaching in Toronto in 1948, but I bided my time for several years and then, well aware there was no graduate course on Hegel, I gathered my courage, approached F. H. Anderson, now the formidable head of the department, with the request, itself formidable, of teaching Hegel, along with other German idealists. "Do you understand Hegel?" F. H.'s question was like an assault. "Yes," I lied and was off teaching Hegel's *Phenomenology* until retirement.

"Till retirement" it would be, for I was, for the first time since 1933, "at home," and, as I have said, philosophy in a hurry is a contradiction in terms.

"The time is ripe for raising Philosophy to a Science." What a promise in the *Phenomenology*'s preface! (I had thought of it since that unforgotten evening—was it in 1937 or as late as 1938?—in the Metzger home, but now I would have to grapple with it.) Philosophy, first, must absorb its own history—*aufheben*, that is, *both* preserve it as it was *and* lift it up—a claim monumental, when it means, as it did for Hegel, "justice" to all past thought at odds, yet never tiring of the "labor of thought," that is, "mediation."[3]

But why Science *here and now*? First, a "beginning" of Wisdom has been made when modernity in philosophy, with Spinoza, goes beyond the "fear of the Lord" of premodernity, itself Jewish, as was Spinoza, to embrace—in modernity no more "fear," no more "Lord"!—Substance; and then, via Kant and Fichte, to reach, with Schelling, nothing less than the Absolute. Although five years younger, Schelling, Hegel's one-time friend and subsequent rival, was already a much-published philosopher and famous in 1801, when his almost unknown friend, Hegel, had written only articles; Hegel's own first book, the *Phenomenology,* appeared only in 1807, when he was thirty-seven years old.

But Schelling's Absolute was merely *asserted,* that is, came "shot from the pistol"; also—although claiming to *comprehend* Totality—it was empty, that is, a "night in which all cows are black." "Labor of thought" was therefore necessary to give it *content,* that is, the Hegelian system; it was also necessary to "give a ladder" to it, namely, the *Phenomenology.*

I have never understood how some professors teach the whole work in a single semester. I never got nearly that far and, after a first few feeble and failing attempts, established a "nasty questions" method. The *Phenomenology* is a difficult text, perhaps the most difficult in philosophy, but—although Hegel may share responsibility for subsequent obscurity in German philosophy—his own text is not obscure. My students were expected to read the text closely, terrified, I hoped, of being bombarded with unexpected questions. The questions, of course, are the work of the instructor, who must first understand the text himself. Just once I sent a friend, at the last minute, into a class already assembled, to tell them I was sick. I had cold feet and needed another week with the text. (Incidentally, I have since read some German philosophy from the Nazi period, and whenever it turns in the direction of Nazism, it slanders Spinoza first.)

I used to warn my students of famous but impatient readers, Marx on the "master-slave" relation, Kierkegaard on the "unhappy consciousness." Marx jumped off Hegel's text into existence in history, the capitalist-labor conflict, and was thus forced to postulate, after the proletarian victory, the end of history. Kierkegaard jumped off into existence of the person, thus into a conflict—with "fear and trembling"—between himself and God.

But for Hegel, "master-slave" and "unhappy consciousness" are forms of consciousness *abstracted from*—and *requiring placement into*—*contexts,* and the context into contexts: what is Hegel's *ultimate* context? Between "right-wing" and "left-wing" extremes, firmly in the middle. "The life of Spirit does not shun death, so as to preserve itself pure from devastation, but endures devastation, maintaining itself in being torn asunder. It finds its truth only when, in being torn apart absolutely, it finds itself."[4]

This is the "context of contexts" in my *The Religious Dimension in Hegel's Thought,* published in 1967 when "home in Toronto" was coming to an end. But I had yet to confront "Planet Ausch-witz." A world of its own, this Planet was hatred, sadism: a whole, to be sure (sought, if also by others, most clearly by Hege-lian thought), but a whole of evil for evil's sake: *No* "Spirit" can *"endure"* it.

After some years of teaching I started on a project for which I received a Guggenheim fellowship. "From Kant to Kierkegaard" would trace the challenge to the "otherness" of the scriptural God, from Kantian "autonomous" Reason to Hegel's Absolute Spirit, the overcoming, finally, of Divine "otherness," or total internalization.

But after Hegel's death the whole enterprise was called into question, first, by none other than Schelling, himself the first to reach the Absolute, and, following him and his "positive" philos-ophy, by Søren Kierkegaard.

So much, for the moment, for one "hat," while I was "at home" in Toronto.

As for the other, Judaism, I must begin with *amcha,* that is, Holy Blossom Temple. On returning to Toronto, after five years in Hamilton, I resumed the relationship to the temple, now im-proved for two reasons. First, mercifully, the war was over and won, although awareness, my own and everyone else's, of what it had done to Jews and Judaism—to the world—was yet to come. The second reason was personal: Heinz Warschauer was now director of education, which he remained until his death. I have written about Heinz, but there is more to say. My friendship with him was close but always difficult, the latter partly because of his position at the temple. He felt—and often expressed his feeling openly, scathingly—that it was appalling for him to spend his life in charge of what he unjustly described as "spoiled kids." But once—at a meeting, in front of his teachers—he had an outburst, saying he was where he was because he owed the Jewish people a debt for having survived. (He had reached that point, much sooner than I.) The relationship was further strengthened many years later when Dow Marmur came to Holy Blossom.

Over the decades I have changed my view of the temple. When I first came back from Hamilton, my main Jewish aim was faith affirmations, and when Heinz entrusted me with the confir-mation class, I remember storming into the first session, asking them to state something about Judaism that they believed. One volunteered "the Brotherhood of Man," another the "Fatherhood of God." Then I asked why they believed as they did and heard "that's what we were told." I then said that others were told differently, in order to come bluntly—perhaps abrasively—to the climax, "then who is right?" I got embarrassment and stunned silence.

I still think I was right in objecting to the textbook. *Modern Jewish Problems* by Roland Gittelson was a "how-to-think" text, shrinking from each and every "*what*-to-think." I have already mentioned Reform Judaism's love affair with Progress and Enlightenment, and in education "how-to-think" reverence was close to it. (I have published essays in criticism of such writers as Gittelson and Rabbi Levi Olan. Olan had attacked the Christian and pro-Jewish—the latter a rarity if not unique—theologian Reinhold Niebuhr for teaching, in the age of Hitler, that sin and not reason rules the world.) In place of *Modern Jewish Problems*, Heinz let me write my own text, which then became *Paths to Jewish Belief*. But I am glad this first book of mine is out of print. It deals with the content of Jewish belief but only prior to Auschwitz.

In those years Gene Borowitz tried to persuade me to write a book for Reform Judaism. His direction "think of Max Enkin as reader!" almost persuaded me. Enkin was a great person, a great Jew, deeply religious, and very much in the world as it was and still is.

But since those days with Warschauer's confirmation class I not only have mellowed, but I also have self-critical thoughts, not only about how to teach, but also about the temple. During those terrible years, Jewish congregations in America—not only Reform ones—tried to shield their children as well as their own morale from the knowledge of events in Europe; sometimes, if these events were mentioned in class, the temple got angry calls from parents. I would not conduct that first confirmation class session now as I did then. And it is hard for me to imagine another "bourgeois" Jewish congregation, either in America or in Canada, with the courage of Holy Blossom Temple to entrust their young to a Heinz Warschauer.

The 1950 theological conference had inspired some of us—Borowitz, Silberman, Schwarzschild, Schaalman, myself—to meet a few times: Jewish faith was in crisis. A few years later a similar group, led by David Hartman, met in the Quebec Hills, now with Orthodox and Israeli participants: the crisis was of the *whole* Jewish faith and—if one can separate the two—also of the Jewish people. At one of those meetings, in 1967, someone said that "mere survival" cannot be the "purpose" of either the Jewish people or Judaism. Milton Himmelfarb exploded: "After the Holocaust, let no one call Jewish survival 'mere'!" I have thought of Milton fondly ever since. Among Orthodox Jews present were Irving "Yitz" Greenberg and Aharon Lichtenstein, among Israelis Harold Fisch and Pinchas Peli; Greenberg and Peli have become lifelong friends. And once Elie Wiesel attended.

From the start Rose identified much more with my Jewish than with my philosophical commitments. Of Hungarian background, she was a Protestant who took Christianity seriously, enough to be well acquainted with Barth's theology. Nobody could deny Karl Barth's theological courage, the more striking because—anathema in Nazi Germany—his Jesus was Jewish. This was partly because Barth was a "theological positivist" (Bonhoeffer), taking the "New" Testament seriously, including the idea that it supersedes the "Old." This was both his strength and his weakness. In 1949, he wrote "The Jewish Problem and the Christian Answer," which recognized the Holocaust as a crisis for Judaism but not for Christianity.

Hence it was extraordinary that in 1963 Barth expressed the wish to meet German-speaking Jewish theologians. I was one who was invited to talk with him in Chicago. But it was too late for him and too early for us. That it was too late for him was evident.[5]

But for us it was too early. Raul Hilberg's *The Destruction of the European Jews* (1961) had just appeared and we were slow in coping with it. At that meeting with Barth in Chicago, Nahum Glatzer thought that the "orthodox" Barth was more accommodating to Judaism than the more "liberal" Paul Tillich; when Barth said he had pondered the cemetery of the Prague Altneuschul, Steven Schwarzschild suggested he should have gone inside, to find Jews studying Talmud. But Jews were not there anymore: even in the early 1960s, Jews and Christians were still talking theology as if nothing had happened; the Holocaust was still too stunning.

But the meeting, if a failure, had a hopeful end, though one that was unplanned at the time. Markus Barth was with his father, quoting Talmud from Strack Billerbeck, a German compendium of rabbinic New Testament parallels. I told this story years later to German students in Jerusalem. They were with Studium in Israel, a German organization that sends twenty-odd students to Jerusalem, year after year, to study Judaism for its own sake: not Strack Billerbeck, but Talmud itself.[6]

But how could Barth understand Judaism as "shutting itself in a Ghetto," away from the Christian *kerygma*, when Jews were being shut into ghettoes by nominal Christians? This had haunted Rose before I ever met her and prompted her and her friend Shirley Dorin to spend a year in Europe. When we became involved and I said I could have only Jewish children, she agreed with me at once: Christian children would be burdened with, and tempted by, anti-Semitism. Later she insisted—since we might move to Israel—that Suzy and David should have an Orthodox conversion, and Nahum Rabinowitz, a member of her *bet din*, now at Ma'ale Adumim in Israel, interviewed her in Toronto. After that interview, he told me she was like Abraham, by which he meant the sacrifice of Isaac, in Judaism called "binding," for the sacrifice did not take place.

I do not know whether Orthodox courts convert children whose mother is not Jewish, but Rabinowitz and his *bet din* did so in Rose's case. Years later, in sending me condolences Rabinowitz wrote: "I recall her as a woman of great integrity and strength of character."

Why was I "at home" in Toronto? I have mentioned my "one hat," philosophy. The other was midrash and my love of it. This love—lifelong since I've known it—was blossoming in Toronto, partly because, even while I was teaching philosophy at the university, I taught midrash in synagogues; I can also say that I lived "midrashically." My philosophical work had to be "objective," that is, purely scholarly, and the philosophers "from Kant to Kierkegaard" are all Christians. But—although the relation became questionable later on—scholarship is one thing, life is another.

My Jewish life found literary expression, mostly in *Commentary,* and my friendship with Irving Kristol, then a *Commentary* editor, and his wife, Gertrud Himmelfarb, lasts to this day. So does a friendly relation with Norman Podhoretz, recently confirmed by him in his *Ex Friends.*[7] *Commentary*'s priorities are not always mine, but at least whenever Jewish existence is at its edge—the uniqueness of the Shoah, the survival of Israel, American attitudes toward both—we always, even after not seeing each other for years, think the same way; of course, I found it easy to side with *Commentary* against its "rival" of recent years. *Tikkun* may have borrowed its title from *To Mend the World,* but it has mostly been conventional leftism, warmed over to make it Jewish and to sound post-Holocaust but only rarely deserving the title. It is boring, and I do not often read it.

Now that I have long been in Jerusalem, my views on *Commentary* have not changed. In its February 2000 issue, Daniel Pipes argued that, after half a century of "non-peace," Israelis are tired. In the May issue he answers two Israelis, one who "refers only to the needs of Israelis, but says nothing about Palestinian readiness to end the conflict," and another for whom Israel's "moral strength" is "sapped" so that such as he can no longer find articles, like Pipes's, "in Hebrew by an Israeli academic or intellectual," hence must turn to U.S. friends. Pipes finds this comment "sad and affecting" and asks "has it, indeed, come to this?"[8]

A newcomer to Israel—as I write in 2000 not all that new, but new enough—I like to think that, while Israeli tiredness is real, it has not "come to this?"

Commentary is on the edge also in its July–August 2000 issue. Efraim Karsh's article "Were the Palestinians Expelled?" states facts: Hanan Ashwari lied when asserting Israel must admit her "guilt and culpability" and that the "real authentic narrative of the Palestinians has to come out"; citing examples of Arab-Jewish cooperation, even friendship, he notes that Haganah, the Yishuv's military branch, had broadcast, even before the British left: "Arabs, we have no wish to harm you. Like you, we only want to live in peace. . . . If the Jews and the Arabs cooperate, no power in the world will attack our country or ignore our rights." But shortly after the fall of Haifa to the Haganah, the secretary of the Arab League, Abd al-Rahman Azzam, declared: "'The Zionists are seizing the opportunity to establish a Zionist state against the will of the Arabs. The Arab peoples have accepted the challenge and soon they will close their account with them.'"[9]

Commentary continues to be with Jews when they are on the edge, hence also with Jewish philosophy on the edge. But it is not

Midstream, whose very name implies that the crisis, minimally begun in 1933, is not over until Hitler's "shadow" is gone.

⁑

My relation with Michael Morgan is in a class by itself: "at home in Toronto" is too narrow a concept. Our friendship began when I gave a lecture on Leo Baeck at New York's Institute for Jewish Religion, before I was "at home" in Toronto. Morgan became, first, my graduate student in Toronto and then my assistant; after that he edited one of my books and has recently edited another. The friendship lasted when Toronto was home no more. He visited me often, recently in 1998 in Jerusalem after—this is written in 1999—I had just been in Bloomington.

Back "at home" in Toronto, I once began a university philosophy of religion course by writing three propositions on the blackboard: "God is omnipotent," "God is good," and "evil is real." The class soon discovered that one can allow only two of these. But for me—unlike for some university colleagues regarding the subject—this question was only a prelude: is it possible that what we have discovered in ten minutes has remained for generations, in living religions, not understood? This question was the real opening of my class, and I may have used as example the midrash that, commenting on Cain's crime, exclaims "Woe unto the Creator *(Yozer),* who calls evil the inclination *(yezer)* He Himself has created!" This doesn't sound much like philosophical "theodicy." (Much academic "philosophy of religion" presupposes that reason is the judge of religion, when "revelation" takes itself as divine, and "reason" is only human.)

Midrash, first, while not to be taken literally, must be taken seriously; both of these concepts are expressed in a technical term, *k'b'yachol* (as it were). Second, while midrash is pluralistic, hence nonauthoritarian, one can speak of a "midrashic framework" into which some, but not all, things fit. Thus one midrash often requires another to disclose the full meaning of both. "Why was the Torah given in the desert?" The desert has no borders, the midrash replies, so when God called, any nation might have come, but only Israel came. But—lest it promote "Jewish arrogance," even merely on behalf of ancient ancestors—this "desert" midrash points to the following "mountain" midrash:

"Why was the Torah given on a mountain?" It provided God with a threat is the reply: "If you refuse, the mountain will bury you." Surely no topic is more delicate—in either Christian or Jewish theology—than uniqueness by dint of covenantal election. (To be chosen is to be singled out, but who wants that? Or can bear it? And what *others* can bear the election of someone else? Only Nietzsche's atheism seems to go further: if God existed, how could he bear not to be Himself.) On the one hand, nothing arouses greater resentment among pagans, familiar as they are with their gods. On the other, none—being only human but facing the dread "otherness" of the scriptural God—can avoid a dialectic in which human freedom, itself real enough, is also overwhelmed by divine power. When Augustine told the pagans of the dying and risen Christ, they knew all about gods dying and rising in nature. But when he said that, having risen, Christ will die no more, they heard of a God they had not known previously, through an incursion that was without precedent.

For midrashic Judaism—the Messiah is yet to come—uniqueness in history is complete with Sinai. God is pictured as bending, for this once-only occasion, the outer heavens, making them touch earth. The midrash also reflects on Moses "ascending" and God "descending": what happens *between* God and Moses in those forty days? The whole Torah is revealed, is the midrashic reply, all 613 commandments. None will ever be superseded, for there is no superseding of Sinai. None, equally, need *ever be added*.

And what of an encounter *directly* between God and the people, the "descent" of the Ten Commandments? "When the first Word descended they all died. Then the Word went back to God, saying 'Thou hast sent me to the living, but I have come to the dead.' So God changed the Word, sent it back, and it found them alive."[10]

The Word has struck these humans *directly:* no wonder they are dead. But since the Word is *commandment* it needs *the living* to perform it; hence, in the second descent, it becomes humanly performable. In Judaism grace is not subsequent to commandment but *in* the commandment *itself,* with Jewish prayer giving thanks for its gift. Sometimes I would joke in class that the apostle Paul studied with rabbis but not long enough.

If Sinai is climax in history, the Exile is its nadir. The Ninth of Av mourns destruction, of the First Temple because of idolatry, of the second because of groundless hatred. Of the day's liturgical text, Lamentations, the second-to-last verse must be repeated after the last. The last verse asks whether God has brought catastrophe to the Jews, that is, the end of the covenant: "Hast Thou rejected us utterly, and art exceedingly wroth with us?" (Lam. 5:22). But the second-to-last verse denies catastrophe: "Turn us back to Thee and we shall turn; renew our days as of old" (Lam. 5:21). This verse is recited after every Torah reading in the synagogue: a God "turning" Israel will "renew her days."

I would often tell a class that others misunderstand Jewish survival when they make it "a mystery," even a divine one. Whenever a minimum of ten men gather for Torah reading—in some miserable hovel in some miserable exile—with them is not only parchment and letters but also the presence of God. In some midrashim God goes even further: He does not send Israel into exile, but goes with them. And Toronto synagogues are not hovels.

But "home in Toronto" came to an end in 1967, for catastrophe was threatening Sinai itself. Also, my work in philosophy was interrupted. I did publish my Hegel book that year. But I had yet to confront Hegel's Spirit with "Planet Auschwitz."

I had struggled with Hegel for fully ten years, a necessity, for his Science affirms an Absolute *beyond* history but also *in* history, an Identity that is Identity of Identity *and non-Identity;* and non-Identity remains real in the System. Hegel required much "labor of thought" for "mediations" doing "justice" to reality, and to do him justice I needed ten years.

Wilhelm Dilthey lost Hegel, but Rosenzweig recovered him and thereafter wrote his *Star of Redemption*—to use his term— *post-Hegel mortuum.*

Nothing is easier for Hegel students than, on the one hand, to soar into a "right-wing" Eternity above History, mystically empty of content; or, on the other, to be plunged somewhere into "left-wing" history. (The former have often been Russians, and F. H. Anderson used to say that when Russians read German philosophy, they get drunk on it; but then they got their vengeance with Marxism.) But, between these extremes, through the "labor" of a "thought" unique to him, dwells Hegel's own thought, firmly in the middle. Precisely that same "labor" is required of Hegel scholars.[11]

Hegel died in 1831, and, ten years afterward, Schelling reappeared from "religious" Munich and caused a sensation in "modern secular" Berlin. Bakunin, Burkhardt, Engels, and Kierkegaard attended his lectures, all looking, each differently, for something new.

Schelling came to assert that the tradition from Parmenides to the Absolute—Hegel's as well as his own—had been "negative" philosophy that abstracted "essences"; and what was demanded now was a "positive" leap into "existence." As early as in 1809—a mere two years after the *Phenomenology*—he had asked whether the Absolute did not destroy him as a free person, that is, destroy his choice of good or evil; and he had speculated on a morally neutral "dark ground" in God that is torn loose from God by human self-assertion. But which is evil, the choice of evil, rather than good, *by* the self, or, more radically, *the assertion of self* that *precedes every* choice?

"Just as there is an enthusiasm for good, there is also an enthusiasm for evil."[12]

One cannot believe that, brooding in "religious" Munich and elsewhere for thirty years, Schelling forgot he once wrote that sentence. Nor that he quoted the mystic Franz Baader: "It is much to be wished that man could fall only to the level of animal depravity. Unfortunately he can only fall below it or above it."[13]

12

Between Toronto and Jerusalem
1967–1983

The date was not lost on the participants: Easter and Purim on the same day. Easter is "the day for Christians to curse Jews": thus Hans de Boer, a German minister and friend of mine, used to begin his Easter sermon in Germany. He did so to shake the comfortably pious, about Easter. Purim is the day for Jews to praise God, for Haman has failed. (De Boer has written several books, one titled *Entscheidung für die Hoffnung* [Decision for hope]). De Boer does not *have* hope; he has *decided* for it.

But on Easter Purim 1967 we were in New York for a Haman who had not failed: called by chairman Steven Schwarzschild. We—Richard Popkin, George Steiner, Elie Wiesel, and I—had come to discuss "Jewish Values after the Holocaust." (Rose was with me, of course.) I had met Wiesel in the Quebec hills, the first Jew I had met who had both faced the Holocaust and had striven to preserve—nay, recover—Judaism. He is still at it.

I have just read *And the Sea Is Never Full,* the second volume of Elie's memoirs. My own *God's Presence in History* (1970) is dedicated to him, as is its 1997 reprint. I am astonished by Elie's stubbornly Jewish memory and, at my age, am encouraged to go on.

Until 1967 I had never faced the Shoah. Berlin was the Nazi capital, but I had been there to study Judaism—Strauss, Buber, Rosenzweig, and, in person, with Baeck, Wiener, Sister—and had not questioned it; nor had I done so afterward, in Sachsenhausen, Aberdeen, the internment camp, Hamilton, or finally, even "at home" in Toronto: the Shoah was always a background threat but had never been central.

But now Schwarzschild was twisting my arm: as a Jewish philosopher, I must confront it. It was the first time I was sick before a talk, on the way to saying what I had not said before, did not want to say now, but had to: there is a "614th commandment." After I had my say, the sickness was gone.

Sinai has 613 commandments, not more even for new situations, new enemies, unanticipated catastrophes. The midrash tells what happened in those forty days when God and Moses were alone on Mount Sinai: until the "Messianic Days," Sinai is Revelation Complete. In Jeremiah, God invokes Nebuchadnezzar as an instrument to punish Israel. But other enemies—Vespasian, Titus, Hadrian—should have their "names wiped out," for they were enemies of Judaism; climactically, Hadrian forbade the practice of Judaism on pain of death.

But Hitler was different. He forbade *Jewish birth*, not a sin but a mitzvah, the first one which makes all others possible. And while, in forbidding Jewish faith, Hadrian had *created* martyrs, Hitler, in killing Jews, *killed also Jewish martyrdom*. Had he won the war, no Jews would be left.[1]

When in 1993 I wrote about the Shoah "never being central," I was thinking mainly of Rosenzweig. But when I reread in 1999 what I had written I recalled two events: In 1938, my third year as *Rabbinatskandidat* (rabbinical candidate), I officiated for the High Holidays in Baden-Baden and got a letter from Dr. Flehinger, the president of the congregation, dated October 9: I had shown the *von tiefstem Leid gequälten* (deeply distressed) congregation *dauernde Werte* (lasting values), thus strengthening them with *frischem Mut* (fresh courage) in their *Hoffnungslosigkeit* (hopelessness).

One month later to the day—during Kristallnacht and from the same pulpit—Dr. Flehinger was forced by Nazi thugs to read from *Mein Kampf*.[2]

The second event, among my last as *Rabbiner*, was in the late 1950s or early 1960s, with a German Jewish congregation in New York, again on the High Holidays. There I said on Yom Kippur that Jews must forgive even Hitler. From the shock permeating every person in the large hall, I knew I had gone beyond the edge.

Herrn
Rabbinatskandidat Emil Fakenheim
B e r l i n.

        Sehr geehrter Herr Fakenheim,

             Im Namen des Synagogenratsmöchte ich Ihnen
für die vorbildliche Art,mit der Sie während der Feiertage in
unserer Gemeinde das Amt eines Predigers versehen haben,unseren
allerherzlichsten Dank aussprechen.
             Sie haben in Ihren formvollendeten Predigten,
die frei waren von jedem falschen Pathos,den von tiefstem Leid
gequälten Menschen den Weg gezeigt in die Welt der dauernden
Werte,haben die Irrenden und Verzweifelnden mit frischem Mut
gestärkt,ihrer Hoffnungslosigkeit die in der jüdischen Lehre
verankerte Gläubigkeit entgegengesetzt und die Wirklichkeit des
geistigen Seins denen entgegengehalten,die nur dem Materiellen
Realität zubilligem wollen.
             So konnte es nicht ausbleiben,daß unsere Ge-
meinde und mit ihr die zahlreich anwesenden Kurgäste mit echter
ErgriffenheitIhren belehrenden und erbauenden Worten lauschten
und der Gottesdienst von Ihrer seelischen Betreuung die dem
Charakter der Feste entsprechende Weihe empfing.
             Wir brauchen Ihnen nicht erst zu versichern,
daß wir uns immer darauf freuen,Sie in unserer Gemeinde zu hören.

        Mit nochmaligem herzlichen Dank und freundlichen
Grüßen

        Ihr sehr ergebener

          N. Flehinger

A letter written to me by Dr. Flehinger, the president of the *Israelitische Gemeinde, Baden- Baden,* to express gratitude for the sermons that I had given during the High Holidays in 1938. Dr. Flehinger wrote this one month to the day before Kristallnacht, when he was forced with beatings to read from Hitler's *Mein Kampf* from the same pulpit while SA men urinated on Jewish prayer shawls. Jews were forced to march through the city and some Germans remarked that they were just like Jesus Christ, but they said this in their houses, watching through the windows. Nobody did anything. I was only a candidate aged twenty-two, and these were my first High Holiday sermons.

Hence there exists, now, this 614th commandment, perhaps for the world, but, at the very least, for the survival of both Jews and Judaism: and without Judaism, can Christianity survive?

In 1968 I amended what I said in 1967:

Jews are forbidden to hand Hitler posthumous victories. They are commanded to survive as Jews, lest the Jewish people perish. They are commanded to remember the victims of Auschwitz, lest their memory perish. They are forbidden to despair of man and his world, and to escape into cynicism and otherworldliness, lest they cooperate in delivering the world to the forces of Auschwitz. Finally, they are forbidden to despair of the God of Israel, lest Judaism perishes.[3]

Thirty years have passed but—other than trivial details, such as replacing "men" with "persons" and omitting "finally"—I would not change a word, even now.

Just how much of a break the 614th commandment was for me may be gathered from my 1965 Bickersteth lecture, "Religious Commitment in the Academic Community," for the University of Toronto faculty and students, Jewish, Christian, and agnostic. In retrospect it reads like a "good-bye."

I began with the idea of the university as agnostic, if not, as Bertrand Russell would have it, atheist, but that the university as such was already a "multiversity." Passing quickly over the "beat" 1950s, I went on to the "sit in, march in, teach in" 1960s.

In the 1960s, University of Toronto president Claude Bissell had four students sit under the table at opening convocation. I do not remember how many of these four were in my first class on German Idealism the following week. But I began that class by asserting their "master-slave relation" had it wrong: I was the slave, for, like a garbage collector, I had not merely to collect their essays but also to read them, whereas they came to class only when they thought it relevant. (Since the 1960s, I avoid the word "relevant" unless I can say what it is for.) Then I wrote one sentence on the blackboard: "The Ego posits itself." This principle was for a course of thought begun by J. G. Fichte, which led to the most radical concept of freedom ever conceived.

The 1965 lecture was a product of those years. The 1960s had already made commitments possible for academics, begun with

Kant but Americanized by John Dewey. (A wit has said that for
Kant "man" was central in the world; for John Dewey it was a
"New York businessman.") Skipping "God is dead theologies,"
themselves then already dead, I focused on Harvey Cox's *Secular
City*. As my spies told me, everybody was buying it; my "spies"
were my wife, Rose, and Bob Miller, the head of the Bob Miller
Bookroom.

I criticized Cox with hesitation, sharply only when he disposed of Nazism as a relapse into tribalism; he did not understand that by comparison all tribes have been innocent, and he
implied, moreover, that our progress had overcome Nazism. I
only hinted in my lecture that metaphysics seemed to have no
place and only briefly mentioned neoorthodoxy, Sartre, Buber,
and Wiesel. I did say, though, that today Barth would not be a
Barthian, and my last sentence was that the Word that had come
to Jews and Christians is "wholly exposed to that wonderful,
hopeful, terrible and desperate reality, which is our present."

‡

Nothing in the "614th commandment" said we should not go on
living in Toronto, only that, perhaps, we should not be so much
"at home."

Events soon intervened, however, all involving Israel. Within
months after the 1967 symposium we had three weeks of Jewish
dread.[4] Egypt and Syria threatened Israel. Nasser blocked the
Gulf of Aqaba to Israeli shipping, told the U.N. peacekeeping
troops to go away, and away they went. Jordan joined Egypt and
Syria. No friendly nations spoke up for Israel. We had every reason to fear a second Shoah, this time in Israel.

More things happened to us personally after the Six-Day
War. Israel's government invited us to Israel; we had never been
to the country, so in 1968 we went. Then, a second time, the
Bergen-Belsen survivors, then headed by the late Yossel Rosen-
saft, wanted us to take part in a pilgrimage, first to Bergen-
Belsen, then to Jerusalem, and we went in 1970.

The symposium in New York had been on "Jewish Values after
the Holocaust." "Values" is a slippery word, for what values one
has "depends on one's view." Leo Strauss would have found that

word unacceptable: for there was truth in facts. I never wrote about a holocaust that might have happened in Israel, but after Bergen-Belsen, could never forget about the Holocaust that *had* happened, hence I am a post-Holocaust thinker still.

Which do you visit first? Bergen-Belsen or Jerusalem? For Rose and myself there was only one answer, aliyah, the answer given to the question asked us by Ya'acov Herzog, an Israeli diplomat.

In Hannover we never left the hotel except for Bergen-Belsen. In Bergen-Belsen itself, Yossel Rosensaft said: "Whenever we come, it rains; God weeps for the sins he committed against Israel." Nobody said a word, including orthodox rabbis.

My concerns about Israel also drew me into politics. Rose conceived of an act of support for Israel, a ship of German Christians breaking the blockade, so I phoned Markus Barth, the son of Karl, who had become a friend. Barth told me not to worry, to give money to the Red Cross. Because of his theology—God would protect Israel—this Christian did not share our anxiety.

Something worse than naive Christian theology or indifference soon followed. A. C. Forrest's *United Church Observer,* the magazine of the United Church of Canada, had ignored the three weeks of threat to Israel. The war was hardly over and won when the *Observer,* under the headline "Injustice," listed sundry Israeli injustices to Palestinians, and the church's general secretary "deplored that Jewish people everywhere seemed to identify the preservation of the State of Israel with the preservation of the Jewish religion." Forrest himself added that Christian churchmen "are concerned with the loss of the Holy Places." Apparently, the holy places had not been "lost" when they were in Muslim hands.

A phone call from Forrest before the article appeared showed us the kind of man he was. We had had a "trialogue" at Beth Tzedek's huge conservative synagogue: my philosophical colleague, lapsed United Church professor Marcus Long; a United Church minister whose name I forget; and myself. Marcus told me beforehand that he would pull a fast one, but not what it would be. After the usual "dialogue" between the other participant and me, Marcus pulled the "fast one," quoting an official United Church book saying the Jews had killed Christ. This left me no choice but, with some heat, to reject this accusation.

Forrest had not been at the meeting, but his next *Observer* accused Long of charging his church with anti-Semitism; his criticism extended to me, but was less harsh since I had always been friendly in dialogue. Shortly afterward, Forrest phoned me, inviting me to be a board member of a new magazine he would head. I reminded him I had never used the word anti-Semitism, and he said he hoped I would not pull the rug from under him.

When I put the phone down, Rose wanted to know the gist of our conversation. She became angry: "You cannot let him get away with that!" She was right, so I phoned Forrest back, asking for a correction, and he agreed to publish a letter from me. In my letter, I said I regretted using the word "slander"; I had used it in the heat of debate, but such was a "common error." Forrest published my letter, but headed it "Regrets the word slander." If students are still interested in Jewish-Christian relations in Canada, they can look up the letter, but they should also know other facts about these relations: that the provost of Trinity College offered me a post, since, in Trinity's view, a Jewish believer was better than a Christian agnostic; that Father John Kelly of Saint Michael's made the crucial motion for Jewish Studies at the University of Toronto (which I seconded); and that the United Church's own Professor David Demson, a deep student of Karl Barth, was an ally, a friend of mine to this day.

That Forrest's "new magazine" never got started was not surprising, nor was I surprised by the *Observer*'s reaction to the Six-Day War and its aftermath.

I got involved with the *Observer*'s reaction because the United Church's own Saskatoon College offered me an honorary doctorate.[5] "Do you wish to co-opt me, or to have me protest against your own establishment?" I asked on the phone. "That's why we're asking you to give the address" was the reply. So, of course, we went to the ceremony, and one-half of what I said in my speech was a challenge to Christian indifference and hostility, the other half was directed to Christian friends.

Saskatoon was not alone among Christian friends. There was Roy Eckardt and also Franklin Littell. Franklin had once been on television with Forrest. After Forrest had gone on about his concern—Christian, of course—for all refugees, Franklin posed a question. "What," he asked, "was the date of the *Observer*'s reporting on Jewish refugees?" There had been nothing, of course. In

1999 Franklin was in Jerusalem, and we reminisced about Rose. He said it took her a while to trust, as a Christian, even him, but then her trust was lifelong.[6]

David Demson, a young lecturer at the Toronto United Church College whom I've already mentioned, was a follower of Barth who, like Rose, had problems with Barth's theology; he had always been fully with us regarding Israel and remains a friend to this day. "Don't stick your neck out too much," I told him. "You might get fired." He replied that when something was right he couldn't ask such questions.

I say so gladly because now, a quarter of a century later, peace between the United Church of Canada and the Canadian Jewish community has been restored, I suspect largely inspired by Johanna Metcalf. In 1995 I gave the first Metcalf lecture, under United Church auspices, "Kristallnacht: Holocaust and Hope."

There were other Christian friends in the Student Christian Movement, of which Rose had been a member. The late Glynn Firth, minister of Bathurst United Church, preached about the Third World and racism. My wife asked him to speak about anti-Semitism; when Glynn said the issue was not serious at that point, she replied "when it is not serious you won't do anything, and when it is serious you can't do anything." No prodding was needed with Bob Miller, the owner of the Bob Miller Bookroom and Rose's employer. Bob is the greatest Christian preacher I have ever heard, but—after he went to Europe and discovered the truth of the Holocaust—he never preached again. I have a chapter on Christianity in *To Mend the World*, to help those like Bob Miller preach again.

I became involved in these and other polemics with Christians, if not happily, with a good conscience, if only because my wife kept telling me not to be "soft on Christians." Her parents were immigrants from Hungary, and she knew Christian anti-Semitism: I must help fight it as a Jew. To give an example of my earlier "softness," I once told a Minnesota Lutheran convention that the Nazis would have carried out the Holocaust even without Luther; it is true, of course, but the wrong thing to say to Lutherans. Not only did Germans follow Luther's suggestions— to burn synagogues and consign Jews to hard labor—but they carried out beyond Luther the practice of *den Spiess umdrehen* (turn the spear around). Luther accused the Jews of attacking

Christianity, when as Jews all they did was circumcise their sons, as they had since Abraham. Hitler accused the Jews of starting the war that he himself started. At the Nuremberg trials, the pornographer Julius Streicher said that he, like Luther, had fallen into the "clutches" of "victorious" Jewry. Lutherans were right to ignore him, but they should have done more. For the time is long past for a universal, public, consciously theological Lutheran repudiation of Luther's *Von den Juden und ihren Lügen* (On Jews and their lies). Had this been done, a few Christians in the Reichstag might have applauded less cordially when Hitler "prophesied" that if "world Jewry started another war" it would be the end of Jews in Europe. Hitler was "turning the *Spiess* around": the "prophecy" was self-fulfilling. Hitler made his "prophecy" in the most public possible place—the Reichstag!—on January 30, 1939. On September 1, 1939, his troops marched into Poland.

For a time Rose thought that, for her to help, she must remain Christian.

Perhaps her doubts about this conviction began when we had the first Jewish-Christian attempt—ever!—to confront Auschwitz, in 1974 at New York's Cathedral of Saint John the Divine. Because it was the first such event, it was quite unfocused and dealt largely with subjects other than Auschwitz, and neither Eckardt nor Littell had been invited. Worse still, when the book *Auschwitz: Beginning of a New Era?* came out in 1977, the whole subject was undermined by Gabriel Habib, a Christian consultant to the World Council of Churches for the Middle East. Habib not only called for a Moslem-Christian dialogue with only non-Zionist Jews, but made the Holocaust into a parochial European-American affair: thus he trivialized it.[7]

Yitz Greenberg (central in inspiring the conference at St. John the Divine) wrote to Rosemary Ruether that Habib had not shared in a dialogue about the Shoah, but Ruether replied that Arabs had legitimate complaints. Yitz's speech had contained this much-quoted sentence: "No statement, theological or otherwise, should be made that would not be credible in the presence of the burning children."

This was Greenberg's working principle. Although worse was to come from Ruether, she, and not only Habib, ignored that principle and trivialized the Holocaust. Then Rose wrote to Yitz, with a carbon copy to Ruether: "Discouraging. It is as if a bystander, during the 'incident' when Jesus rebuked the woman at the well, came away saying 'he obviously hates and is trying to silence the Samaritans.' The pain comes with the knowledge that the bystander is not a 'Pharisee' or even a Roman, but one of the disciples." Her letter ended: "Is dialogue, after all, a costly illusion?"[8]

In 1977 we again became involved with politics, this time intra-Jewish. We decided to visit the Soviet Union, to offer moral support to *refuseniks*. They needed support, for the Soviet system was repressing Jewish culture and was openly hostile to Zionism. In Riga we visited Salaspils, a huge Soviet propaganda concentration camp. When we asked to sign the visitors' book in the office, we saw, among other inscriptions, an Arab one, praising Soviets for "their opposition to Zionisms wherever they are found." My inscription was "Let nobody distort what happened here."

From Salaspils, a showpiece of anti-Nazi Soviet ideology, I asked our Intourist guide to take us to Rumbula. (The *refuseniks* had told us Jewish victims are there, perhaps from Germany, even from Berlin.) Although the place is not easy to find, the Intourist guide knew where it was. It is an insignificant place, marked with just a small sign saying "saboteurs etc.": Jews were the "etc."[9] As I mentioned earlier, this is when I remembered Hans-Georg Hanff, sadly, the colleague, with whom I had discussed war and peace in 1935. If Berlin Jews were here, he could be too.

In Moscow we met Benjamin Fain. Moscow was difficult, for we had been warned there was no place—a hotel room, an apartment—that was not bugged, but Fain arranged a "party." He must be an outstanding physicist, for the Soviets had spoiled him, and he had no reason except love of Judaism to risk aliyah. Now long at Tel Aviv University, he recently told me that only since he came "West" (as he calls Israel, although he has also visited America) has he known real life.

In Minsk we met Colonel Lev Ofsischer, once a hero of the Soviet Union—he had downed many Nazi planes—but then a hero no more; once a colonel, he had been demoted to private, for he wanted to go to Israel and had become a *refusenik*. He had heard of *B'rera* (choice) in America, a Jewish organization urging Israelis to find Arabs with whom they can negotiate. His own *b'rera*, Ofsischer told us, was between being a colonel and a private, the latter with a good conscience.

On VE Day all Russians come together to celebrate victory after the terrible Nazi onslaught that threatened them with defeat. But the Jewish ordeal had been even worse, and for several years Minsk Jews had observed the day separately, with Ofsischer not only arranging it, but also giving the main speech. I asked Ofsischer to tape it, so that it could be translated and played in Toronto, code-named "Mozart." ("Mozart" was for spoken material, "Schubert" and "Beethoven" for music.) At the Moscow airport—though one official protested that it was no music hall—others, the KGB, had to play our tapes and then confiscated the spoken material. But they mixed up the tapes, and we managed to get out with Ofsischer's speech. The KGB have one of our Schubert or Beethoven tapes.

Although it occurred at the beginning of our Soviet visit, I have left the most thrilling, thought-provoking incident to the end. Riga moved me, for there we saw our first *refuseniks* on Soviet soil, about twenty of them, none older than eighteen, none looking brave, but most wearing, bravely, a Star of David necklace. I asked Arkady Zinober, their leader, what he wanted me to speak on. He replied: "Jewish philosophy." Asked for a definition, he answered, "All of us want to be Jews; Jewish philosophy will tell us why."

This must have been—at that place, at that time!—the deepest definition of "Jewish philosophy" in centuries, perhaps since Sinai and, moreover, in accord with a midrash about Sinai itself. The ancient Israelites might have said, "Let us hear what Sinai says and then decide whether we want it." But the midrash makes much of their saying the opposite: "We shall do it and hear" (Exod. 24:7). A repressive regime had robbed Soviet Jews of all Jewish knowledge, for decades. Then the Nazis invaded, were pushed out, but left few Jews alive. Now a "remnant of the remnant"—naked, without Jewish knowledge!—wants "Jewish philosophy" to explain why they should be Jewish.

Our first visit to Israel offered two experiences that I will never forget. The first: a gas station with Hebrew signs. One Zionist promise—Jewish normalcy after two millennia—fulfilled. (Before

1933, "Jewish normalcy" meant almost nothing; now, almost everything.) Gas stations in Israel have long ceased to excite me. Also, after more than a decade in Israel, Zionism is not as "normal" as once it was, to put it mildly.

Quite different was my other memorable experience. Our driver—his name was Elijah—did not take us to Jerusalem for several days, but the closer we came the more my heart pounded, till we got to the Wall. I let a photographer monopolize me and take my photo with tallit and tefillin. I had not used tefillin since my bar mitzvah and then, for a little while, in Berlin.

I am at a loss to explain my feelings. For German Jews, Jerusalem belonged to a past that no longer mattered, and we never had the pseudo–American Jewish kitsch—Washington, their Jerusalem!—of calling Berlin ours. I can only guess that our "religious" prayers had greater "secular" power than I once thought. Including Psalm 126, recited on Shabbat, which speaks of Jews "laughing when they returned to Jerusalem."[10]

But in 1970 it was Bergen-Belsen, more than Jerusalem, that affected me. In an address to us in Bergen-Belsen, Norbert Wollheim, a German Jew I became friends with, called Hitler a *Spottgeburt von Dreck und Feuer* (a "monstrous offspring of feces and fire," taken from Goethe's description of the devil).[11] He made me wonder how the greatest German—like Shakespeare in England—could have described so accurately the most depraved, at a time when Hitler was still unimaginable. But even more important, I keep thinking about Wollheim's reference to the murdered as *k'doshim* (holy ones). This pronouncement is unprecedented; for, alas, with Jewish martyrdom murdered, they were not martyrs—*al kiddush hashem* (for the sanctification of the Name)—but victims. Yet—on this of all subjects!—can the gut reaction of survivors be wrong?[12] Certainly not their motto—"Holocaust and Rebirth."[13]

No matter how often I quote this, I know I shall keep thinking about it, not only as a Jewish philosopher, but also as a philosopher in general, for the issue involves the experience of absolute evil (Wollheim), the possibility of imagining it (Goethe) and the possibility of relating the two to each other (Hegel).

But paradox and despair stayed with me from Bergen-Belsen. "Earth, cover not the blood shed on thee!" These are the words on the memorial. But grass covers it all.

Such experiences in the hectic 1970s may explain why, eventually, we moved to Israel. But—I keep stressing—I would not be writing these memoirs if they were merely a personal story. Universal, normative reasons for aliyah came during six summers in Israel, then with our children Suzy and David and the support of the Canada Council. Moshe Davis and Yehuda Bauer became friends, but it was Pinchas Peli, together with his wife, Pnina, who became our *Shaliach*.[14] These "messengers" are sent by Israel to cities—New York, Chicago, Toronto—to make it easier for would-be *Olim*, with advice about housing, taxes, pensions. But our *Shaliach* did more; he tried to help us decide whether, for us, aliyah was necessary. In *Jewish Philosophers and Jewish Philosophy*, my late friend Pinchas is listed as the last of seven Jewish philosophers. But I expect philosophers still will not accept him.

One summer the Pelis took us to Kibbutz Yad Mordecai, named after Mordecai Anielewicz, the leader of the 1943 Warsaw Ghetto uprising, who fought and perished in it. Before his death Anielewicz wrote: "My life's aspiration is fulfilled. The Jewish self-defense has arisen. Blissful and chosen is my fate to be among the first Jewish fighters in the Ghetto."

Five years later, in May 1948, the kibbutz named after Mordecai warded off Egyptian forces for five days that may have saved Israel. Anielewicz's hope for a future Jewish self-defense was not fulfilled, for SS General Jürgen Stroop boasted of having vanquished Jewish "bandits," with flame throwers and machine guns, against a few pistols and home made Molotov cocktails.

But the battle for Yad Mordechai—for Israel—began in the streets of Warsaw. To this day, the justly larger-than-life statue of Mordecai dominates the kibbutz. Behind it stands the water tower smashed by the Egyptians, a mute reminder that—even after climactic Jew hatred and Jewish powerlessness—Jew hatred has not vanished. But this stands behind the statue. Before it lies what the real Mordecai Anielewicz longed for but never despaired of: green fields, crops, trees, birds, flowers, Israel.

These and similar experiences led to our decision to move to Israel. But more than personal experience, there was at least one thought—I insist against all, adversaries or woolly-headed friends—that is philosophical. While "at home" in Toronto, I had considered November 29, 1947, the day to celebrate. The U.N. had responded to events by voting for a Jewish and an Arab state; if Jews deserved a state in Palestine, so did Arabs.

But I did not know what had happened between November 29, 1947, the day of the U.N. vote, and May 14, 1948, the day on which Ben-Gurion proclaimed the State of Israel.

Arab attacks on Jews increased in Palestine, and, with irregulars invading, the country was at war, even before the British military left. No Arab, within or without Palestine, had thought of accepting the U.N. decision.

On March 18, 1948, the U.S. delegate to the U.N. General Assembly, Warren Austin, proposed that, since Jewish statehood could not be established peacefully, it should be postponed and be replaced temporarily by a U.N. trusteeship for all of Palestine.

U.S. Secretary of State George Marshall, no mean military expert, urged Jewish acceptance since, if Israel declared itself a state, Arab armies might crush it. Undersecretary of State Robert Lowell added a political point: if Jews accepted the offer and Arabs still attacked, the U.S. could send troops. But if Israel declared itself a state, the Jews would be on their own.

Accept trusteeship—for how long? Maybe forever? That patient Zionist, Chaim Weizmann, phoned Ben-Gurion to say "declare the State, now or never," and he was right: a few years later would have been too late. They could not celebrate in Jerusalem— it was under Arab siege—but danced in the streets of Tel Aviv on May 14, 1948. With the future uncertain, Ben-Gurion felt like a mourner at a feast. Later he said: "We did not fight in 1948 to establish the State. We fought to defend it. The U.N. gave it international sanction and then ran away. We brought it about ourselves."[15]

A "world conscience creating Israel," then, if not a fraud, is a pseudoliberal illusion, bound to create other illusions, such as Israel was "born in sin" and "exploits the Holocaust" and in general the current "post-Zionist" mentality. One finds this mentality even in Israel; using it but going beyond it—something that the woolly-headed find hard to resist—are Arab media, who join neo-Nazis in asserting that the Shoah never happened.

Worse than an illusion, it is obscene. If November 1947 is the date and "the world's bad conscience created Israel," then the one creating the bad conscience is none other than Hitler, the "grandfather."[16]

In contrast, if May 1948 is the date, the grandparents are Mordecai and his desperadoes in the Warsaw Ghetto, who fought without hope of surviving but did not despair.

I have used the word "philosophical" earlier: this was deliberate. Jew hatred, though no longer remembered any more than
the Warsaw Ghetto uprising, will diminish with peace in Israel
and may even disappear; but "SS Colonel Stroop versus ill
armed 'bandits'" must be described as *"radical evil in history,
viewed by the perpetrators as redemptive."*[17] *Both that* the perpetrators did it *and the way* in which the victims suffered it elevate it
to the level of *weltgeschichtlich* (world historical).[18] And the fact
that the Third Reich lasted only twelve years does not mean that
ruptures are gone. (For the rupture of at least three histories—
German, Christian, Jewish—see in the appendix my inaugural
lecture in Kassel, 1997.)[19]

From 1973 on we spent six of seven summers in Israel, except
for the summer of Rose's pregnancy; in five we climbed Mount
Sinai. Each time we looked for a Word, and the first time we heard
it before ever climbing. A man came rushing into our tent, looking for "the philosopher." I identified myself, and he said just
one thing before rushing out again: a painter from Netanya, he
wanted to paint these mountains when he had been here as a soldier; but a painter must be alone, and until he read Nietzsche he
was afraid. Back in Toronto, I read *Zarathustra,* now with Exodus
next to it; Exodus scared me, but Nietzsche was sound and fury,
not signifying very much. Moses spent forty days on Mount
Sinai, with God. We were up there; there is no food, no water.

Our next trip discouraged attempts to find present significance in Sinai. Our companions belonged to the Club Med, complaining about too much hot sun, drinking too much wine every
night, and when we came down again, they wanted to crown
someone "Miss Sinai."

While the last two ventures to Sinai are not worth mentioning,
the third brought the Word. This time our guide was a leftist.
(Leftist Israelis are said to love every religion except their own.)
Rather than rush to the top for sunrise, we stopped at every holy
place, including the monastery of the thirty-nine martyrs. The
monastery takes its name from the story of thirty-nine monks
who were killed by marauding Bedouins; a surviving monk,
knowing that thirty-nine is not a holy number but forty is, committed holy suicide. Thus we heard the biblical "choose life." My
teacher, Leo Baeck, had heard it, when Kristallnacht caused Gandhi to urge German Jews to commit suicide—this, Gandhi

thought, would wake up world conscience—but like Buber, Baeck, the last great spokesman of German Judaism, spurned his advice. It is sad to think of how Gandhi failed to understand German Judaism vis-à-vis Kristallnacht-Nazism, but it is sadder yet to think of Baeck's "choose life" and of what happened to it.

After summers in Israel, we spent two more years in Toronto, but my "two-hat" existence—scholarship in philosophy, midrash in thought and life—was already nearing an end.

I had done my best to keep the two apart, for two decades and, counting my Ph.D. period, almost three. But in 1973, I published *Encounters between Judaism and Modern Philosophy*.

This book is about modern philosophers, but here I had best stick to Immanuel Kant. Even Jews who are only formerly German love Kant. Hermann Cohen was a neo-Kantian before he became a Jewish philosopher; and as late as 1970, I myself had still written that, while Kant's suggestion of Jewish "euthanasia" "sounds obscene" today, his intentions at the time were "benevolent."[20]

But if *Encounters* demands mutuality of modern philosophers, this includes also Kant. If Kant can accuse Abraham, vis-à-vis God in Isaac's case, of a "heteronomy" that obeys the divine will, however repugnant, why not wonder, as does the midrash, how this same Abraham can behave as he does—surely, minimally, "autonomously"—in the case of Sodom and Gomorrah? Again, if Kant did not find a concept of a "hereafter" in his Old Testament—for him a sine qua non in religion—why not ask friends about post-Biblical Judaism? He corresponded with the Jewish physician (and lay philosopher) Marcus Herz, and Herz must have known "Sayings of the Fathers" (they are in the daily prayer book); in them the "world to come" is prominent.

If such "encounters" were needed, even with Kant, not just the past was catching up with me, but especially the Holocaust: my "two-hat" existence, as a whole, was coming to an end.

Or only partly, as I would discover in Jerusalem: the two would be two, even there.

If, as a once-German Jew, I have focused on Kant in *Encounters*, in *To Mend the World* I focus on Hegel, the thinker I have thought with longest, struggled with most deeply. In 1967, I had published *The Religious Dimension in Hegel's Thought*, but in that year the crisis about Israel had made me stop short of "Planet Auschwitz."

Now, still in Toronto, still in Canada, I could postpone it no longer. With a two-year Killam Fellowship, it was the best, longest period of leisure I ever had; there would be little of it, little of "home" in Israel. Such as it is, *To Mend the World* will remain my magnum opus.

✝

"I raise myself in thought to the Absolute . . . thus being infinite consciousness, yet at the same time am finite consciousness. . . . *Both aspects seek each other and flee each other . . . I am the struggle between them.*"[21] This passage from Hegel must have provoked my thought, even back in Berlin. (Certainly Metzger, a former Husserl assistant, would have made much of it.)

If "the age" is *really* "ripe" for Science, Hegel *both* rises to the Absolute *and* remains with his finitude; and since, unlike Kierkegaard, he does not remain geared to a self, viewed by him as petty—let alone make it *existenzial* and *existenziell*, as, following Kierkegaard, Heidegger does in *Sein und Zeit*—the unfinished "struggle" is between his Age in History and Eternity, and a *struggle it remains: then can* either *Science* or *the Age get to "Planet Auschwitz"*?

I quote Hegel again: "The Life of Spirit does not shun death, so as to preserve itself pure from devastation but endures it and maintains itself in being torn asunder. It finds its Truth only when it is torn asunder absolutely."[22] I also paraphrase my comment in the same chapter: "But Auschwitz *is* a 'Planet,' a world of its own, but 'unprecedented in hatred and sadism': '*no* Spirit' can 'endure' it."

In 1967, this was just an assertion: how to go beyond assertions? There is only one way: a philosopher must plunge from *theories* about evil into *evil itself,* that is, expose his thought to *Dreck und Feuer* (feces and fire)—the Auschwitz reality. "Auschwitz" is itself a "Planet" of its own. How better to face it as such than with a philosophy insisting that the Whole is the Truth? And what to do, thereafter, philosophically?

In the quiet of the Robarts Library at the University of Toronto I could, of course—other than remembering Sachsenhausen, slight in comparison—only *imagine myself* in the Holocaust, that is, I could read about it in survivors' reports or works of scholarship; however, I found even the worst credible.

To begin with, *wherever thought looks, evil is somewhere else.* Thus, to cite examples in Claude Lanzmann's *Shoah*, Treblinka's Jewish women, lining up to get killed, are naked and hence are cold in winter; so is *Unterscharführer* (noncommissioned officer) Franz Suchomel, for he has no winter uniform.[23] If *Schöne Zeiten* is, rightly, the title of a book about *Täter* (perpetrators) and *Gaffer* (onlookers), and this is a good time for robbing and killing Jews, the *Täter* and *Gaffer* may as well have a *schöne Zeit* (good time) of it.[24] If an *Erntefest* (harvest festival) is celebrated for Jews wiped out in Poland, why should the murderers not "celebrate"?[25] If Eichmann is a *Hanswurst* (Hannah Arendt's term for "clown"), his "evil," famously, is "banal."[26] Finally, if Eichmann is near the bottom, the one at the top surely is Hitler, if only as author of the Weltanschauung requiring a "problem's" "solution," none short of the "final" one. Thus one is *just compelled to* ask: surely Joachim Fest knew, before he wrote his book, not only about meat hooks for the July 20, 1944, "traitors," but also about movies for Hitler to watch, so as to miss none of the carnage.[27] Why then does he assert that Hitler *does not want to watch it* in the *Jewish* case and hence why does he postulate—absurdly, after Hitler's Reichstag speech—a "striking" führer "silence" about Jew hatred, thus further postulating, more absurdly, "some support" for the "conjecture" of a "remnant of bourgeois morality" in Hitler?[28]

Fest is a respected historian and hence cannot be taken as sharing Hitler's own view that—despite "crimes" that Jewish babies are "born with"—death in the gas chambers was a "kinder" punishment than Jews deserved.[29]

Fest's personal observations appear toward the book's end. Perhaps a clue is found in its beginning, where he wastes five of the book's almost eight hundred pages on "Hitler and Historical Greatness," thereby showing himself to be another German unable to face the fact that a *führer once considered "great"—by nearly all, in Germany if not elsewhere—was radically evil.*

In his prologue Fest asks whether Hitler had "historical greatness," but his last sentence is "can we call him great?" Before that he writes: "If Hitler had succumbed to an assassination or an accident at the end of 1938, few would hesitate to call him one of the greatest of German statesmen, the consummator of Germany's history. The aggressive speeches and *Mein Kampf,* the anti-Semitism and the design for world dominion, would presumably have fallen into oblivion, dismissed as the man's youthful fantasies."[30]

Which "we" does Fest write about? I have already cited Leo Baeck's prayer on Kol Nidre in 1935: by the standards of Fest's "we" it would have fallen into oblivion three years later. Moreover, by then the Kristallnacht had occurred, the last chance for the world—nay, Germans themselves—to bring down the Hitler regime, avoid the war, avoid fifty million dead, avoid the Holocaust.

In the inability to cope with Hitler and Hitlerism, historians are not alone; witness Albert Speer's testimony. Gitta Sereny wasted time asking whether Speer had lied in claiming ignorance of Auschwitz, for if so he was like many others.[31] In contrast, Speer's knowledge of the führer, as he himself showed, was virtually unique. He writes: "What he loved about fire was not the Promethean aspect, but its destructive force. . . . Fire itself, literally and directly, stirred a profound excitement in him. I recall his ordering showings in the Chancellery of the films of burning London, of the sea of flames over Warsaw, of exploding convoys, and the rapture with which he watched those films. I never saw him so worked up as toward the end of the war, when in a kind of delirium he pictured for himself and for us the destruction of New York in a hurricane of fire. He described the skyscrapers being turned into gigantic burning torches, collapsing upon one another, the glow of the exploding city illuminating the dark sky."[32]

In every civilization worth talking about the innocent *remain innocent*, resisting even the devil. But, despite his puny efforts at the end—to stop Hitler from destroying Germany—Speer could resist Hitler only when he was dead.

But where, in all this, is the "Planet"? If Hitler's Weltanschauung is "abstract"—banal because of "abstractness" and abstract because of his "bourgeois morality"—the actions of the *Täter* and the *Gaffer* are banal also, for, under the circumstances, their actions are only those for which it is a *schöne Zeit*. The unity of the "Planet" thus falls apart into two parts: the "abstract" Weltanschauung—the *führer* says what the *Anschauung* needs, but wants no "details"; and the *Täter* and the *Gaffer*—who obey suggestions, if not exactly orders, whatever the "details," when this time may be the one and only *schöne Zeit* for their deeds. *Thus the evil vanishes: it is in neither part, nowhere.*

But a Hegelian "whole is the truth" thinking cannot let this happen, for such thinking is *circular*. Unterscharführer Suchomel did not *have to* join the SS or *become* an *Unterscharführer*. The *Gaffer* and the *Täter*—already common thieves since the 1938 Kurfürstendamm episode (which was, in reality, no "episode")—were free to say "no" to the mass-murder escalation, a "no" for which they would not have been punished, and, of course, they could have said "no" to their own sadism. Arendt's *Hanswurst* made decisions beyond a *Hanswurst* 's banality, first, when he joined the SS, second, when he took this job. They *all created* the "Planet," but the Planet also created *them*.

I read about the so-called ordinary men in the *Erntefest* who did not feel badly about killing only children, since they would not long survive without adults: the Holocaust whole was more than the sum of the parts: in the *Erntefest* ordinary men killed children.

There is no need to hark back to Nazi origins, but only to Kristallnacht, the last possibility for Germans to overthrow the regime. (After that came the war; then it was too late.) If, at the lowest level, Kurfürstendamm citizens had remained law abiding; if, higher up, the police had done their job, and defended the *Rechtsstaat*; and if, at the highest level, Roman Catholic Father Bernhard Lichtenberg had not been alone, but if many others had also protested honestly like Lichtenberg, not like Bishop Wurm, half-heartedly, with reservations, themselves half-Nazi— then there would have been neither war nor *Erntefest*, for there can be no *Fest* without *Ernte*.

During Kristallnacht, Lichtenberg had prayed for Jews at his Berlin *Hedwigskirche*, had gone on doing so for two years, until he was betrayed, arrested, and jailed for two years; old and sick, he died on his way to a concentration camp. Had just a few hundred of others, Catholics or not, Christians or not, done likewise and, like Lichtenberg, taken serious action—say, in front of burned-down synagogues—the regime would have collapsed. Earlier I cited George Mosse, who maintained that "the night of the long knives" in 1934 was the last chance for Germans to overthrow the regime. But now, as a philosopher, I disagree with this historian: he speaks about "the possible," I about the "not impossible"; Kristallnacht was not necessary, not inevitable, but contingent.[33]

That even at Auschwitz evil was contingent was shown by SS officer Flacke.

It is true that if "God is dead" "everything" is "permitted," but, surpassing Nietzsche, in the *Dreck und Feuer* of "Planet Auschwitz" *evil was commanded.* This even Hegel's "Spirit" cannot grasp, although it goes beyond Nietzsche and mediates evils in wholes and the death of God, in *the absolute* Whole. But with "Planet Auschwitz" *all* mediation is impossible: the more radically the attempt to mediate is made, the more starkly it collapses into a "surprised acceptance and horrified resistance."[34] Thought must—ever again—"accept" with "surprise" that Auschwitz *did* happen, hence *could* happen, and thus it must be *doubly* surprised that *we are still here, yet "resist in horror" understanding it:* Auschwitz is a rupture, of *thought* and *life.*[35]

Dr. Ella Lingens, a prisoner, recalled at the Frankfurt trial that there was one island of peace at the (Auschwitz) Babice subcamp, because of an officer named Flacke. "How he did it I don't know," she testified. "His camp was clean and his food also."

The Frankfurt judge, who had heard endless protestations that orders had to be obeyed, was amazed.

"Do you wish to say," he asked, "that everyone could decide for himself to be either good or evil at Auschwitz?"

"That is exactly what I wish to say," she answered.[36]

But "Planet Auschwitz," a *factum brutum,* is *not* necessary, *not* inevitable, but contingent.

13

On Icons and Radical Evil
A Bit of Philosophy

I must interrupt my narrative here for a bit of philosophy and repeat what I said at the start, that those who wish can skip this
next chapter. I have written that post-Holocaust Judaism needs
not only reflection on evil but also philosophical, even metaphysical, reflection; even more so because philosophy since Plato
has no concept of *radical evil*—his famous image of the cave has
only lesser imitations of a lesser Good. I must, on an enormous
subject, be brief.

A few years ago I wrote:

Two extant pictures of Schelling give an inkling of the
contrast [between his youth and old age], the first a painting of the young man, the second the only photograph of
his old age. What the old Schelling sees, we can see in his
eyes. These are the eyes of a man, who has been struck, almost physically, by brute facticity. . . . As a philosopher,
what has struck him is not this or that fact, but facticity as
such, its bruteness as such, so that, if he is an "empiricist"
of sorts, his is, as he says himself, occasionally, a metaphysical empiricism.[1]

Schelling had come far from the youth identifying Truth with
Beauty. But, back in 1954, I had already written on the aged Kant
concerning "radical evil"; and Schelling, also in old age, depends
on him. My last sentence had been: "Nothing in heaven or on
earth is more important than the moment in which a person—any

person—makes him or herself good or evil. . . . And whenever anyone makes such a decision, the universe, so to speak, holds its breath."[2] Or is what is seen in Schelling's eyes only *what I see* and have seen for many years?

Had Hegel been alive in 1954, he might have replied that evil in Kant and Schelling, while real, is, in Hegel's *Weltgeschichte*— honestly, with all the strenuous "labor" necessary—*aufgehoben* (suspended, sublated). Hegel is the only Western philosopher audacious enough to "mediate" between Eternity and History; or one could call him humble because he merely comprehends what, according to him, history *has already* done. The startling thing is Hegel's view that Eternity and History have met in his own time, that in some sense, if no other, Eternity and History are one. But, Hegel does not deny the difference although, at the same time, he does deny it. Thus he reaches the concept of *Weltgeschichte*, understood by Reason not merely human, but human-Divine. My book on Hegel, *The Religious Dimension in Hegel's Thought*, had only one ultimate aim, how Hegel, a human being with merely human reason, can rise to a Reason that is absolute.

Why, for Hegel, is "the time ripe" here and now? And how can he be audacious—nay, presumptuous—and also humble? Two revolutions have occurred in modern history, a secular one, the French Revolution, which was humanity storming Heaven, and a religious one, the Reformation, in which divinity touched the heart on earth; these two revolutions need each other. Yet a third revolution has taken place in modern *thought:* begun by Spinoza, continued by Kant, with their difference already partly mediated by Fichte and Schelling. Hegel had been humble: he merely completed in Thought what was *already there* in Life and potential in Thought.

But of the mid-nineteenth century Winter and Bagett have written: "One of the icons of the twentieth century, the gas chambers of Auschwitz, brings us to the limits of language, perhaps to the limits of human reason itself. Hell came to the surface in Auschwitz and left a taste of ashes for all of us who live in its shadow."[3] Although historians, Winter and Bagett philosophize when they use "icon," for this says something was essential for the twentieth century, even beyond it for the twenty-first century.

Winter and Baggett follow this passage in their book with a photograph of Jewish women and children in the Auschwitz of

1944. One takes for granted that the SS and the generals who were "following orders" had also shared in the murder of others, but of whom else did they not merely take photographs but also keep them? Winter and Baggett must have used pictures that were recovered from the SS men when they were captured. The SS kept them to the end, for victory to the end, crucial for their own *Weltgeschichte*.[4]

If Auschwitz is an icon today, Malcolm X was yet another icon yesterday, and others doubtless will emerge tomorrow. For Rosenzweig this process was "historicism." It was a predicament from which he was rescued despite and because of Hegel: the *Star of Redemption* was possible *post-Hegel mortuum*.

The possibility existed *because of* Hegel, for his Reason—absolute, final—could not flee to a "postmodern world," as reason once had, in Plotinus, the Stoics, the Epicureans, to a world after ancient paganism and its emperor gods; the possibility existed also *despite* Hegel, because absolute Reason liberates humanity for an *einfältiges Wandeln mit deinem Gott*, a "simple walking with your God" (Rosenzweig, quoting Micah 6:8). The liberation is for Jews and Christians and ultimately for the world.

Hegel knew, of course, that evil exists in the modern world as it does in all worlds, but it is "accidental," alongside the "essential." But he did not know radical evil: "Planet Auschwitz" could not be coped with by dismissing it as accidental beside the two revolutions in modern life nor by absorbing it by *Verstehen* in thought. Nor could Hegel, like those such as Winter and Baggett, reduce his Reason to "limitation," that is, to finitude after all, and be destroyed by "Planet Auschwitz." Rather—if I understand "Hegel Today"—in facing radical evil, his Reason would have shown an ultimate freedom, a hitherto unsuspected self-destruction. (This concept does not yet appear in *To Mend the World:* self-destruction of Reason confronting "Planet Auschwitz" emerged after nearly two decades of reflection after *To Mend the World*.)[5]

This facing of radical evil would have included Reinhard Heydrich's "particularly fiendish trick": as historian Klaus P. Fischer noted, "Jews were to organize their own destruction and pay for every penny of it—a scheme worthy of the worst of sadists." Elsewhere Fischer reports that only a small number of Heydrich's followers were clinically classifiable as sadists.[6]

As self-destruction, the final freedom of Hegel's Reason, transcending both Heydrich and his "fiendishness" would have pointed to a post-Holocaust future. Have philosophers, rather than medical doctors, ever defined sadism? Now it is no longer confined to the Marquis de Sade, but is *weltanschaulich*, "metaphysical"; for what once was actual is possible ever after.

On "radical evil" I am still, philosophically, involved with the Hegel-Schelling controversy. But for the Holocaust, Schelling's "metaphysical empiricism" is not enough.[7]

14

To Jerusalem

In 1983 our family moved to Jerusalem, but for me personally, this was not the end of Toronto. In 1995 I was asked to give the keynote address at a university symposium, celebrating twenty-five years of Jewish studies. I viewed the celebration as a memorial to Father John Kelly, who had been its prime mover, and I was invited by his successor, Professor William Dunphy, now also deceased.[1]

I could not speak on this subject and omit the negative. I could not speak about Judaism, philosophers, and universities and be just positive, of course not about German and even European universities, but also not about American ones, including even the University of Toronto. Why, in the nineteenth century, had Leopold Zunz, the founder of *Wissenschaft des Judentums* and a man who was proud of *Wissenschaftlichkeit* (scholarly / scientific discipline), asked for just one chair, and yet was turned down by the Prussian government? Why, in the twentieth century, had philosopher Jean Paul Sartre, though compassionate about French Jewish Holocaust survivors, written that existentialism was atheist or Christian? (As if Buber and Rosenzweig did not exist.) If "prejudiced *Wissenschaft*" is a contradiction in terms, surely so is "prejudiced philosophy." Why, even at the University of Toronto, was the subject only twenty-five years old?

But the Toronto affair was a celebration; hence my main theme was not past defeats, but a present victory, in Toronto and elsewhere. Of past defeats I mention only two causes. One is that some say that no people has a history without a state and the other is that the State of Israel came into being just after the most radical attempt to "solve" the "Jewish problem."

At the end of the "between Toronto and Jerusalem" period, we were visited by Will Herberg, a Jewish theologian and an old friend. He came to lecture on Sinaitic Judaism. But when he claimed that "by the logic of their position" secular Jews should "stop being Jews," I protested. "What about survivors? Israelis? Auschwitz survivors on aliyah to Jerusalem?" Herberg replied his commitment was to Sinai. He had no use for "novelties."

For us the Holocaust and Israel had ceased to be novelties.

Part 3

Israel

15

A New Job

"Where are you from?" the woman asked. She belonged to the "Absorption Ministry" of the Israeli government, welcoming newcomers to the country. "Toronto." "Did you have a good job?" "Yes." "Do they have much anti-Semitism?" "No." "Then what are you coming here for?" She had the wrong job.

Once I would not have thought so. When we were first invited to Israel, we had lunch in Jerusalem with Jacob Herzog, who, we guessed, had suggested inviting us. When he asked, "Why are you not coming?" it was the second time in my life that I had no answer to a big question. The first time was in the Halle jail, and it took me fifty years to answer that question, in my book *What Is Judaism?* This time, it took us—Rose and me—thirteen years; we answered it when we came to Israel.

Or perhaps the absorption person, after all, had the right job.

I do not recall whether Israel's government in 1983 was Labor, Likud, or National Unity, and whether, despite the Law of Return, they wanted such as us. But since, next to the state itself, this law is the only *real*, albeit radically inadequate, Jewish response to the Shoah—"no more Jewish homelessness, no more Jewish refugees, exile is over!"—it did not seem important, and it was not.

Like the welcoming official, I had the wrong job, or, rather, it was wrong for me to have a job: learning Hebrew should have been my sole occupation.

Learning and forgetting languages often seems the story of my life, in my youth, Greek, and now Hebrew. Despite Rubenstein and Sister, now at age sixty-eight and hard of hearing, I should have attended an ulpan for fully six months.[1] For Rose, then in her late forties and without Hebrew, it would be hopeless. In Toronto her jobs had been charity and/or charity related. In Israel, without Hebrew, even employment by a charity was ruled out. But, despite Yossi's being in the "terrible twos," Rose stuck it out until she got sick.

In 1983 I had been invited to serve as a professor at Hebrew University for three years, but I doubt I would have gotten the position without the Institute of Contemporary Jewry. A part of the university, the institute had been founded by Moshe Davis and, after his retirement, was directed by Yehuda Bauer. (The university itself was represented at the institute by Nathan Rotenstreich, but although I respected, if not stood in awe of him for translating Kant, we had no real relationship.)[2] With Davis a relationship was real, because of his interpretation of Mordecai Kaplan's "Jewish Civilization."[3] Having made aliyah, Moshe applied that concept within the academy but also against it (first in Jerusalem, later worldwide), that is, against scholarly infatuation with the past, the further away the better, and the scholarly conviction that for contemporary affairs journalism is enough. (In 1974, although long on record as a critic of Kaplan's theology, I spoke in tribute to Kaplan at a New York "Reconstructionist" dinner, mostly because of Moshe.)[4]

My relation with Bauer was different. He introduced us to Abba Kovner, who had led the resistance in Vilna. Kovner told us of his speech at the end of the war to the "last ones" among Jewish resistance fighters, before they all went away: now the enemy knows how easy it is; it has happened to Jews once, and will happen again. When I argued it hadn't, and Kovner replied that Stalin had died just in time, I had nothing more to say. Rose and I visited him several times before he died.

In introducing us to Kovner, Bauer was not waving an Israeli "flag," posthumously, for armed Jewish resistance in the Shoah. He knew as well as Hilberg how relentless and cunning the Final Solution had been—"relentless," for no Jew must stay alive, "cunning," with devious schemes to make armed Jewish resistance near-impossible. Hence it was a harrowing debate, when, once in Boston, I was the third participant, together with Hilberg and Bauer. Hilberg argued that armed resistance alone counted, but Bauer maintained that, under the circumstances, stealing food or medicine, hearing lectures, even attending religious services also mattered. The audience, mostly professors, sided with Bauer, but when Hilberg asked, "Who in this room owns a gun?" there was a dead silence.

As the third participant—also a professor, as well as a one-time follower of Buber and Baeck, both steadfast in Judaism, even in face of the worst adversity—I was in the middle, but while Hilberg's truths had begun to sink in, my position was still closer to Bauer's: he knew the difference between the post-Shoah Jewish "Emergence from Powerlessness" (the title of a book of his, for which I wrote a preface) and Jewish impotence in Nazi Europe.

But there was and is a difference between Bauer's views and mine. When writing "against mystification," he may have included me among the mystifiers. That this is a misunderstanding was clarified when, in the 1980s, Ron Rosenbaum came to Jerusalem to ask Bauer, a "historian," about "theology" and me, a "theologian," about "history."[5] (Rosenbaum thought the time was ripe, not for yet another explanation of Hitler, but for putting the spotlight on the explainers.) For Bauer, Hitler is *in* history, that is, he is "explicable in principle, but that does not mean that he *has* been explained"; but for me "the closer one gets to explicability, the more one realizes that nothing can make Hitler explicable." I should have added—and in conversation probably did—that historical explanation must first go as far as possible. (After my three months in Kassel, Germany, I would have used the word *betroffen*, which translates roughly as "stunned.") Our difference is the difference between a historian and a philosopher. "Planet Auschwitz" and "Planet Third Reich" are *in* history, but the attempt at *radical* explanation—that is, philosophy—discloses a *rupture of history in history.*[6]

The opening page of Rosenbaum's *Explaining Hitler: The Search for the Origin of His Evil* has four quotations, one by the well-known Hitler historian Alan Bullock and the two quotations already mentioned, Bauer's and mine. Rosenbaum's fourth and final quotation was ignored in reviews by the *Jerusalem Post* and *Commentary,* yet for me it is pivotal; it may even have inspired Rosenbaum's book as a whole: "He [God] owes me answers to many questions" (Holocaust survivor at Auschwitz, 1985).[7]

But I do not want to give the wrong impression about Kovner: a resistance fighter, he was also one of Israel's great poets. Once

Rose and I visited the Tel Aviv Diaspora Museum. In Israel *dati* (religious) and *lo dati* (not religious) Jews used to be rigidly distinct, and now that some *dati* Jews are in politics, the state is both better and worse. (Once, wearing a kipa, I hailed a taxi on Shabbat and earned scorn and laughter.) A left-wing *Hashomer ha Tzair* socialist, Kovner was *lo dati*.[8] Yet he created a display in the Diaspora Museum that has "religious" festivals on one side, "secular" ones on the other, Purim, the "Festival of Trees," the Ninth of Av and others: what, Rose and I wondered, will he do with Yom Kippur, place it in the middle or at the end of the passage? For there is nothing "secular" about Yom Kippur. In a description in the museum Kovner quotes the Talmud: "The gates of prayer are sometimes closed, but the gates of *T'shuvah* are always open."[9]

I quoted that passage in *To Mend the World* (326). It has a crucial place in the book's argument, not only the Talmudic passage itself but also Kovner's use of it: after the destruction of Jerusalem, the Talmud was meant for *the whole* Jewish people, including Rabbi Elisha ben Abbuya, called *acher*, "the other" because, with the temple destroyed and exile begun, he could no longer believe, *but he was not excluded*. Neither does Kovner exclude those who, after the Shoah, cannot believe; yet he lived and died in Israel, as if exile had ended. Kovner did not merely quote the Talmud; he also spoke to *amcha* now.

Since the institute was part of Hebrew University, I asked Dean Aaron Singer about my role there. Surely teaching in Jerusalem should differ from teaching in Toronto or at Harvard: the "here and now" should be part of it, nay, *in* it. But the dean said: "You can get away with it, but none of us can." I got it: I was not just another rabbi, retired but still preaching. (There are plenty of those in Jerusalem.) In Toronto I had ceased to be a "two hat" philosopher: in Jerusalem I still was. Or was again.

Sometimes I could do justice to both "hats," scholarship and the "here and now." They were building at Hebrew University, with rubble and dust everywhere. Once I was teaching Yehuda Halevi's *Kuzari* and had just ended a lecture by quoting him: "Jerusalem will be redeemed only when Jews love her stones and dust." Then I got carried away: "What are you waiting for? There are plenty of stones, there is plenty of dust." With this I walked out of the classroom.[10]

But mostly my "two hat" philosophy was less dramatic. My students belonged to three groups, Germans, one-year visitors, and Israelis. The Germans were the best students, but they had been selected in Germany. (I will have more to say about Studium in Israel later.) The overseas visitors were hard to classify, their experience was varied, and their knowledge ranged from expert to zero. But when I first arrived, my chief interest was the Israelis. Since they worked during the day, and my classes were in the evening, they were often tired. Also, I had been warned about their impatience; since they were in the midst of ongoing Jewish history, they philosophize—they have to!—on their own.

Although my first course was on Jewish philosophy, it began, not with Hermann Cohen, but with Kant. In Toronto one spends a whole semester on the *Foundations of the Metaphysics of Morals*, but in Jerusalem, I had been advised, one evening would have to do. The "expert" (as I invariably call students whom I assigned the responsibility of being prepared to hold forth) that first evening was finished in twenty minutes. I said hers was a fine summary, but *why* did Kant say what he did? "That's his opinion!" It did not look good for philosophy.

In Biblical studies Moshe Greenberg, whom we communicated with when we first arrived, had similar experiences: he too had to lower his expectations. But both of us were initiating a new period in Jewish history, and the lowering of standards was necessary but worthwhile. Israeli cab and bus drivers listen to the news every hour on the hour. But for students—at least of the Bible and philosophy—their field of study is subject to daily tests: in Bible, whether they defend the state or seek peace (most want both); and philosophically, they have "opinions."

With Toronto University committees, I sometimes had to defend Hebrew University; some colleagues viewed it as "colonial," others as "Third World." In 1981, the philosophy department honored five retirees, and each of us said a few words about his plans. But even my friend John Hunter (who introduced me) was just personally pleasant; only Bob McRae understood, for he had been in a Nazi POW camp.[11]

When I arrived in Jerusalem in 1983, my job at Hebrew University was neither "colonial" nor "Third World." I had a book on Hegel under my belt, hence I was regarded as scholarly but was permitted to sermonize, provided I didn't do so often.

My three years as professor were no great success, at least not with the Israelis. I had a Catholic student from Spain who believed in two kerygmas in Christianity, the second being the Jewish state, but he just said this privately. An American Jewish student of mine organized a symposium at the University of Oregon, "Ethics after the Holocaust"; but that was in 1996 and he too was from overseas. Just one session in Jerusalem—this also with overseas students—sticks in my memory, for it could happen only in Jerusalem. The subject of the session was "Jewish identity." I arranged for three "experts" to carry on, while I just sat and listened. One was a German woman, who had missed Hitler's definition of "non-Aryan" by one generation and had come to convert to Judaism. Another student, she too a woman, also wanted conversion; she was an American Episcopalian. The third was a Catholic priest, who had converted from Judaism as a young man, had twinges of conscience now, and was sent by his U.S. superior to Israel. There were, of course, Israelis in the class, probably the majority of the students; but how it struck them I do not know.

When first in the "Land of Promise"—if only to double-check that aliyah had been no mistake—new *Olim* such as we look for indications that it was indeed as the word says an "ascent," and although we expected the worst, we had some surprises. Before Sukkot, the "feast of tabernacles," I went to Mea Shearim, the orthodox quarter in Jerusalem, to buy a sukkah and then look for decorations; I found Christmas ones. When I mumbled something about Christmas decorations being odd in Mea Shearim, the salesperson replied: "Christians have their *simchah,* and we have ours."

This surprise, from a supposedly "close-minded" "ultra-Orthodox" Jew, was preceded by a contrasting one, in a Reform Jewish kibbutz. The first festival that occurred after our arrival was Pesach. Our daughter Suzy was working for six months in Kibbutz Yahel (near Eilat), then the first Reform Jewish kibbutz in Israel. (There now is another.) We were invited for Seder.

The Seder was disappointing: too much confusion, too much noise, too many children—their presence can be inspiring, of course, but it is not good for attention to the text. Then someone announced that next evening we would go into fields to count the *Omer*.

The *Omer*, no longer observed in Reform Judaism, has long been a meaningless ceremony in Orthodoxy: counting one day each day, from one to fifty, the kind of ceremony that is equally meaningless, surely, in Christianity, for what is Pentecost? But to count *to a harvest* is different. That second evening we sang and danced, to the sound of guitars.

I gazed at the arid surroundings: can *anything ever* have been made to grow here, even in Biblical times? Then I gazed at the fields, the vineyards, the Western youngsters who had made them grow, and I was filled with awe, of the land, of the people, but most of all of a mitzvah that, once moribund, has been brought to new life.

Sukkot that year was also surprising, but in a different way. During this festival, Jews are to dwell in booths for a week, originally out of respect for Nature—the harvest—later also out of respect for History—the forty years. Israeli weather is clement enough not just for eating in the sukkah but also for living in it, even sleeping and surely, with the knowledge of "the Land here-now, desert-uncertainty past," Israeli sleep should be sound. But apartments in Israel are small, earning a living is hectic, and—most important—when we first came, peace was still just a hope; even in 1999, I had to write to my friend Fred Krantz and his Canadian Institute for Jewish Research in Montreal that we in Israel after the Shoah are in the desert again, without signposts, but that his institute, fortunately for us, is a good one.

Hence not only Sukkot is different, but also Shavuot, "the feast of weeks." Once, with the post-Pesach "fifty days" behind them, Jews received the Torah and could understand it as "given whenever they receive it." But now we are in the midst of a "Jewish return into history."

With my three years at Hebrew University over—the Toronto house sold, a Jerusalem apartment bought, aliyah definite—Dean Singer said I could continue as long as I wanted, in the School for Overseas Studies, as *moreh min ha-chuz*, "external teacher," the lowest in rank and pay.

In explaining rank and pay, he said: "Now you are really one of us. You get treated like dirt, like everybody else."

I was glad to be like everybody else and accepted the position, of course, but my main reason, to begin with, was Rose. She could no longer eat without help but amazingly—for a while encouragingly—could still follow a lecture, and with Leon Barshaw taking us to the lecture hall at the university, and sitting with her in class, we went to my lectures. Leon has long been my best friend in Israel. The most civilized engineer I know, he worked for Westinghouse in Switzerland, Spain, Egypt, other countries, until he retired in Israel. An American, he has moved from Trotskyism all the way to Zionism and Israel. Whenever I "get soft," usually liberal, he keeps me honest.

When Rose could no longer come along with me to the university, I went on teaching.[12] But when, in 1996, I made what seemed a small decision—one, however, that was much bigger than I thought at the time: to teach for three months in Kassel, Germany—it resulted in the end of my teaching. When I returned to Jerusalem, I found Hebrew University's schedule all arranged for the next year; it was a sign that eighty is a good age to quit. Even at eighty, I needed an excuse to stop teaching.[13]

16

Mostly Unfinished Business

A few years ago the *Canadian Jewish Review* invited me to write a monthly column. (The period is over now.) Readers in Canada may have thought my columns right-wing, but American and Canadian former liberals often move to the "right" in Israel, "right" meaning with a concern for the state's safety, even its survival, which is part of the reason they have come to Israel. (I sometimes tease my friend Shirley Olman, once a prominent Washington Democrat, who, when widowed, made aliyah and has moved "right"; her son works for Daniel Elazar's soberly realistic Jerusalem Center for Public Affairs. I will have more to say about Elazar later.) None of us ever loses sight that Israel can only win wars, can afford to lose none, for loss now involves the grim thought of rogue states seeking—even having—arms of mass destruction.

My column opposed Oslo, less because of the unknown professors who had engineered it, less also because of Shimon Peres's dream, too hasty, of a "new Middle East," but mainly because of the much advertised (and actual) irreversibility of a process that would have Israel do all the giving—including accepting unpredictable Palestinian statehood—and leave her with little with which to bargain when, at last, the sought-after "peace" arrives, and along with it the still unresolved fateful issues: borders, water, refugees, Jerusalem. (The easiest issue is water, for, as it took no politician but an intellectual, David Horowitz, to point out: the sun has all the electricity, the Mediterranean enough water; desalinating is just for politicians—after peace.) And all this in a democracy, without elections. The United Nations often acts as if it regrets having voted for Israel; if enemies still want to push Israel into the sea—in stages, of course—they have long learned not to say so, and the world just wants peace, without questions asked.

I now side with the decision of the late Daniel Elazar's Jerusalem Center for Public Affairs to accept the peace process, for, to me at least, Israel is still under siege; not even Churchill (who helped his people endure under siege for a year) could have done so for fifty.

Vis-à-vis Oslo, while the Jerusalem Center for Public Affairs is firmly Zionist, its focus is broad enough to include the right and the left. Thus I recall Manfred Gerstenfeld's *Israel's New Future,* which interviews optimists and pessimists, the left and the right, Abba Eban and Abraham B. Jehoshua, who are more or less doves, as well as Moshe Arens and David bar Illan, who are more or less hawks, the "more or less" because, with Israel under siege, neither term applies; moreover, Gerstenfeld's organization has internal as well as external problems. Those on the outside are the United Nations, Europe, America, the Vatican, the "permanent threat, Islamic fundamentalism," and the "loaded dice of the foreign media," are all here to stay: these factors had been among the reasons why we came to Israel. Gerstenfeld's book got me interested also in "inside" problems: "Returnees from the army, as officers, have had important responsibilities. They have traveled the world as well, and then they come home and are offered jobs selecting chicks in the kibbutz hatchery."[1]

When in 1938 in Berlin we considered a kibbutz, we never thought of this.

With two elections gone—one with Netanyahu, the other with Barak as prime minister—and the process not reversed, I mention only two of my columns for the *Canadian Jewish News,* for I still view them as correct. As I wrote in 1999, Israel had just moved to the final compromise in the sought-after peace, ending a tragic conflict, between "right" and "right" (Hegel). In one column, I compared two heroes resisting tyranny, but Nelson Mandela is at home, while Nathan Sharansky is still on the way. My other column celebrated Jerusalem: not the first return, after the Israelites had retained hope in Babylon, but the second—after hope was annihilated and then recovered.

Other business, once intractable, had been left unfinished much longer: "What does Judaism say to us now?" I had been asked that question on November 11, 1938. I published my answer almost fifty years later, in 1987. *What Is Judaism?* is for a new generation of *amcha*.

The Holocaust is *a fact;* hence *as a possibility* it will always be built into *amcha's* Judaism: this is why—for me as a theologian and philosopher—not only survivors but post-Shoah Jewry as a whole are *amcha;* it is also why I had no answer to Abba Kovner when he had said that Stalin died just in time.

Hence, I could also *begin What Is Judaism?* only with the minimum—bare Jewish survival and fidelity to it, *itself* minimal—and *end* it, as its *maximum*, only with its Shoah extremity—the absurd, paradoxical, there and then only midrash of Warsaw Ghetto Rabbi Kalonymous Shapiro: a God "far" from Israel precisely because God loves Israel, that is, is near: because God's love, were God *with* Israel, would destroy the country, through the infinity of God's pain. God is not indifferent, remote, for he loves Israel; yet the extremity of Auschwitz and His own suffering in it makes him distant; the extremity of His pain, were it close to Israel would destroy it.

I published *What Is Judaism?* in 1987, but in 1996 also published midrashim of Return. Seeing "earthly" Jerusalem "in bondage with her children," the apostle Paul made his followers rise above destroyed, captive Jerusalem, on earth "below," in a Jerusalem "above," "free," and "in heaven," the "mother of us all" (Gal. 4:25–26).

But the midrash sounds as if its author knew the apostle's view of Jerusalem and contradicted it. It *resists* abandoning "earthly" Jerusalem, has its *God resist* abandoning it, has God refuse to dwell—as it were, in unconcerned luxury—in Jerusalem "above" (*Bab. Talmud, Ta'anit* 5a).

Another midrash has the *Shekhina*, "God's Spirit," "never stir from the Wall": Why act that way when, with the people in exile, it is alone with stones? The *Shekhina* waits for their return (*Shir ha-Shirim R.* 2:9). But since June 7, 1967, the *Shekhina* does not wait any more: such, at least, are the words of a Jewish song—almost an anthem—second only to "Hatikvah," "the hope," Israel's national anthem: "Jerushalayim shel Zahav," "Jerusalem of Gold."

Today the "politically correct" have forgotten that "Jerusalem of Gold" was once second only to Israel's national anthem. Even so, on every Ninth of Av thousands of Jews come to the Wall, there both to lament and to rejoice. The lament, 2000 years old, is more extreme because there was no Jewish state during the Holocaust; but so is the wonder at having returned.[2]

The winter 1999 issue of *Azure* had one theme: "The Jewish State: The Next Fifty Years." Of over fifty contributions, mine was shortest and hence can be quoted in full:

What sort of "Jewish State" should Israel be? To answer decisively, it may still be fifty years too soon. For a catastrophe has happened that Herzl never dreamed of, and for Ben-Gurion it had yet fully to sink in. However, Ben-Gurion knew there must be a Jewish state, and Weizmann's judgment was "now or never." Too terrible had been the Holocaust in Europe, and too terrible Jewish helplessness everywhere else.

The decision "a Jewish state now" had been secular-religious. Without the secularists, the religious would have been waiting for the Messiah, alas, in Europe. Without the religious, secularists might have built a state elsewhere; but they would never have made it to the Land of Israel.

Two years after its founding the Knesset passed the Law of Return; had it failed, it would have been to their lasting shame. Another seventeen years later, Israel returned to Jerusalem. Others have compared it to the Crusaders, who came, left, and left behind ruins. But Jews came back to stay, rebuilding Jerusalem.

Recovery takes patience and time and, being short of both, Jews at one extreme forget their quarrel with God and lapse into ultra-Orthodoxy, while Jews at the other make Germans exterminating Jews into a quarrel between "people" and "people."

Will there be an end to patience, even after fifty years? Jews have returned once before and, had they not done so—had all the tribes been "lost"—neither Christianity nor Islam would ever have arisen. Perhaps one day two words of the "Hatikvah" can be changed, and "Jewish soul" can be replaced by "soul of Abraham." The Christian God, too, is God of Abraham, Isaac and Jacob; and when Abraham died, "Isaac and Ishmael buried him together" (Gen. 25:9).

Of course, the other "children of Abraham" *would have to mean* what they sing, the exile, the Shoah, the return to Jerusalem.[3]

I wrote this only two years ago, but I now think my "fifty years" were too soon, not only for Palestinians but also for Israel itself. Ever since Oslo, the Palestinian authority has exploited education to its ends, has texts denying the Hebrew Bible's Jewishness; for example, a fifth-grade text begins "Abraham was a Muslim monotheist and was not among the idolaters." More seriously—this involves the threat of war—May 15, Israel's Independence Day is widely mourned as *Nakba*, a "catastrophe," implying that, despite Oslo, Israel's very existence is not accepted, such that after every Oslo "peace for territory" step, the Palestinians want more. But most serious is a problem in Israel itself: in its own Knesset, Arab members waver as to whom their loyalty belongs, to their country or to the as yet undeclared Palestinian state.

What I feared when I opposed Oslo has become real, but I still hope for the change in the "Hatikvah." I now think, however, that fifty years are not enough.[4]

17

Germany

In 1958 we visited post-Hitler Germany. It was my first time, thirteen years after Hitler's fall. Rose and I had married in 1957; the next summer I took her to meet my father in Aberdeen. (My mother had died; he had remarried Trude Silberberg, known from Halle's HTV 04.) Since we were in Europe, we went to Germany for a week. There we became friendly with just one person, a young, enterprising American black man, who was in Mainz to study racism. It would take me thirty more years, until 1988 in Fulda, to reach the view that I should visit Germany, speak with Germans, listen to them, even find allies and friends there.[1]

I had meant to omit personal reactions from my narrative, considering them unimportant, but since this memoir is also personal, and this part of it is about Germany, I have changed my mind.

In 1958 we arrived in Germany without even knowing it. The rest was a mixture of the new and much too much of the old. My getting out of Germany had been hostile, abrupt: we arrived now without even knowing it, and the immigration official was soft-spoken and polite. (Now they always are soft-spoken and polite.) We barely boarded a Rhine boat just as it was departing, but the person on the boat, a staff member, made a fuss about getting the ticket outside, at a ticket booth on shore. The boat itself displayed a poster about the Rhine being international, but the music played on board, while not exactly "Die Wacht am Rhein," was martial. What is worth telling is our first encounter with Germans, as it were, "on German soil." (In Canada, Germans had been no problem.) I had promised Rose and myself two things, that I would take no nonsense from anyone, and that I would ask questions. My first inquiry was to a waiter on the boat, where to go in Mainz, and he suggested the pub of the Holy Ghost, but urged me to bring my papers: once he had gone there without his and was arrested. Thus my second question: "As a German you must carry papers?" This was enough for an outburst: "Germany is still a *Polizeistaat* (police state), and if I were young enough I would leave for Canada." (I had told him we were from there.)

I returned to Rose and told her she had to meet this guy. Meanwhile the waiter had been joined by another, who told us he had been in Canada—as a prisoner of war, of course; after the war he had applied to immigrate but had been refused. I said nothing, but no more was necessary, for he spilled out that he had been in the attack on Crete, but he was no longer a Nazi, unlike his brother in East Germany who was still an idealist. But he recognized that Hitler had made "mistakes," with the churches and the Jews, for they were too powerful.

I said: "Perhaps the churches are powerful, but the Jews were murdered." "But they have all the money." Such was the end of my first "dialogue" with Germans "on German soil," for, of course, I ended the conversation: "You say you are not a Nazi anymore, but you still are." During all this the first waiter said not a word.

With this incident—except for our encounter with the enterprising young man studying racism in Germany—our first visit to Germany was finished. Not much else happened.

Our next visit was to Bergen-Belsen in 1970, with survivors. We went to the camp, but otherwise Rose and I never left the Hannover hotel. She never came with me to Germany again.

I had participated in Jewish-Christian "dialogues" before, but when, in the late 1970s, I was invited to one with Christians in Germany, I replied I would come when the subject was the Shoah; invited again, I accepted and went to Aachen and Krefeld in Germany, Simpelveld in Holland. It was Holland because of Emanuel Levinas, who had sworn not to set foot in Germany.

I met Levinas also in Israel, and we found we had Rosenzweig in common. He invited me to Paris, but Rose's Alzheimer's was just beginning, and I could not go.

Additional Jewish participants at the conference included philosopher Werner Marx, who had left for America in 1933 but returned to Germany to accept the Heidegger chair.

When the dialogue was published, it showed that the discussion had been a failure. *Damit die Erde Menschlich Bleibt* (So that the world remains human) states that Jews and Christians, while "not simply deaf" to one another regarding Christology, must speak to one another in post-Hitler Germany, then speak together, each with the ethics of his or her faith, for the future, on behalf of an "earth habitable for humans."[2]

As I wrote to the editors of that volume, Wilhelm Breuning and Hanspeter Heinz, at least two incidents showed that the dialogue we had hoped for had failed. One Jewish participant had reported how the SS had given a Jewish woman the choice between picking one son, who would be allowed to live, and refusing to do so, in which case all four sons would be killed; how a rabbi had told her she must refuse, for she could not have a share in murder; and how she obeyed, with a "heavy heart" but "comforted." The editors speak of a "thoughtful listening silence" (163), but they do not seem to know there are many kinds of silence, from Helmut Gollwitzer's refusal to preach on the first Sunday after Kristallnacht, to Friedrich Wilhelm Marquardt's five hundred pages of it, in *Von Elend und Heimsuchung der Theologie* (On the misery and affliction of theology).[3] But the editors make the cited incident into a case of "bottomless ethical choices for humans in our time" (153). *For humans!* Trivializing the Shoah, ignoring its "scandalous particularity," falsely universalizing it.

That the Shoah had been evaded in this dialogue was still more obvious in another case: "The hybrid distinction between seemingly innocent witnesses and a world full of guilt is not permitted." Thus participant Richard Schäffler of Bochum University, but the failure was less his than the editors', who thought there had been a consensus (162). Four years after this book's appearance, I spoke at Schäffler's university and quoted Primo Levi: at Auschwitz the perpetrators had "robbed the victims even of their innocence"—a unique guilt of these perpetrators and, of these victims, surely an unprecedented innocence.

Nevertheless, I am glad I went to Aachen, Krefeld, and Simpelveld, because of Hans Hermann Henrix and Martin Stöhr. On meeting me at the airport, Henrix had said, "Jewish Christian hostility will not end until Christians relate positively to Jews, not despite Jewish non-acceptance of Christ, but because of it."[4]

This introduction—as well as Henrix as a person—remained with me through the dialogue, the presence of a friend.

Stöhr responded to my talk in Krefeld. He began: "We Christians have lived alongside Jews for nearly two millennia. But we have never listened to them, and our Christian faith, in this respect, has not helped us. Then why do we want to listen now? Not because of our Christian faith, but because six million Jews were murdered."

Then followed a relentless critique of Jew hatred in the religion of love, making me wonder, even worry, whether any Christianity would be left, until he said: "We Christians must begin again with the first two questions of the Bible 'where are you, man?' And 'where is your brother?'"

Thus I first heard—in Germany of all countries!—about "a new Christian beginning," with an "Old" Testament now called "First."[5]

But only thirty years later, since 1988, was I made to feel I must return to Germany again. It was on March 6, my older brother's birthday, and I was in Fulda despite, but also because of, him. Had Alex not died of sickness (one account) or committed suicide (another) in Nazi Berlin, they would have carted him to Treblinka: thus I was in Fulda despite him, but because of him to give the *laudatio* for Studium in Israel. This is a German-sponsored organization that annually sends twenty-odd theology students to Jerusalem in an attempt to bridge the Nazi abyss. If there were no such attempt, even for the next generation, Hitler would laugh in hell. I told my Fulda audience there was no better way to bridge the abyss than for young German theologians to study in Jerusalem. This effort would also cope with time-honored prejudices, to ensure that they be honored no more.

Why am I critical of Buber going to Germany, speaking to Germans, when I went as well? All I can say is that he went fifty years too soon, that most Nazis are now dead, some by hanging, most through a peaceful old age, and, of course, some like my schoolmate Rossmann, even in 1933 or 1934, never wanted the "damn thing," the swastika in the *Turn und Sport* medal.

Thus Fulda was crucial for my visits to Germany: if an invitation to "genuine dialogue" (Buber) came from the German side, I must respond on mine. (See my first address in post-Hitler Germany, in the appendix.)

But then came the Historikerstreit, leaving me unwilling to return. Just to read about it was like "thinking" of Germany "at night" and "losing sleep." But I had done enough of that, with Heinrich Heine, as youth leader of the Halle Bund deutsch-jüdischer Jugend.[6]

But despite the Historikerstreit I just *had* to come, in 1986, to an international congress on Franz Rosenzweig's hundredth birthday, in Kassel, the city of his birth. But it was with pain of thought like no other I know of. Since my Berlin years, Rosenzweig had kept me steadfast, more even than had Buber and Baeck; his life and death inspired. His *Star of Redemption* had ended with a stirring "Into Life," possibly Christian, certainly Jewish, but so soon after his thought and his death came Jewish mass murder.

Wolfdietrich Schmied-Kowarzik's effort was Herculean, first in arranging the congress, then in editing the two-volume *Der Philosoph Franz Rosenzweig*.[7] But I cannot have been the only one at that Kassel conference to consider it as also quixotic, not only because of the grim Auschwitz and Treblinka end, but also because of Nazi efforts, both before and after his death—so long as they could, with lasting effects—to erase every trace of Jews or Judaism that had ever existed in Germany.

But Schmied-Kowarzik's effort, if Herculean and quixotic, was also truthful, an aspect that made me come back to Kassel in 1997 and become a friend. By chance or not, in that year he published *Vergegenwärtigungen des zerstörten jüdischen Erbes*, a record of the "destroyed Jewish heritage."[8] The book contains lectures by ex-pellees, now invited back, one per year. I was the eleventh annual lecturer, for three months living in Kassel, teaching German students in Germany.

I describe the content of my courses in my inaugural lecture in the appendix. Two of my three courses were obvious, based on my books, on the *Problematik* of Jewish faith after the Holocaust, my *What Is Judaism?* as text for beginners, my *To Mend the World* for the advanced. The third course was conventional: Hermann Cohen, Martin Buber, Franz Rosenzweig. But I wanted to open it unconventionally: after the Holocaust, can Jews relate to Kant as Hermann Cohen did before? After this epoc-making event, can

Jewish philosophy be the same? German philosophy? Philosophy as a whole?

But if, back in 1983, my Jerusalem students had one problem with "Kant and Hermann Cohen," unprepared as they were for philosophy, in 1997 my Kassel students had another, in that they were not of the *Volk der Denker* (people of thinkers) anymore. This is just my impression: "Hitler as philosopher" has destroyed not only, rightly, the proto-Nazi nineteenth-century *Fichte Bünde* but also, surely wrongly, the "golden age" of philosophy as a whole: my "unconventional" session on Kant and Hermann Cohen in Kassel was a failure.

I spent much of my three months in Kassel preparing a lecture I would give at a Rome conference and hence had little time for life in post-Hitler Germany.

Even to live in post-Hitler Germany was not easy: I was unable to take trains, so they took me by car; my right arm was lame, and my son David joked, Biblically, about forgetting Jerusalem. My memory of the three months in Kassel is thus mixed up, sporadic, and fragmentary. I will write about just three persons from that time.

Christoph Münz has published *Der Welt ein Gedächtnis Geben* (To erect a memorial for the world), a volume of nearly six hundred pages about Jewish *geschichtstheologisches Denken* (historical-theological thinking) after Auschwitz.[9] The "thinking"—as it must be in Judaism—is "historical" *and* "theological," both together, the people and the faith. But since, with a few recent exceptions, *Geschichtstheologie* does not fit into the German academy, in either departments of theology or of history, neither his book nor Münz himself has a place in German universities.

The second person is a young student—she cannot have been more than eighteen—who once came forward after a lecture, gave me an envelope, and rushed off. (I looked for her but never saw her again.) The envelope contained a poem about me, "this old man" comes in with his "tennis shoes"—no German professor would wear them to class—and gives us in this "godforsaken country" a new "image of God." She had added her own theology: "God made a mistake, sending the rainbow."

This made me change my metaphor about "bridging" the "abyss": bridges are built by humans, but after the Shoah there is a high wall between Germans and Jews, especially German Jews;

it needs flying over, and this requires—is sometimes given— more than human help.

My third person is Eva Schulz Janner. A Jewish refugee in America, she had met German professor Burkhard; they married and returned to Germany. (I stayed with them in Kassel.) Eva is secretary of the local Jewish Christian society for *Zusammenarbeit* (cooperation). In everyday life she constantly meets people who have tried to forget, do their best to, have long forgotten. But her work is with those who remember, wish to remember, seek to re- cover, are *betroffen*. Eva taught me this word in its current Ger- man usage. It means more than "stuck," is more like "shaken." And it goes with an *Ahnung*, or "hunch," which must be, will have to be, will be something more—said, done, happen.[10]

18

Return to Halle

In 1993 I returned to Halle. In my first chapter I have described how I went to the *Stadtgymnasium*, was reminded of Reinhard Heydrich, and got the shock that made the past come back, like a close-up in the movies. It was after my return home, to Jerusalem, that I started these memoirs.

In 1937–1938 I had attended Halle University as a student. In 1993 I was back as a professor, speaking on "Auschwitz as Challenge to Philosophy and Theology." I published this lecture only with hesitation: it was too tough and left no impact I know of. In 1937–1938 philosopher Paul Menzer had shown, as a person, with his courage, that in morality one "imperative" is "categorical"; but in 1993 what philosopher could explain how its Hitlerization by Adolf Eichmann had been possible? (Eichmann quoted Kant at his Jerusalem trial, in explanation of his obedience to Hitler.)[1]

And theologian Otto Eissfeld had cited Isaiah, that the "hut in the cucumber field" of the "daughter of Zion," if frail, still stands; but in 1993 what theologian, Jewish or Christian, could face the fact that at Auschwitz *both* "huts," the Jewish and the Christian, had fallen?

In 1993 my Halle listeners must have been stunned, *betroffen*; so, on reflection, was I.

So long as Halle was communist, I had given no thought to the city, let alone to a return to it. Hence when, sometime in the 1980s, Ilse Strauss, the daughter of Curt and Hannah Lewin, visited

Rose and me in Jerusalem, I did not understand what she was trying to tell us. After Kristallnacht—with my father in Buchenwald, myself in Sachsenhausen, my mother alone—Ilse's mother had telephoned mine and told her to move in with them. Why? Curt was the only Jewish male in Halle at home, unmolested: he was protected by their neighbor, none other than Reinhard Heydrich. (Later, with Heydrich assassinated, and none to protect them, Curt and Hannah Lewin were murdered.) I assumed Heydrich had been their neighbor still and I had once published that my mother, for a few weeks, had lived "under the same roof" as him.[2] That he headed the SD office in Berlin; that this was both fomenting and practicing Jew hatred; that utter ruthlessness had gotten Heydrich where he was; above all, that this one-time neighbor of my parents' friends would soon admit his former "mistake"—to expel Jews was not enough; from oldest to youngest, they must be murdered—of this I knew nothing, *had wanted* to know nothing.

But after my return from Halle to Jerusalem, I took a few steps to find out. I had heard that in 1935 Heydrich had made a policy statement; in 1993 or soon after, I got the document and also Shlomo Aronson's book, for most scholars the best on Heydrich still; published in 1972, it was written when reliable contemporaries were still alive.[3] Most important of all, I contacted Ilse Strauss in London and got answers to my questions.

Heydrich's "Wandlungen unseres Kampfes" is a crucial article in *Schwarzes Korps*, the notorious SS magazine, published in 1935. Its timing was obvious: Hitler was rearming. So was a crucial Heydrich motive, a boundless ambition. This much I got from the document itself: in it he argued that *Wandlungen* (metamorphoses) were necessary, and he wanted a large share in the *Kampf*. But why, in 1935, his claim that leaders of Jewish organizations—such as my father's Reichsbund jüdischer Frontsoldaten—were "sparing no effort to get Jews to enlist"? Why a Jewish "plot" against military "purity"? Since Heydrich had been a Lewin neighbor—in 1938 had still acted neighborly still—why not, through Curt, ask my father? He would have told him there was no such RjF "effort," let alone a "plot."

But, with the *Schwarze Korps* document full of anti-Jewish paranoia and Jew hatred, this is, of course, an absurd question.

Yet the hatred and paranoia themselves are puzzling, for even before 1934, Heydrich already enjoyed power and had "widened exceptions" to "prohibitions" for Jewish organizations, expressly allowing the RjF to exist. I got this information from Aronson's book, but did not need it for this, for the BdjJ was still legal in Halle, when I left in 1935.[4] More, my father wrote for the still existing *Schild*, the RjF periodical, as late as in January 1938. (When I visited Halle in 1998, they gave me an essay he had published, urging his *Kameraden* to be faithful to the memory of their dead, as well as to each other. His advice lasted for just ten months, until Kristallnacht.)

So why that sudden switch, from 1934 to 1935? Saul Friedlaender explains that Eichmann had supplied Heydrich with a report, "most astonishing" in its "imaginary concreteness," about Jewish organizations in Paris, Amsterdam, and elsewhere, all existing and supposedly plotting. (The organizations existed, but the plots did not.) In Friedlaender's view Heydrich and his men "probably" thought it "inconceivable" that Jewish organizations existed and did not plot.[5]

But Joachim Fest has a different theory. Heydrich's "almost frenzied emphasis" on fighting and defeating the "Jewish enemy" and his "shrill tone" in *Wandlungen* stem from his own fear of having himself "Jewish blood." I once thought Aronson had discredited this theory. (An SS official had asked about it, publicly, in 1932, before Hitler was in power and hence—so Aronson argued—unable, if he wanted, to keep Heydrich in the SS, for he still lacked the power to suppress the truth.) But now Ilse tells me she once met Heydrich's grandmother and that she was Jewish. Still, Ilse was not more than five years old at the time and writes that she was more interested in the grandmother's candy. So Fest may have a point, even his assertion that the rumor of "Jewish blood," psychologically upsetting, was enough; Heydrich "was teased about it even as a school boy." But nobody commits mass murder because he was teased at school.[6]

Thus neither theory explains what happened between 1934 and 1935 to account for the document's sudden viciousness. Later scholars describe SD's "satanic cleverness," with Heydrich its presumable author.[7]

But on Heydrich as an adult, Ilse herself was of little help. She sent me a letter a former maid who knew both families had written: as a child Heydrich had beaten his younger brother with a whip, and the maid had to stop him, but children do such things. Why did Heydrich, as an adult in power, behave like a neighbor to her father? In view of what happened later, Ilse must have thought about this long and hard. But she had no answer.

As we have seen, Joachim Fest has a hard time with "Hitler and evil": no wonder, Hitler had once been führer and the führer could do no wrong. In contrast, he finds it easy enough to compare Heydrich to "the great criminals of the Renaissance, with whom he shared a conscious awareness of the omnipotence of man." But even these criminals lacked the "courage" to murder children. The "courage" for that was Himmler's boast, but Fest *can* cope with him: *der treue Heinrich* (loyal Heinrich) betrayed Hitler, tried to "bury the hatchet" with Jews, disguised himself as an ordinary sergeant, and, when captured, committed a coward's suicide with a pill. Fest writes: "'My behavior is more important than what I say', [Himmler] had declared at his Poznan speech. . . . Now his behavior contradicted it all. There is no legend."[8]

But Fest's first sentence suggests he is unable to cope with Heydrich, whose "fiendish trick" must cause philosophers to redefine sadism: "In Reinhard Heydrich, National Socialism seemed to be confronting itself."[9] What is confronted was evil.

Only two persons of any fame were born in Halle; the other was Georg Friedrich Händel. Among the world's great composers, only Händel loved post-Biblical Judaism. (Way back in the past, for the Hallel in synagogue, we had used a tune from Judas Maccabaeus.) Händel spent most of his life in England, but the city of my birth had once been proud of his birth, enough so to memorialize him with a statue on the *Marktplatz*.

But this was long ago. In 1942 the music director of the Berlin Propstei (provostry), in charge of Christian oratorios, protested that Germany could not afford Händel's "glorification of the Vengeance God Yahwe, at a time when World Judaism was mobilizing mankind to annihilate the Aryan race," and in 1944 a certain Johannes Klöcking, still believing in Nazi victory, "translated" Händel's Israel in Egypt into *Victory in Walstatt*.[10]

I was in Halle again in 1998 to give a second lecture, this time long enough to go to the *Marktplatz*. I went not to see other

Sehenswürdigkeiten (places worthy of being seen) such as the Marienkirche or the Roten Turm, but just the Händel statue. The Nazis might have done what they did in Dresden to Mendelssohn, smash the statue; but the Händel statue is still there.

19

Before and After My Return to Halle

In Toronto, in 1979, I had read Eberhard Bethge's biography of Dietrich Bonhoeffer and decided to write to the author. In 1938–1939, Ernst Tillich, brother of Paul Tillich, had been in our "block" in Sachsenhausen, a Christian Gentile among about sixty Jews, but evasive on why he was there; now I learned the reason from Bethge's biography: Bonhoeffer and others had written to Hitler, complaining about the treatment of Jews, but Tillich and Werner Koch had leaked the letter to the foreign press. Had Tillich's arrest made Bonhoeffer politically active, made him join the anti-Hitler conspiracy, thus leading to his eventual martyrdom? An important question about the past, but still more important was another, about the future: if Bonhoeffer had lived, would he have developed a post-Shoah Christian theology? Bonhoeffer had been Bethge's friend, and his biography was such a tribute to him that I thought it right to trust him, posthumously, with so weighty a question. And, of course, I trusted Bethge.

But I never expected so painstaking a reply, detailed, serious, with so much honesty about his friend and, above all, his own sense of urgency: the problem needs study; despite advanced age he may do it himself, for an epoch in Christianity has ended. However, Bonhoeffer himself had known only about Jewish expulsions, not about the Shoah.

Then this man, surely indispensable for future Christianity, German and worldwide, Protestant and Catholic—he had just finished his big biography—went through his papers again and found one unequivocal sentence: "The expulsion of the Jews must lead to the expulsion of Jesus Christ, for Christ was a Jew."

On this slim basis and other findings, Bethge lectured on "Bonhoeffer and the Jews," also wrote, "Nichts scheint mehr in Ordnung" (Nothing seems in order any more).[1] Bonhoeffer would have found it "unimaginable," how "seamlessly" Christian theology returned in 1945 to where it left it in 1933. The *Erschütterung* (shock) of the Shoah was not behind Christians but still ahead: "Die 'Judenfrage' von 1933 war angesichts von Auschwitz nun total zur Christenfrage geworden" (The 'Jewish question' of 1933, because of Auschwitz, had become a Christian one).[2] Such was his lecture in 1979.

For me, still in Toronto in 1979, this was, for the moment, the end of my relations with Germans and Germany; but Bethge himself was well past his beginning. The Protestant church in the Rheinland had set up a committee called Zur Erneuerung des Verhältnisses von Christen und Juden (For the Renewal of the Relationship between Christians and Jews). It had met for two years, not another Christian committee *about* Jews, but one *with* Jews. It arrived at a resolution, and when it was passed, Bethge was regarded as one of its "fathers." About the Shoah, it asked: "Who is *betroffen* by this monstrous event?"[3] It answered:

The answers of Jews are difficult because of a *Betroffenheit* of their own which, rightly, refuses to make the incomprehensible comprehended, the unspeakable speakable thus, as it were, with speedy comfort stealing from the dead even their death.

Christian answers are difficult because of the danger of abuse as escapes from their own implication. This danger exists with every premature interpretation, such as a speedy invocation of the Crucifixion, or a quick assertion of the Resurrection that is not preceded by lengthy repentance; or as an abrupt "nonetheless" without any testing of comparable situations of suffering.[4]

The key sentence of this—the most difficult part of the committee's "resolution" was: "Theological answers to the question of theodicy must guard against robbing God of Divinity, and against distorting the abandonment of the murdered."[5] This was a crucial statement, made by Jews and Christians together.[6]

An enormous statement, for theology and philosophy, and it happened in 1980 in Germany. Although there were Jews in Germany, those few in attendance must have been deeply honest.

The courage, honesty of these Jews—it had taken all these years to reach this point—is amazing: they must have faced, in bitter truth, *both,* the innocence of the victims *and* Hitler's Weltanschauung, which holds that Jews are born guilty: their innocence cries to heaven as well as against it. But no less amazing are the courage and honesty of Christians who have faced the "scandal of particularity" *for Christianity:* after Auschwitz, Christianity needs a reformation, more radical than the one that once made Germany famous. The Jewish-Christian dialogue Buber wanted, needed, did not get before the Holocaust, has become indispensable. Or—to complete my essay on "icons and radical evil"—Hegel's self-destruction of Reason has not only negative consequences, warning of dangerous possibilities, but also demanding necessities, and among them surely is the "death and rebirth" we found at Bergen-Belsen.

Perhaps these Jews and Christians remembered Chaim Kaplan, writing almost forty years earlier; but they cannot have known David Patterson, who wrote only in 1999, recalling Kaplan. The Warsaw Ghetto diarist had died in Treblinka in December 1942 or January 1943, but the last line of his *Diary* is: "If my life ends, what will become of my diary?"[7]

With this question Patterson opens his book: after that he recalls how the doomed man wrote, not knowing whether anyone would find it and read it.[8]

To hark back to Bethge's 1973 statement, he, in *Konsequenzen,* quotes Franklin Littell and me a few pages earlier. If Littell wants to retain his "alpine" image, from now on it means that Jews and Christians would meet at the top, and that, after this, any lesser Jewish-Christian "dialogue," is backsliding.

Perhaps, by whatever name, a reformation is necessary also for world Christianity. This is shown by Patterson's title: the extremity of the Auschwitz *Sonderkommandos* was beyond "the edge of annihilation" but, even so, a "recovery of life."

Germans such as Stöhr, von der Osten-Sacken, and Henrix prepared the Cologne conference. But much of it was also implied when Pope John Paul II came to Jerusalem, the Wall, and *Yad Vashem.* Yet without disturbing Catholicism and prior to the conflicts sure to come regarding Jerusalem, he might have spelled out that, after the Holocaust, Jews just *had to* return to Jerusalem.

"How doth the city sit solitary that was full of people" (Lam. 1:1). Lamenting—but also rejoicing that the city had Jews again—the pope might have cited this "Old Testament" passage, that is, that after the Holocaust, this "testament" is no longer "old."

We made aliyah in 1983 and were in Jerusalem for ten years. Then came 1993, the year in which I went to Halle; our marriage was ruptured, and I would live alone, write these memoirs.

The year that began sadly ended with joy. On December 31, David and Wendy got married, he from Toronto, she from Glasgow, both having met in Jerusalem. For me there was further joy. Wendy's folks in Glasgow are friends of the Goldbergs, the family that had sponsored my parents in 1939 and had helped them to leave Nazi Germany. The Goldberg granddaughter was at the wedding.

In March of that year we had to find a place for Rose and discovered Sheila Mark. I used to think of *Olim* as two kinds, those who must come (refugees from Russia or Iraq) and those who want to come (such as ourselves). Sheila Mark made me think up yet a third category: *Olim* who come, find the country needs improvement, and stay to do it. A nurse from England, Sheila found Israeli nursing homes inadequate and set up her own. So long as Rose was at home with Alzheimer's, her old friend, Shirley Dorin, on a farm near Calgary, visited, once with Herman, her husband, as a friend and caretaker when I lectured in America. Nobody ever had a better friend. Now Sheila Mark's people took care of her, until 1998, the year Rose died.

Now that I have that new category, I include in it Zvi Ehrenberg, my lawyer from Melbourne, and my doctor, Ted Miller from Toronto; also Moshe Davis, who died in 1998, and Daniel Elazar, who died in 1999. Both have founded lasting institutes in Jerusalem.

But most newcomers have friends, who "make the country better." Davis and Elazar were special. With his Institute for Contemporary Jewry, Moshe changed the university world, for from now on universities that care must have, or soon will have to offer, Jewish Civilization courses. And with his Jerusalem Center for Public Affairs, Daniel changed the Jewish world, for he has brought the Biblical concept of covenant into present political action.

One kind of Israeli, *Oleh* or native born, we still await to bring a genuine peace, with justice as close as practicable between "right" and "right." (A tragic conflict is not between right and wrong but between right and right. Compromises are necessary.) But this does not depend on Israel alone. As Charles Krauthammer has written, only one election ago—not all that much has changed—large nations may suffer defeat and even when occupied cannot disappear, but Israel is small. I have quoted this before, but now add one sentence: not many Jews are left; Hitler murdered one third.

20

A Theo-political Decision by a Jewish Philosopher

In 1992 Louis Greenspan and Graeme Nicholson edited a *Festschrift* (memorial volume) entitled *Fackenheim: German Philosophy and Jewish Thought*.[1] I am indebted to the two editors, also to the other contributors, five my former students and yet a sixth a student of a former student. I mention one, Michael Morgan, without whom, it often seems, I would not have lived so long; also I have similar feelings for John Burbidge, in Michael's case because he has long been with my work, in the case of both, because they edited books of mine, when my wife Rose was sick with Alzheimer's and I was not up to it. The *Festschrift* got it right: German philosophy and Jewish thought have been my work.

I had best sum up decisions that made me both a philosopher and a Jewish one, and the kind I still am.

The first was in 1935 when I decided to study Judaism, which later brought me to philosophy: without this not only mine but our Berlin struggles for a divine Presence—of all places, for Jews in Berlin, the Nazi capital—would be unintelligible. We were *seeking access* to Judaism, in pre-modernity with Yehuda Hallevi and Maimonides, in our age with Buber, Rosenzweig, Baeck: we were not born—or "born again"—"fundamentalists." Reflecting on pros and cons in the Jewish heritage, we did not jump into, presuppose Jewish faith, just because of Hitler. As is well known, people become religious in adversity. Aware of that, we avoided it: after all, we were in the Hochschule für die Wissenschaft des Judentums.

All of us looked for a Judaism to hold on to. But at least I could not read Rosenzweig without also thinking about Schelling and Hegel. Of course, we also heard of Heidegger, read Jaspers's *Die geistige Situation der Zeit,* "the Spiritual Situation of the Age," although I learned only later these were *Denker in dürftiger Zeit,* "thinkers in a [philosophically] meager age" (see Karl Loewith's essay).

With this decision presupposed, my second was much later, the 1967 "614th commandment." In itself, this was not a decision for Zionism, let alone for a Jewish state or Jerusalem, but seeing in Nazism a new threat, not anticipated by Jewish tradition, I saw Jews and Judaism as requiring a new commandment. (Traditionally, 613 were given at Sinai, to Moses in his forty days.) In *To Mend the World* and other post-1967 writings I could come to no other conclusion.

How was Hitler's threat new? The last important one, informing all subsequent others, had been raised by Hadrian, the ancient Roman emperor who, bent on nothing bigger than keeping his empire, had forbidden, on pain of death, *Jewish faith,* which he saw as endangering Rome and who, through this prohibition, though of course unwittingly, created Jewish martyrs. There were ten rabbis who practiced Judaism, defied Hadrian, were caught and put to death; their martyrdom is mentioned in the most solemn part of the Yom Kippur liturgy. (My Uncle Adolf used to point this out to me.) Where is Hadrian's empire now? But Yom Kippur, hence Judaism, still exists.

In contrast to Hadrian, Hitler sought world conquest for the "Aryan master race," implying that "sub-human 'non-Aryans'" such as Poles and Slavs were too numerous and, making *Jewish birth* a crime deserving death, thereby killed not only Jews but also Jewish martyrdom. If *birth,* not *faith,* is the Jewish "crime," Jews in Buchenwald, by fasting on Yom Kippur, eating only bread with no other kosher food available, were not martyrs: they merely facilitated Hitler's job.

Much of this was shown in *To Mend the World.* But the book's core emphasis was that, *irresistible* though the assault was—on Germans-hostile-to-Nazism, on "sub-humans," and, always, on Jews—it had *nevertheless been resisted.* Today Christian theologians should ask whether Christianity has survived the Holocaust; when, as mentioned before, only one high prominent

Christian, Berlin's Catholic *Domprobst,* Bernhard Lichtenberg, had resisted, in Kristallnacht, that is, before the war, when resistance was still possible. What if hundreds, nay, thousands of Christians, led by well-known leaders like Lichtenberg, had prayed before burned-down synagogues? Would the Nazi regime have collapsed? From the impact of Lichtenberg on the regime, this is not impossible. If so, no war, no millions of dead, no Holocaust.

But while the Holocaust troubles Christian theologians, for the perpetrators had once been baptized, yet now murdered every Jew and would have murdered Jesus also, they need not despair of Christianity: at least there was one.

Philosophers similarly troubled need not despair of philosophy. Professor Kurt Huber's intended address at Roland Freisler's *Volksgericht,* though he was prevented from giving it, was resistance as well. But in philosophy, too, there were only few, mostly Huber's students of the Munich "White Rose." If Christians think of Lichtenberg, philosophers should think of Huber, as they already do of Socrates.

And Jews? Females and males were "punished," "religious" as well as "non-religious" Jews, all not for crimes but for their birth. But to Nazis, neither Jewish birth nor death was innocent, for after birth Jews were circumcised, and before death they could say Sh'ma Yisrael. In cutting off both, the one by murdering Jews at birth, the other at Treblinka and Auschwitz, they cut off the Jewish-Divine covenant radically. This ought to concern not only Jewish theology but the Christian as well. It also ought to concern philosophy, at least if it takes history seriously.[2]

The Holocaust thus was a total rupture; clear already in Kristallnacht before the war, *total* because for *Humanity*—with perpetrators doing everything wicked, victims able to do little—and *Divinity* because for both it was the God of Abraham. Even so, many of the victims have died with faith in God, itself resistance in extremis, perhaps greatest of all.

At my age, I cannot make any more theo-political decisions. But I *can* stay in Israel, for after the Holocaust, Jews need a state, and there is, can be no other: this is *political.* And what is *theo*-political? I *can* stay in Jerusalem for, even though this is far from the Messianic Age, with many considering "Auschwitz" its refutation, hope for Jerusalem survives.

Epilogue

Post-Holocaust Antisemitism in Europe

A Double Shock; and, On German Guilt after the Holocaust (Jerusalem, 2002/3)

When I started *An Epitaph for German Judaism* I did not plan to write about myself at all. But one of my personal catastrophes was shared by all survivors, even those of Auschwitz and, so one hopes, much of the world. That no human being is innocent is a belief shared by Jews and Christians, which is why Jews have Yom Kippur, Christians the Crucifixion.

But guilt after the Holocaust is *particular:* did I, personally, do enough for my brother left behind, think enough of my murdered uncle? Did *the world* do enough for the six million, countless Russians, Czechs, Poles?

The real guilt, of course, belongs to Germans, yet others, too, have no mere *feelings* of guilt, for psychologists to deal with: *the guilt is real.*

Theologians and philosophers must cope with this fact, and the first to do so was the German philosopher Karl Jaspers. It was brave and responsible of him to write so soon, for the need was urgent and immediate but, as we shall see, it was much too soon.

Jaspers distinguished between individual and collective guilt but, beyond both, asserted German guilt about Hitler Germany as "metaphysical" and this, he asserted, consisted of being alive.[1]

That this was wrong I knew from personal experience. My high school teacher of Greek and religion, Adolph Lörcher, could have escaped to Switzerland, for his wife was Swiss; also, like Bonhoeffer, he could have joined a plot on Hitler and risked getting murdered. However, his duty was *to stay alive,* teaching high school boys like us that there was a true Christianity and a better Germany. And if he was one German innocently alive, there were others, of course, and it is basic to know, even fifty years later, what kind they were. Was fleeing into the army "internal emigration," that is, into innocence? But one would still fight Hitler's war.

‡

I cannot cope with this question without first dealing with antisemitism and, shockingly, this after the Holocaust. (I once was naïve enough to consider this impossible.) I learned from James Parkes, a Christian pioneer in Jewish-Christian relations, that "antisemitism" is a codeword for something else; that it cannot be got rid of; and that the least we should do—lest people think there is such a thing as "Semitism"—is spell it without a hyphen.[2]

Why not replace it with *"groundless* Judeo-phobia"? I add "groundless" for the first Jewish response to so long a hate is, naturally, that it must be their fault. "There are too many Jewish lawyers, doctors, left-wing politicians, i.e. 'communists' in the Diaspora, in Israel too many right-wing politicians, i.e., 'fascists.'" Without the adjective "groundless," Jews blame themselves or other Jews. But European Jews were lawyers, doctors, businessmen because they could be nothing else, farmers, army officers only in America, essential as both in Israel; there, however, they "colonize" land belonging to others. Zionists may stress that "Palaestina" was invented by a Roman Emperor who, having conquered the land, named "Philistines" its true owners; but this stress on an ancient fact only proves Jews are behind the times, in the Diaspora when they pray for Jerusalem, Zionists when they *actually move* to the Land, even reestablish a long-outmoded State: no Jew, religious or secular, accepts that something "New" has happened, the New Testament for the religious, Progress for the secular.

Nobody disputes that Diaspora and Israeli Jews can justly *be criticized, Israelis, the State itself, if they* actually behave *like fascists, lawyers if, prior to the revolution, they are crooks or overcharge.* But this is

<table>
<tr><td>1</td><td>Staat/État/Country
Bundesrepublik Deutschland</td></tr>
<tr><td>2</td><td>Standesamtsbehörde   Weimar ---
Service de l'état civil de
Civil Registry Office of</td></tr>
<tr><td>3</td><td>Auszug aus dem Sterbeeintrag Nr. 747/1942 Weimar-Buchenwald -/-
Extrait de l'acte de décès n°
Extract from death registration no.</td></tr>
</table>

4	Tag und Ort des Todes Date et lieu du décès/ Date and place of death	Jo Mo An 02 04 1942 Weimar-Buchenwald --------------------------
5	Name Nom/Name	Goldberg --
6	Vornamen Prénoms/Forenames	Adolph --
7	Geschlecht Sexe/Sex	M --
8	Tag und Ort der Geburt Date et lieu de naissance/Date and place of birth	Jo Mo An 21 09 1898 Marburg an der Lahn -------------------
9	Name des letzten Ehegatten Nom du dernier conjoint/Name of the last spouse	Goldberg --
10	Vornamen des letzten Ehegatten Prénoms du dernier conjoint/Forenames of the last spouse	Erna --

	12	Vater Père/Father	13	Mutter Mère/Mother
5	Name Nom/Name			
6	Vornamen Prénoms/Forename			

11	Tag der Ausstellung Date de délivrance/ Date of issue	Jo Mo An 30 11 1998	Siegel/Sceau/Seal

Unterschrift/Signature/Signature   Reimann

SYMBOLES/ZEICHEN/SYMBOLS/SIMBOLOS/ΣΥΜΒΟΛΑ/SIMBOLI/SYMBOLEN/SÍMBOLOS/ISARETLER/SIMBOLI
Jo: Jour/Tag/Day/Dia/Ήμέρα/Giorno/Dag/Dia/Gün/Dan
Mo: Mois/Monat/Month/Mes/Μήν/Mese/Maand/Mês/Ay/Mesec
An: Année/Jahr/Year/Año/Έτος/Anno/Jaar/Ano/Yil/Godina
M: Masculin/Männlich/Masculine/Masculino/Άρρεν/Maschile/Mannelijk/Masculino/Erkek/Muški
F: Féminin/Weiblich/Feminine/Femenino/Θήλυ/Femminile/Vrouwelijk/Feminino/Kadin/Ženski

This is the death certificate of my uncle, Adolf Goldberg, husband of my father's sister Erna, which I obtained in 1998 at the suggestion of Volkhardt Winkelmann, for only a relative could obtain it. The document does not state correctly the date or cause of his death. He was actually murdered in the "Sonderbehandlung 14f 13" prior to April 2, 1942 (most probably on March 13, 1942), in der Landesheil- und Pflegeanstalt Bernburg where he was gassed upon arrival under the category "Straefling." On October 7, 1940, he had been imprisoned, in *Schutzhaft genommen,* in Halle under the category "political—Jew"; from there he was brought to Buchenwald on December 18, 1941. The last transport left Buchenwald for Bernburg on March 12, 1942. Bernburg had been a *Heil- und Pflegeanstalt* for a long time, but they had transformed into an institute for gassing the "politically infirm and insane" and lied even about this. They asserted my uncle had died of a heart attack. When I read of his death on my first visit to Halle in 1993, the book *300 Jahre Juden in Halle* did not mention this, so I did nothing except send a letter to the *Mitteldeutsche Zeitung, 'Der Dank des Vaterlandes'* ("The Thanks of the Fatherland"). But since I have heard the truth I think of my uncle every day.

not why my father, a lawyer, was robbed of the right to appear in court in Nazi Germany, and why his *Heimatstadt Universität* stole his doctorate. (Germans, always thorough, were never as thorough about antisemitism before.) In 1999 the current *Rektor* of the *Universität* apologized, and they gave me, the only surviving son, an honorary doctorate. After the Holocaust, an apology is rarely enough. But in this case it was the best the Martin Luther Universität, Halle/Wittenberg could do, for my father died in 1970.

The word antisemitism, then, can be replaced by "groundless Judeo-phobia." This may be awkward, needs explaining, but so does antisemitism. Then why not substitute it? One reason is bimillennial, the other, unique since the twentieth century. In Bar Mitzvah lessons I learned that Judaism has two "daughter religions," Christianity and Islam, and I wondered soon after, ever since, why the "daughters" are so often nasty to the "mother." Now, however, the Christian "Religion of Love" is widely getting rid of its "oldest" hatred, seeks to rid itself even of "contempt," with some Christians even loving the Jewish state, visiting her, while the other, Islam, is insulted when called antisemitic, even as it escalates it. Once one was called, called himself an antisemite if one disliked Jewish noses; now if one wants to kill Jews. Quite an escalation.

Why have the two daughters changed, in diametrically opposite ways? Because of the Holocaust. No other explanation makes sense. True, Karen Armstrong may have taught at London's Leo Baeck College, but paid no attention to Baeck's protest, mild but clear enough, published in *Merkur*, a respected German magazine, that the ghosts of murdered Jews still haunt the world, including the Jewish state. But she wrote two best-sellers accusing Jews of "remaining stuck" with the dead 1930s. Philosopher Ted Honderich was born in Toronto, probably heard me lecture about the Jewish dead, but learned only that further Jewish dead are needed, for Palestinian liberation. Who says Auschwitz is so extreme that no escalation is possible? The SS did only what it was ordered, but suicide-bombers must surely ask their parents, father or mother, for they also kill themselves. Of course, such as Armstrong and Honderich presuppose that even after the Holocaust, Jews have no right to *Eretz Yisrael*, the Land of Israel.

It took many years for Christians, Protestants and Catholics, to repent of their "contempt" for Jews, for what it has done, much or little, to make the Holocaust possible; it took even longer for Intifada II to exploit it: since Nazis killed Jews, "Muslim extremists" can do better, can even be religiously inspired.

Astonishing it is that few Jews listen when Anne Bayefski calls the 2001 UN conference in Durban antisemitic, and that only Zionists pay attention when Edward Alexander writes that antisemitism is being stolen, in every issue, by Michael Lerner's magazine *Tikkun*. But everybody can see Yassir Arafat on TV steal Winston Churchill's two fingers, his sign for Victory. Churchill's was over Hitler, Arafat's over Sharon, the "Israeli Hitler."

True, the thesis "two-daughters-and-the-Holocaust" is confusing because Europe's Christians are confused themselves, for while the French, though democrats, handed Jews over to Hitler, still act like Vichyites, Franco, though a fascist, turned Hitler down. This upset *den Führer* so much he would rather have his teeth pulled than argue with Franco again.

Even so, the thesis applies in Europe. Spain may hate Jews normally, more so now since, having behaved better than France, it has them still, the rest of Europe because it is sick and tired of hearing about Auschwitz.

Hence the real questions concern Germany, after all, and me as philosopher, also after all. Once Yehuda Halevi was concerned because, with Muslims and Christians fighting each other, Jews were crushed between them: now Arafat tells Palestinian children, Muslim and Christian that, when they are old enough, they should act as comrades-in-arms. As Jewish philosopher I worry more than my medieval Jewish predecessor. As scholar in German philosophy, I must ask whether *ultimately* antisemitism *is* the fault of Jews: would even Hitler's Germany have tolerated Jews maligned, done nothing when they disappeared if Jewish innocence, through millennia, had been total?

Do Jews and Judaism fit into modernity? Into modern philosophy? Jaspers thought Kant was the greatest German philosopher, but Hegel, if not greater, was more relevant. In the early nineteenth century Hegel wrote:

Es ist dies der merkwürdige, unendlich harte, härteste Kontrast. Einerseits ist der allgemeine Gott, Gott des

Himmels und der Erde, und zweitens ist der Zweck und das Werk dieses Gottes in der geschichtlichen Welt so beschränkt, dass dieser Zweck und das Werk dieses Gottes nur diese Familie hat.[3]

[This is the thought-provoking, infinitely harsh, nay, harshest contrast. On the one hand, God is universal, God of Heaven and Earth, and secondly is the purpose and work of this God in the world of history limited, so that the purpose is only one family.]

This is, of course, the divine-Jewish covenant, restated as a philosophical problem: *Universalism vs. Particularism.* Hegel has a problem with the "Old Testament" because he takes it seriously. Even so, "harsh" though he considered the problem, Hegel tries to do justice to Judaism, even in his "World History."[4]

What would Hegel think today? Such as Franz Rosenzweig thought World War I was the End of Hegel's influence. With the Holocaust the essential part of World War II, the shock would have been radical, and antisemitism after the Holocaust—in Europe of all places!—would have been a double shock.

This, though evident, is guesswork. For something else Hegel can be cited *verbatim.* He wrote that, while Muslim monotheism is "fanatical," Jewish monotheism is "admirable":

Diese Zuversicht des jüdischen Volkes ist das Bewunderungswerte, das in den Schriften dieses Volkes, und unter anderem bei so vielen Siegen zum Vorschein kommt[5]

[This confidence of the Jewish people, that among every thing else, appears also in its many victories, is admirable.]

Hegel wrote this late in life, close to his death; but as early as in the *Early Theological Writings* he had written the following:

Nachdem es [das jüdische Volk] alles getan, was höchstbegeisterter Mut leisten kann und nachdem das grauenvollste Elend ertragen hatte, begrub es sich und seinen Staat unter der Ruinen seiner Stadt. . . . Der zerstreute Überrest der Juden hat zwar die Idee seines Staates nicht verlassen, aber ist damit nie mehr zum Panier eigenen Mutes, sondern wieder zur Fahne einer trägen Messiashoffnung zurückgekehrt.

[After doing everything the most enthusiastic courage could achieve, they [the Jews] endured the most appalling of human calamities and were buried with their polity under the ruins of their city. . . . The scattered remnant of the Jews have not abandoned the idea of the Jewish state, but they have reverted not to the banners of their own courage, but only to the standards of an ineffective messianic hope.][6]

With so long, so persisting an understanding of the Jewish people, he would have been shocked by Jewish "calamities" he thought unthinkable and viewed Jews today, with a "courage" as desperate as "enthusiastic," with a hope not "ineffective," restoring their state and rebuilding their city.[7] "The Idea is not so impotent to be mere Idea." This applies here: the State will survive against all odds, and: Jerusalem will never be ruins again.

✝

Klaus P. Fischer's *Nazi Germany: A New History* has been called, rightly, the best one volume history of the Third Reich. It was published only fifty years after. Yet on German guilt it still quotes Jaspers: not many philosophers seem to have tackled this question.

Fischer illustrates Jaspers with a metaphor. Nazi crimes are like a rock dropped into a pond. There are big ripples nearby, lesser ones further away, but in due course the pond is quiet again.

This metaphor is inadequate, nay, contradicts Fischer's own work, for this pond, though after fifty years, has not been "quiet." Indeed, Fischer's book may have been too soon.

It was too soon to ask the big questions: Frederic the Great was the "first servant of the State"; and every German child still knows how the king wanted to confiscate a mill that disturbed his sleep, but how the miller took the king to court, won and the king had to remain sleepless. Also, every lawyer, certainly my father, knew that Bismarck made the *Rechtsstaat* firm like a rock. Hitler, in contrast, did with the state what he wanted, called Roland Freisler his Wyschinski, for he had learned from communists what a *Volksgerichtshof* was, yet now was a Nazi.[8] Hitler's use of Frederic and Bismarck was not an ordinary use by a politician of his predecessors. It was nothing less than a rape, and German guilt was for letting it happen.

Unscientific Postscript: The Modern "Dejudaising"
in Germany and Its Sequel, Memory and Understanding
(Jerusalem, March 30, 2003)

Like Søren Kierkegaard, I call this postcript *unwissenschaftlich*
(unscientific), for how could a memoir be objective, *wissenschaft-*
lich, when it has been about lives and deaths of those dear to me,
family and friends? As an article, it has appeared in Germany,
but in that country, in which I was born and educated, I know
now only few, whereas in the English version I can think of many
who, having read the book, will read this postscript.[9]

In 1819 seven young Jews met in Berlin for a question. It was
serious enough to found a *Verein* (club) that lasted five years:
"Club for the Culture and Science of the Jews." *How was Jewish*
existence possible in the modern world? This was the question. For
the seven, the "modern world" was Europe, mainly Germany.
Even America was far away, to say nothing of other continents.

The question had already occupied the previous generation.
But "the Enlightenment" had understood Jews only in the abstract, as "human-beings-in-general," with the result of a "Baptismal Epidemic" (Dubnow). Yet neither could one remain stuck
with tradition; this was too old-fashioned, no longer possible.

One of the seven was Eduard Gans, still young but already a
Hegelian, who made speeches saying that Judaism should *auf-*
gehen (dissolve) in Europe but not *untergehen* (perish). Consequently the *Verein* had two principles, that as Jew one must not
be baptized, and that, "if we feel that that being a Jew in the modern world is necessary, it must be possible." Now one would call
this principle "existential."

Among the seven were three who later became important.
One, Gans, already mentioned, became an editor of the "bliss-
fully remembered" deceased Hegel. Already in 1819 he had inspired the "club," was famous for a short time, but is known now
only among Hegel specialists. The second is famous still, should
not just be here and there cited, but be viewed as crucial by
Germans caring about Jews, and German Jews caring about
themselves, for he understood not only German-Jewish hope for
Modernity, but also its tragic aspects. He did not, however—as
some seem to think—anticipate the German catastrophe in the
next century. (Nobody did or could have.) It was none other
than Heinrich Heine. Not until recently did they name a street in

Jerusalem for him. I think he would not have responded with one of his sarcastic poems, but with genuine joy.

The third of the seven was Leopold Zunz, the arch-patriarch of the *Wissenschaft des Judentums* (Science of Judaism). He had important followers like Heinrich Graetz, among them my own teachers Ismar Elbogen and Leo Baeck. Elbogen taught Talmud but mainly Jewish history. I wanted to study this subject from an "eagle" perspective, its meaning and purpose, but he taught it from a "frog" one: how did Jews in ghettoes make a living? How did they survive persecutions? I was too young and understood him only later, much later. Elbogen had been a great teacher.

Baeck, like Elbogen, taught at the Hochschule für die Wissenschaft des Judentums, but unlike him till its very end; I was no longer there, for I was arrested by the Gestapo on November 10, 1938, one day after Kristallnacht, and carted off to concentration camp Sachsenhausen for three months, after which they released me and I, luckily, escaped, to Aberdeen, Scotland. But as my teacher from 1936 to 1938 Baeck taught Judaism, Midrash, and homiletics, undeterred by the hostility around us, this in Berlin, the Nazi capital. One of his last students has reported that he saw Baeck desperate only once, when in 1942 the *Hochschule* was closed. Till the end he believed that, just as Judaism, Jewish *Wissenschaft* must survive, if "remote" from Germany then elsewhere.[10] It had originated in Germany, but that Germany no longer existed. Did he think it would exist again in a future Germany? I do not know, but a Leopold Zunz Research Institute exists in Halle a/S *Universität*, of my *Heimatstadt*.

Of course, it can deal only with what has been, but is no more.

The "elsewhere" for me was Canada. I taught till retirement at the University of Toronto, at first philosophy, later also philosophy of Judaism, medieval like Yehuda Halevi and Maimonides, but mainly Rosenzweig, Buber, and Baeck. Rosenzweig had died in 1929, but Buber wrote and Baeck taught in the midst of an hostility, whose climax was unforeseeable and which also—as I argue elsewhere—despite research that could fill a library, still remains unintelligible. I remember reading in 1933 or 1934, Buber writing that all depends, not on what happens to Jews, but on how they respond.[11] But how does one respond when murdered in a gas chamber, without prior warning? This Buber could not foresee in 1933 or 1934.

Elbogen's specialty was liturgy, and Franz Rosenzweig once

said that Jewish theology is in the *Siddur*, the daily prayer book. I never forgot this, and took a *Siddur* with me even to Sachsenhausen. "That fellow brought the whole Talmund along," said an SS officer. I almost felt like laughing but, being in "KZ," I did not laugh. But the man really said "Talmund," and of it as a many-volume work he had no idea.

Returning to my "elsewhere," I was in Toronto long enough to be at home. This ended suddenly in 1967, when Israel was in mortal danger. Colonel Nasser did not merely utter threats; he had made a pact with Syria, and even with Jordan, had closed the Bay of Aqaba to Israeli ships, by any international law a *casus belli*, and had ordered UN General Secretary U Thant—whose soldiers were to guard the peace—to move, and move they did. Israel was encircled and alone.

This happened in June 1967. A few months earlier I had been invited to a symposium in New York, on "Jewish Values after the Holocaust." It was less an invitation than a challenge, even a provocation. I had argued for years for Jewish faith, with the Holocaust only as background—because of it, even despite it. Chairman Steven Schwarzschild was therefore fully entitled to urge me into the symposium, leaving me without excuse with this question: *what, after the Holocaust was still believable in Judaism?* So I participated. We did not think about Christianity at the time.

The other participants in the symposium were Richard Popkin, George Steiner, and Elie Wiesel. I had met Wiesel before. He still is special for me, was then the only one confronting the Holocaust *wie er wirklich war* (as it really was; Ranke), yet stubbornly remained with his Jewish faith, exploring it even in new depths. As a philosopher, I was especially struck by his stress on how they died. This is crucial for theology, not only Jewish theology. When Roman Emperor Hadrian forbade the practice of Jewish faith on pain of death, Jews, among them Rabbi Akiba, despite him, practiced it, thereby risking and suffering martyrdom. This is even part of the Yom Kippur service. Where is the Roman Empire today? However, Judaism survives.

But for Hitler the Jewish crime *was birth*, not faith, and Hitler's Germany was consistent in making Jewish martyrdom difficult and, in Auschwitz, quite impossible. How can one be a martyr when one is killed, not with familiar weapons like guns or revolvers but an unexpected gas-chamber? I say "unexpected" for they were cunning enough to pretend these were showers, even gave them soap and towels. I must keep on stressing this, for even Jews, while not forgetting "the 6,000,000," often have given no thought to *how* they died. "They would anyhow be dead now." But that there are many ways to die was known at least to one philosopher, Martin Heidegger, the most prominent in Nazi Germany. Heidegger declared—of all years in 1933!—that Albert Leo Schlageter's death was unique, for the French occupiers of the Ruhr had executed him when he had resisted, he alone. But even after the end—after the "thousand year Reich" had ended in twelve—Heidegger never faced death at Auschwitz. Yet the death of each and every one exceeded Schlageter's in at least three respects. Schlageter was single; at Auschwitz Jews had children, who were murdered with them; he had a grave, theirs was the clouds; his death was meaningful, not only to himself, with them they did their best to blot out memory, that they had ever existed.

This ought to *force* Christians, radically, into *theological thought.* Do they really think Nazism, had it existed two thousand years ago, would have let Jesus die on a cross, slowly for him to experience it, publicly for the faithful to remember? Are they foolish enough to follow Heidegger who, himself foolish, viewed gas chambers as a mere "postmodern" product of impersonal "technology"? Is blotting-out-death not possible in many ways, for persons in their human wickedness?

Unless Christians give up on Christian faith, the Holocaust requires a post-Holocaust Christian theology. Not also a post-Holocaust philosophy? After all, Socrates thought about death; Heidegger, arguably, about nothing else.

I once thought highly of Heidegger for, subjecting all metaphysical claims to "historicity," he seemed to flatten out all of them, as a truly impartial critic.[12] But this was before I knew enough about Hegel's "middle," between "right-" and "left-" Hegelian extremes.[13] To understand this middle took me ten years.

What I said at the New York symposium would become decisive for me, but does not belong here. After it was over, my wife and I were invited to a pilgrimage to Bergen-Belsen and then to Jerusalem. About this there would be much to tell. I confine myself to a monument in Bergen-Belsen on which the languages of Polish, Russian, French victims were inscribed, but not of Jewish. Only when the Jewish survivors protested did they add Hebrew and Yiddish. German "Dejudaizing" was therefore also present in Bergen-Belsen, even after death.

I have borrowed that word in my title, "Dejudaizing," from Zalman Rubaschoff, who used that word in the title of an essay in Berlin, then almost took the train back to Russia, but gave his ticket to someone else. As "Zalman Shazar" he became Israel's third President, still concerned with the sequel of German "Dejudaizing," still fighting it.[14]

In Jerusalem in 1970 I gave a lecture on our pilgrimage in the presence of distinguished critics, the late Arthur Morse, Manes Sperber, Piotr Rawitz, Alfred Kazin, who criticized my lecture mainly because I had been too harsh on young American Jews, who were concerned about Vietnam without being less concerned about Auschwitz. The critics were probably right, for how can one be *on this* pilgrimage without being overwhelmed? The chairman was none other than President Zalman Shazar.

In the article published in Germany, mentioned above, I had much more to say. But here, in this postscript, for those who have read the book, I can be brief. When we came after 1933, also young Jews, also to Berlin, not only Berlin but all Germany had been changed, more radically than we could understand. But our principle was still the same: "If we feel Jewish existence is necessary, it must be possible."

Appendixes

Documents

Books by Emil L. Fackenheim

Notes

Index

Appendix: Addresses in Germany and Essay in 2002

These memoirs were finished before Rosh Hashanah 2000, that is before September 11, 2001, and before the Second Intifada, the one an epoch-making event for the world, the other at least for Jews. I have resisted the temptation to bring the text up-to-date, for I want to state things truthfully as they were, and were perceived by me, during most of my life.

But we are still in the midst of Intifada II and, in a way, it escalates Auschwitz. True, suicide bombers cannot kill thousands, only a few dozen at a time, but the Nazi perpetrators could act without thought, without a decision, killing like robots: press a button one day, another the next, just as ordered, directly or indirectly, by the Kommandant. But to kill him/herself a suicide bomber needs a decision: Shall I do it? What does father think? Mother? Moreover, with a decision he/she needs an ideology, even a Weltanschauung—hope for him/herself in Heaven, hate for the victim on Earth.

Thus in 2002 I just had to write two essays, one theological, the other political, together they may be called theo-political. They are at the end of this book.[1]

A

Laudatio for the Study Circle Studium in Israel

Fulda, March 6, 1988

The sixth of March is important for me.[2] It was the birthday of my older brother, Ernst Alexander, who would be seventy-five today if he were still alive. But he was the only one among my closest relatives who could not flee from Nazi Germany in time. I do not know even how he died. One version is that he fell ill and died in hospital. The other is that he went freely to his death in 1941. Never did the word *Freitod* (voluntary death) (instead of *Selbstmord* [suicide]) have a deeper meaning than at that time. In either case he evaded the SS, who would have carted him, like other Berlin Jews, to Treblinka.

I am here today despite my brother, which is evident to everyone who is honest and faces what has happened. Such people do not talk about *Wiedergutmachung* (overcoming the past) or fall back on the German proverb that the "thousand-year *Reich*" was "so long ago" it is "no longer true." For those who had to suffer the twelve years that were to them, in fact, like a thousand, an abyss was opened that has no likeness. It exists between Germans and Jews, especially German Jews. The Jews of Poland and Russia were murdered by enemies; the Jews of Germany by those with whom, as it were, they had sat on the same bench at school, and whose fathers had served with theirs in the war.

I am thus here despite my brother. It is also because of him for, despite the abyss, there must be ways of bridging it. If the attempt were

236

not made, Hitler would laugh in hell. And his laughter would be especially hellish because the abyss, torn open in those years, was not only between Jews and Germans but also between Jews and Christians.

This is not to say that Christians as such were guilty of the Holocaust. But no thoughtful Christian can doubt that, had it not been for a tradition that now, rightly, is condemned as "teaching contempt" for Jews and Judaism, the Holocaust would have been impossible. Just consider one simple fact: I am speaking to Germans and Christians, but the term *Deutsche Christen,* "German Christians" is impossible and will never be possible again.

The task then is to bridge an abyss that was torn open, on the one hand, between Jews and Germans, on the other, between Jews and Christians, especially those who are both Germans and Christians. As regards the abyss between Jews and Christians, I have done my share to bridge it through much of my life. But when four years ago we moved from Toronto to Jerusalem, I did not dream I would enter into conversation with young people who are Germans and Christians and who spend a year studying in Jerusalem. For a Jew in our time to live in Jerusalem is incomparably meaningful. But after four years I can say that nothing has been comparable to these conversations; without them I would not be here today. For these young Germans and Christians seek, from their side, to bridge the abyss. They are in no way responsible for what happened in the time of their grandparents. But they voluntarily take responsibility upon themselves, for, hopeful for the future, they know there is ground for hope only if one takes upon oneself the burden of the past. Thus one can, on the part of Germans, not have Goethe and Hegel and certainly not Heine unless one takes also Hitler and Heydrich. (Händel was born in Halle, but so also was Heydrich, one of the worst.) Among Christians, one cannot have Augustine or Luther without also accepting the burden that Augustine fell prey to the calumny that Jews were children of Cain and that Luther was a hatemonger who suggested, centuries before Kristallnacht, that synagogues should be burned.

How can young Germans and Christians bridge this abyss? In no better way than that attempted by those with whom I have been in conversation these four years. These days one hears often from Christians that anti-Semitism is un-Christian or even that the "old" Israel still has a role in the age of the "new." But in view of such a long tradition of calumny, Jews are right to be skeptical, and unfortunately this skepticism is often justified. Thus, for example, there was Vatican II and, years afterward, a Vatican audience for Kurt Waldheim. Anti-Semitism on the right is condemned by the church, then reappears on the left, disguised as anti-Zionism. What can be done on the part of Christians, within the religion of love, to put a final end to the miserable tradition of Jew-hatred? Nothing better, in my view, than what these young people are doing, namely, studying Jewish texts. Through the centuries Christians have imagined that Jews spend their time rejecting the Christ of Christianity or, worse still, kill him again, as they are supposed to have done originally. But if Christians study Jewish texts, they discover with astonishment that, while Jews are sometimes serious about Christ in their dialogues with Christians, otherwise Christ is not in the teachings of Judaism. Have Christians ever studied the Talmud except to slander it? Rarely. Why was it so necessary to slander it? Were Christians, including honored professors, so insecure in their faith that they needed these slanders? If so, it does not say much for their faith.

Studium in Israel, which has been sending students to Israel for ten years, does not have these fears, for students come to study Talmud itself, for its own sake. And what do they discover? For one thing, that God created only one human pair, so that no one can say his forefathers were better than others. A great example of antiracist thinking! Or the passage adjuring heaven and earth that it does not matter whether someone is man or woman, Jew or Gentile, that everything depends on whether he or she directs the heart to heaven. Does this not sound like Paul, despite the fact that Jews do not go through Christ? Should a Christian not rejoice over the fact that his "older brother" found this truth without Christ, so that other non-Christians can do likewise? Perhaps this view could liberate Christians from the narrow Augustinian doctrine that makes life hard for Christians, the belief that there is no salvation outside the church.

That this is only abstract thought these young people must know themselves. Thus tonight they heard speeches about tolerance of "the other," but, having lived in Israel, they know that accepting the "other in general" is much easier than grasping the nettle of anti-Semitism, especially if no Jews worth speaking of live in Germany. Can there be Jew hatred without Jews? Remember Shylock, and in Shakespeare's England there was not even Hitler. After Study in Israel, after their return to Germany these young people have a big job.

But if it is cause for hope that these young people study, as Christians, Jewish sources, it is also cause for hope that, as Germans, they do so in Jerusalem. This is even necessary, for in this respect there is no choice. For if, after what has happened, there is Jewish faith at all, it is because a Jewish state arose after the great catastrophe, and because, through the centuries, Jews have not forgotten Jerusalem. After the Holocaust they would have lapsed into despair had they not returned to Israel. Never was statelessness so great a catastrophe as during the Third Reich, and at no time was the rebirth of a Jewish state as great a blessing as it is in ours. There are today people in many countries, Germany included, who no longer want to see this, and certainly Israel has many problems, including the Palestinians. But they must not confuse the insight, as German theologian Johann Baptist Metz has put it, that the State of Israel is a house against death. There are many Arab countries, houses for life. Israel is the only Jewish house, and it still is against death. If it were destroyed, Hitler would have the last victory. It would also be, after four thousand years, the end of the Jewish people. But here too hope must have the last word. Once Israel will be a house, not against death, but for life. But people of insight know this is not yet the case and probably will not be in our time.

The circle Studium in Israel knows all this. The young people who belong to it learn this through Dr. Michael Krupp. They build a twofold bridge to the Jewish people, as Christians and as Germans. They are witnesses to hope. Hence it is a great joy for me, a Jewish refugee from Germany, to return to Germany in order to honor the circle, for creating hope for a Jewish, Christian, German future.

Hegel, the greatest German philosopher, once said the wounds of Spirit heal without leaving scars. He could no longer say this today. Scars remain, and "healing" is not the right word. But it is possible to alleviate the pain, and this is why we are here.

B

Inaugural Lecture: Franz Rosenzweig Memorial Lecture Series

Gesamthochschule Kassel, April 24, 1997

This is the first important time I have given an inaugural lecture on German soil, introductory to a whole term in a German university.[3] I am aware not only of the importance of the event but also of its timing. When an action is important, so is its timing.

The timing was important also when I gave my first major address, ever, on German soil, in 1937. It was Yom Kippur, the highest Holy Day in Judaism. I was twenty-two years old, a rabbinical candidate, and these were my first sermons. Only one had preceded it, in Halle.

I no longer remember what I spoke about, but on Yom Kippur one speaks about God, Jewish sin, *t'shuvah*, "repentance," and at the end of the all-day worship the community experiences reconciliation with God. On these topics no modern thinker has written more deeply than Franz Rosenzweig, born in Kassel, to whose memory this lecture series is dedicated. After his death and after what happened in Germany later, nothing better could have been done than to establish this series. Rosenzweig died in 1929, and the catastrophe in Germany began less than four years later. My first sermons were in 1937, already in the midst of the Hitler regime.

The place of the Yom Kippur service befit the times, Berlin Weissensee, the largest Jewish cemetery in Germany, an external indication that Jewish dying in Germany had become more appropriate than

Jewish living; moreover, in addition to the location, there was a theological problem, especially for Yom Kippur, especially after the Nuremberg laws of 1935. In the Talmud it is said that nations persecute Jews because of their faith, and that persecutions are permitted by divine love, are even divinely ordained, to lead Jews to that true *t'shuvah* to God and Humankind that will eventually lead to Messianic redemption, in which "everyone will sit under his vine and fig tree," without fear of others.

According to Rosenzweig, Yom Kippur anticipates redemption and thus keeps awake hope for Christians and, through them, indirectly, for the world.

But the Nuremberg racial laws of 1935 did not deal with what Jews did or failed to do, believed or did not believe, but *with birth*, and birth happens to everyone without his or her action; hence it is not something for which *t'shuvah* is possible. In 1937, did I understand this difference? I think not.

I was born on June 22, 1916, in Halle. After matriculating in 1935 at the Halle *Stadtgymnasium,* I went to the Berlin Hochschule für die Wissenschaft des Judentums. I sometimes ask myself whether I would have gone to Berlin had the Nazis not come to power. At matriculation I listed as my planned field of study Greek philology, in addition to Jewish theology. Without Hitler might I have become a professor of Greek philology, possibly at Martin Luther Universität Halle/Wittenberg? This I shall never know.

Essential for my decision to study Jewish theology was resistance to the Nazi assault on Jews and Judaism. My purpose was less to become a rabbi, for about authority I had Kierkegaardian doubts, than to find answers for what had happened to German Jews since 1933. Essential was the fact that, although I knew little of Judaism before I went to Berlin, I was convinced—a priori, as it were—there was an answer in Jewish tradition. In the following decades, this led me to wrestle with the tradition, especially with midrash, as well as with the Jewish Bible, and I was not disappointed, for I found veritable treasures. But after many years, I reached the awful insight that the tradition, even the Bible, has no answer to what happened after 1937, was unpredictable even then. For the Nazis, what was to come was the "final solution" of a "problem." For survivors among Jews, it was a crisis of their faith without precedent. We are still wrestling with the uniqueness of the Holocaust. References to genocides elsewhere, even if comparable, are still evasions. Jews have existed with the Jewish faith for four thousand years.

Did Hitler fail to exterminate Jews but succeed in destroying the faith of Jewish survivors?

This, of course, is unacceptable, but it is the basic issue in these lectures.

The Holocaust was unpredictable in 1937, but a connection existed with what had preceded it, for events in 1942 followed from the 1935 Nuremberg laws. The war was on, German Jews were being deported to Riga, and the *Generalkommissar* for White Russia, Wilhelm Kube, was not only an old party member but also a convinced anti-Semite, was yet horrified that among the deported were not only "Aryan-looking" girls but, worse, men wounded in the Great War, even wearing medals, hoping this would save them. Thus he treated them as exceptions to the mass shooting on March 2, 1942. But for this he earned the wrath of no less a person than Reinhard Heydrich, who wrote him on March 21 that it was regrettable that six and a half years after the Nuremberg laws were adopted, their meaning still had to be explained. I am not suggesting Kube was a nice man or not an anti-Semite or a Nazi; but with exceptions German Judaism was over: they were all murdered.

This I could not have anticipated in 1937, and what was true of me, was true also of other Jews and, to be fair, also of countless Gentile Germans.

It was generally true that the Nazis' intentions regarding the Jews were underestimated; after 1933 it was often heard that the soup is not eaten as hot as it comes from the kitchen. Even the 1935 laws were often trivialized: not many would have predicted how Heydrich would soon apply them. Instead, some thought that legal regulation of the so-called Jewish problem was better than SA or SS violence in the streets. Some Jews even thought these laws were the last attack; especially if they were old or sick and had no country to which to emigrate, they comforted themselves that one could live with these laws. But one could only die with them.

My studies at the Berlin *Hochschule* were abruptly interrupted—nay, terminated—by the Kristallnacht, after that, the concentration camp Sachsenhausen, hasty exams for the rabbinate, flight to Scotland, one year's study there, internment in Scotland and Canada, and, finally completion of the Ph.D. at the University of Toronto in 1945, with a dissertation titled "Substance and Perseity in Medieval Arabic Philosophy, with Introductory Chapters on Aristotle, Plotinus, and Proclus." Thereafter I was a rabbi for five years (1943 to 1948) in Hamilton, Canada, and following that a member of the Department of Philosophy at the University of Toronto until my retirement in 1983. Then we moved to Jerusalem, where I still teach.

My main work has been—still is—the problem and fate of revelation in modernity, except that in more recent years the Holocaust has replaced modernity. "Revelation" I understand as the incursion of the "Divine Other" into the human world and hence include Christianity as a religion of revelation, a necessity if only because the most significant thinkers in modernity were Christians. Under the influence of Leo Strauss, I first tried to go back to the Middle Ages, which also explains the topic of my dissertation. But after a few years I turned to modernity, and not only because it was impossible to avoid modern philosophy.

Until 1967 my work fell into two parts, which remained separate because of the objectivity required by scholarship. One of my "hats" was scholarship, the other was my commitment to Judaism.

The scholarship was devoted to philosophy from Kant through Fichte, Schelling, Hegel, and Kierkegaard: is it possible to embrace Kantian "autonomy" and hold fast to the "Other" of Biblical revelation? In my opinion "From Kant to Kierkegaard" is the deepest development of the theme "Revelation and Modernity," although—an insight that came later—it is not radical enough for "Revelation and the Holocaust."

This radical insight came in 1967 and was produced by the crisis preceding the Six-Day War. The world Jewish community feared a second Holocaust, this time in Israel, and, with this fear, I had to face the Holocaust that had happened. And since it is impossible to face a unique catastrophe and then turn to other subjects—as it were, as if it had not happened—I am still a Holocaust thinker.

In 1939, the real motto of the times was *rette sich wer kann*, "save your skin." As one who was able to do that, I am here now, almost sixty years later; between this and my first address in Germany lies an abyss that—despite attempts even in Germany—defies efforts to find its like, and it concerns not only Jewish and German history but covers much more, for if Nazi Germany had won the war, it would have ruled the world and made it *judenrein* (free of Jews). But since Germany lost and reached its aim only in part, the abyss exists in at least three histories, the German, the Jewish, and the Christian. (And also the European? Thus it seems, in view of what is coming to light now.)

In all history, was there ever an attempt to exterminate every member of a people, as if, on the one hand, they were vermin of which not one may remain, on the other, as if they were devils who deserved capital punishment? Even the concept "genocide" must still be distinguished from "extermination," for if one is obsessed with the idea that Jews are vermin, as a matter of their nature, the tortures are still unexplained: one gets rid of vermin but does not torture it. Hitler claimed he was merciful to Jews, for he got rid of them without needless pain. So he said, but that is not what the Nazis did.

If one really wants to explain these two aspects of the crime—the Jews are vermin and devils—it is probably possible only through the Nazi Weltanschauung. In *Mein Kampf,* Hitler writes that the conflict between Jews and humankind is cosmic, and if the Jews were to win, the world, as it was thousands of years earlier, would be lifeless. In a footnote he even corrects himself and says "millions of years." Was he insane? If so, how did he become führer? And were all the *little Hitlers,* who carried it out *insane also*? The scholar Raul Hilberg has said he has always answered only small questions—the typewriter murderers, the special trains, and so on—for fear of giving too small an answer to the big question: why it happened at all. Insanity, of one or some or all, is one of many answers that are too small. Joachim Fest says Hitler was a metaphysician. This answer is big enough, but it is doubtful whether it can be maintained.

Thus it is in German history. How is it in the Jewish? Where else were Jews not only defined by birth but also persecuted? Birth is choiceless, and Jews were systematically robbed of choice; even in extremis people usually have a choice, between heroic resistance and martyrdom. But the Holocaust was different. By elaborate schemes of deception, everything was done to make resistance impossible, and, as regards martyrdom, the great examples in Jewish history were inapplicable. The Roman emperor Hadrian, until Hitler the worst enemy of Jews, forbade the practice of Judaism on pain of death and thereby created Jewish martyrs. (Ten became famous and to this day renew Jewish faith; they are mentioned in the Yom Kippur liturgy.) But while Hadrian created Jewish martyrdom, Hitler not only murdered Jews but also Jewish martyrdom. Hadrian forbade Jewish faith, Hitler, Jewish life.

And Christian history? The "Aryan Christ" is mostly a German affair, arising in the nineteenth century, and I am not sure whether Christianity or Germany is done with it. (If people now are largely against racism, they are not necessarily pro-Jewish.) But even before this aberration, Christianity had long been anti-Jewish; the positive attitude toward the "older brother" is still recent and must raise Christian doubts about the Christian past. In my view, this is a tragedy of world historical significance, for hatred invaded the religion of love with hatred of Jews.

This is why the Holocaust is a new challenge for Christianity. So long as anti-Semitism targets only some Jews—in the old version, they are too stubborn to recognize Christ, in the new, they are parasites, unpatriotic, conspirators—there are always, beside these "bad" Jews, some good ones, or at least one. But if the criterion is birth and the aim a world *wholly judenfrei*, there is *no good Jew*, including the carpenter of Nazareth.

We are thus dealing with three histories, the German, the Jewish, the Christian. Then how do I move, in this inaugural lecture, from Jewish history (in Jerusalem, where I live) to German history (in Kassel, where I visit)?

For me this question had already become an issue in 1939, on the Kristallnacht after which they took me, with about twenty thousand others, to concentration camps, in my case, to Sachsenhausen. After three months they released me, with the warning that if I did not leave Germany within six weeks, they would take me back there, this time permanently. *Rette sich wer kann* was therefore the call of the hour, and I was successful.

I have already been back to post-Hitler Germany several times, but this is my first time for a whole term. Can I explain this, in the context of my life?

Am I following an old teacher's request before I fled Germany, to return and help rebuild Germany? No, this can be done only by people living in Germany. And had my teacher, Dr. Adolph Lörcher, known in 1939 what would follow, he would not have asked me.

For Germany, the problem is deeper than many want to recognize. For example, what am I to do with the report, which appeared in the *International Herald Tribune* on November 7, 1992, that one-third of Germans still believe Hitler had a "good side" and that Jews are partly to blame for having been persecuted so often? People who live here, not visitors, have to cope. All I can do is bear witness, as of November 10, 1938, the last day I was German. (On the next day the Nazis arrested me.)

A friend and I walked all over Berlin to look at the damage of the previous night. On Kurfürstendamm we saw honest *Bürger* climb over broken windows and leave Jewish stores with coats, dresses, shoes. In 1935 they had made Jews *vogelfrei*. (To a *vogelfrei* person, one can do whatever one likes.) Only three years were needed to transform honest citizens into common thieves. This was one side of the destruction of the *Rechtsstaat* of which Germany had once been proud. Another was the police. In celebration of the 1935 Nuremberg laws, a Jew had been led through the streets, carrying a sign saying he would never again complain to the police. In 1938 the police only watched as the synagogues burned.

The destruction of the Jews thus was also a self-destruction of Germany, that is, of the German *Rechtsstaat*. This had already been turned against Germans themselves once before, in the "night of long knives" of June 30, 1934, when the SS had murdered three hundred people, some political rivals but others harmless people. That this was the beginning of the self-destruction of Germany for Germans Hitler himself announced publicly a few days later in the Reichstag, through a law whose sole purpose was to declare these murders legal, retroactively. (He also made a speech in which he called himself the highest judge of Germany.) If this was the beginning, the end came on April 26, 1942, when the Reichstag handed the power over every German to Hitler and then, consistently, dissolved itself, in effect, committed suicide.

Hitler had a "good side"? Not for Jews. For Germans? Without Hitler's total defeat, Nazism wholly destroyed, Germans too would have been *vogelfrei*.

To this I can bear witness, but help rebuild Germany? I cannot understand my task as such. I see it as building bridges over the abyss that has been torn open. My own bridge is in philosophy, the German and the Jewish. Once there was a "Golden Age" in German philosophy, from Kant to Hegel, and it is no accident that Jewish philosophy also flourished under its influence. The task is to recover the past, or what of it is worth recovering, and this includes not only Hermann Cohen but also Kant, not only Buber and Rosenzweig but also Schelling and Hegel, without whom Rosenzweig would not have been possible.

But recovery is possible only within limits. So radical is the abyss that philosophy, too, is affected. Is it possible for philosophy not only to build a bridge but also to look into the abyss? Honesty demands this, of philosophy and of religious faith. The attempt is necessary, for even in failure there can be truth.

For building bridges one needs hope. From the German side, the Rosenzweig guest professorship is an expression of it. From the Jewish side, I say that the hope that died in Auschwitz was reborn in Jerusalem. It is still in danger, but I am here as witness that we are not allowed to let it die a second time.

C

Assault on Abraham: Thought after Fifty Years, Address on Receipt of an Honorary Doctorate in Theology

Ruhr-Universität Bochum, Bochum, May 20, 1998

Only once in forty years of lecturing was I unable to go on. What I had to say had shaken me, and I needed a few minutes of respite.

In Toronto I had had a regular course on the "Golden Age" in German philosophy. I was fond of it, for it was German philosophy but also far enough from our century. I saw no reason for change after we moved from Toronto to Jerusalem.

There was need, however, for a new emphasis, for while the age had been "golden" for German philosophy, it had not been so for German Jews, who were still struggling for emancipation in Germany and also for self-emancipation. Even Moses Mendelssohn—admired, nay, celebrated as a "modern Socrates"—needed permission to live in Berlin and presumably got it because of his "Reason." A wit has said the Jews of Berlin esteemed reason, more so than Christians, for Christians could live in Berlin without it.

Lecturing in Jerusalem, I came to Schleiermacher's 1799 *Addresses on Religion*. He had a Jewish friend, Henriette Herz, with whom he would discuss his lectures beforehand, and when he reached Judaism he said the religion had long been dead.

"Those who at present still bear its colors are actually sitting and mourning beside the undecaying mummy and weeping over its demise and sad legacy."[4]

Perhaps he had discussed it with Henriette and she had agreed, for she was baptized soon afterward.

This was the point at which I could not go on, for I had to think of two Americans, Will Herberg, a Jewish socialist who became religious and asked Reinhold Niebuhr to convert him, and Niebuhr himself, who sent him away to Jewish sources, of which Herberg knew nothing. He would become a significant Jewish theologian. I knew him well.

Judaism was just beginning its nineteenth-century renewal, and Henriette Herz could have had a share in it. I still experienced its renaissance myself, in the early Hitler years. But by then it was of short duration, till the Kristallnacht of November 9, 1938. When they set the synagogues on fire, they murdered it.

What a tragedy that even in its Golden Age *Schleiermacher* could not do for *Henriette*—German philosophy for Judaism!—what *Niebuhr* did for *Herberg*! Would history have been different? Probably not, for Hitler had a Weltanschauung of his own. Even so, this in no way alters the tragic flaw in German philosophy's Golden Age.

But "golden" it was, and for that reason I think it would be good for German philosophy—perhaps for Germany—if there were a recovery of it. This might be a better way of discovering what Germany once was, is today, can be, than what showed itself in the *Historikerstreit*.

But the Schleiermacher example is enough to show that a recovery could not take place without major changes. Thus even Hermann Cohen could not have Kant today and ignore his advice of "euthanasia" for Judaism, nor would it have been hard for Kant himself to do, for example, via Ezekiel, what he did for liberal Christianity.[5] Or—to give an ominous example—what of Fichte's German *Urvolk* (primal people), requiring a *Zwingherr* (tyrant) for enforcement? In itself ominous, this example is more so because it is too close to Heidegger's German "metaphysical" *Volk*, proclaimed when a *Zwingherr* was already in power.[6]

But the radical problem of "recovery" of the "Golden Age" is that it cannot evade the twelve years that now, at last, are recognized as years of dread. A book titled *Thinking about the Holocaust: After Half a Century* has just appeared.[7] "Half a Century" is much longer than Hegel's "Owl of Minerva," philosophical thought rising to flight, when the "day" of life is done. But this is not the first time Jewish thought needs more time. Perhaps the very first was back with Exodus and Sinai, events of great moment that still require thought today, and recent is the expulsion from Spain in 1492, finding thought in the Lurianic Kabbala, only fifty years later. This, however, is not the most recent instance, and the Holocaust is incomparably worse: the Jews expelled from Spain lived and could tell their children; but the Holocaust victims were murdered, their children with them.

Paradoxically, the extreme nature of this most recent catastrophe gives rise to the illusion that "healing" of what, evasively, is called "the loss" is already present, indeed, has not been necessary. Thus *Thinking about the Holocaust* has an essay by Anita Shapira in which she writes that in 1945 Fischel Shneerson, a Jewish psychologist in Palestine (i.e. Israel), reported during a writers' convention at *Ma'aleh Hahamisha:* "There is a very paradoxical psychology at work here. . . . I would say that the Jewish people still doesn't know what happened to it." Shapira adds to this: "[Schneerson] saw it as a reflection of a traditional Jewish behavioral pattern for coping with catastrophe." Schneerson said: "The Jewish people evades facing up to its calamities. We have encountered a historic phenomenon—the Jewish people distracting itself from its afflictions. This is our habit—after a massacre there is a fast day, [we set up] a pogrom relief committee, and then we go on with our business." To which Shapira adds: "The Holocaust did not infuse a new perception of reality."[8] The same can also be said of the Diaspora. Thus one reads *The Diary of Anne Frank* or Victor Frankl's *Search for Meaning* and finds comfort where there is none.[9] Then how can one recover the Golden Age in German philosophy and not evade those twelve years of dread?

I put this question to Hegel, first, because he took history seriously, second, because of his integrity. On its account, he never quite managed to place Jewish history into his thought. Perhaps this was one reason for his support of Jewish emancipation.

The following passage is found in Hegel's *Early Theological Writings:* "After doing everything the most enthusiastic courage could achieve, [the Jews] . . . endured the most appalling of human calamities and were buried with their polity under the ruins of their city. . . . The scattered remnants of the Jews have not abandoned the idea of the Jewish state, but they have reverted not to the banner of their own courage but only to the standards of an idle messianic hope."[10]

What can philosophy say today? What else but that, after "calamities" grotesquely more "appalling" than Emperor Hadrian's, the Jews returned to the "banner" of their "courage" and restored their state! Hadrian prohibited Jewish faith on pain of death, thus creating martyrs, and Rabbi Akiba's martyrdom inspires Jewish faith still; but

Hitler prohibited Jewish life, thus murdering both Jews and Jewish martyrdom.

This distinction sums up Hitler's Weltanschauung, but does so too neatly, does not begin to exhaust it. Even before the 1923 putsch, this Weltanschauung knew all there was to know about Jews. "The Jew" destroys the nation and socialism: "remove the Jew" and you have National Socialism. "The Jew" started the Great War and ended it, with a stab in the German back: the Jew is Germany's archenemy. Indeed, "the Jew" is *the world's* enemy: World Enemy Number One. The Jewish Bible teaches work as punishment, and "the Jew" is the prime parasite. As early as in Hitler's much-quoted letter to Adolf Gemlich, Judaism is described as "racial tuberculosis"; and by 1941, Hitler had been promoted—had promoted himself—to its discoverer, equal to the great Pasteur.[11] But rarely quoted is the following, from 1920: "We are unshakably determined to root out this evil, to annihilate it root and branch. We shall use every means to reach this goal, even an alliance with the devil."[12]

With the *Machtergreifung* (seizure of power), "annihilation" became possible, and with Auschwitz actual: Jews were vermin, although one rids oneself of vermin without torturing it. The torture of Jews began spiritually, with the Star of David Jews had to wear, became physical in Auschwitz, and climaxed with the *Sonderkommandos:* Jews themselves had to cart the gassed corpses into the ovens. Primo Levi has called this the most demonic crime of National Socialism: "One is stunned by this paroxysm and perfidiousness: it must be the Jews who put Jews into the ovens, it must be shown that the Jews, the sub-race, the sub-men, bow to any and all humiliation, even to destroying themselves."[13]

Since 1958, Levi had borne witness for the victims, but not until 1988, fully thirty years later, could he bring himself to write of their destroyed innocence. Then he either killed himself or fell to death. (Scholars still legitimately disagree about the cause of his death.)

Now more than another ten years have passed: is the time yet ripe for "Minerva's Owl?" Historians dare not yet answer why it was done; but the result is clear: this was the *most radical* assault ever made, on the *very beginning* of Jewish history, Abraham's Exodus. Abraham believed, and Jews to this day circumcise their sons; but the beginning, with its promise of "life" and "blessing," found its end in Auschwitz—death and curse.

The curse of the *Sonderkommandos* is *more radical* even than death. The death of the gas chambers was meant to end Jewish history, after four thousand years of much blessing. But the curse was to destroy, retroactively, *its blessings also,* including the birth of Christianity, of Islam.

This terrible insight takes us back to the courage that was recovered when the state was founded. "The Jewish people does not know yet what has happened to it": thus it was in 1945, and surely not much different three years later, when the state was founded. Was their courage mixed with doubt? Or even the courage of despair? Or, after all, mixed with hope?

After fifty years, is philosophy ready for *Weltgeschichte*? Unless we let Hitler use it, the concept has vanished from philosophy with Hegel; but the time may be ready for a restoration—one of sorts—once this much is understood: the Star of David was raised from its deepest humiliation ever and made the banner of the restored state.

Today this is widely forgotten or misunderstood, even by Israelis. But when the time is ripe for world-historical thought, with it will come also world-historical hope. The God of Abraham is also the God of Christianity, and Ismael was Abraham's son. The assault on Abraham was also an assault on church and mosque, but neither church nor mosque understood. The hope is that one day they will understand.

Abraham must have had questions. Who are you? (This was God's first speaking to him.) What is the blessing? Why choose me?

But Abraham asked no questions and went, as God wanted, in the innocence of faith.

D

On the SS Murder of My Uncle Adolf Goldberg, and in Memory of Leo Baeck

Martin Luther-Universität, Halle/Wittenberg, October 22, 1998

My life could be summed up in three trips, from Hamburg to London on May 21, 1939, from Toronto to Tel Aviv in October 1983, and from Halle to Berlin in May 1935. All three were important: the first to escape from the SS; the second, to reach Jerusalem; but—although I had then no way of knowing it—the decisive one was the train trip to Berlin.

When I left Halle for Berlin in 1935, I knew a few things about Jewish history and religion, enough to realize they were now subject to assault and defamation without precedent. For this I needed but to look through the window, from our house, Wettinerstrasse 17, at the church across the street, with a swastika flag hanging there. I decided to study at the Berlin Hochschule für die Wissenschaft des Judentums. I knew the calumnies were false. I went to Berlin to learn the truth.

What I learned in Berlin was decisive also for my other two significant trips. The one to London was, despite the need to flee, by no means a case of *rette sich wer kann*, "save your skin," but rather "existential." There were three of us in Berlin, and we were sure which Jewish decisions to escape were "authentic," either to Palestine, to build the land and rebuild the people, or westward to rebuild Jewish thought. Martin Heidegger's philosophy had produced a joke in which a student walking out of a lecture of his, says, "I have already decided but not yet what for." Then came 1933, and Heidegger decided for Hitler. But even now, fully half a century later, I think our "existential situation" was more "authentic"; Heidegger's was merely the world in general, but ours, life-or-death *ernsthaft*, "seriously," was Nazi Germany in particular. Nor were we open to any "what for": instead, whatever our decision, it was for Jewish renewal.

What I learned in Berlin also affected my second trip, from Toronto to Jerusalem, for it was caused by a crucial event, the three weeks of dread before the Six-Day War, when we feared a second Holocaust, now in Israel, that neither Jews nor Judaism would survive. In 1967 I wrote, and in 1969 reformulated, a "614th commandment." (On Sinai, traditionally, 613 were given.) The new commandment has four parts: Jews must survive; they must remember the six million; they may not despair of mankind; they may not despair of God.

The feared dread did not happen, but one need only think of Oslo and its yet unfinished consequences to realize that danger for Israel is not past. Water; borders; Jerusalem; refugees, to say nothing of Iran and Iraq: all these pose potentially terminal dangers, and without Israel, Jews and Judaism, after four thousand years, would be where Hitler and his Third Reich wanted them to be, finished.

What did I learn in Berlin? I will concentrate on my teacher Leo Baeck, the last spokesman for German Judaism.

1. He was among the earliest to say that, after one thousand years, the history of German Jews was ended.

2. He vowed, also early, that he would remain in Germany, as long as even a minyan was there, a quorum required for a religious service. He kept his vow, too, and was deported to Theresienstadt.

3. Then there is the remarkable, often overlooked fact that he taught at all. As head of the *Reichsvertretung* of German Jews, he had to meet the Gestapo, perhaps once or twice a week. Yet he seemed to take teaching the ten or twenty of us just as seriously, if not more so, and this was no mere appearance but a fact. No wonder we listened.

4. Nor was this our only reason. Before I had come to Berlin, in the fall of 1935, Baeck had distributed a prayer for Yom Kippur, to be read in Berlin synagogues; part of it was as follows: "We stand before God. With the same resolution with which we have confessed our sins, personal and collective, let us say that we perceive with revulsion the lies uttered against us, the false charges made against our faith and its defenders. Let us trample these abominations beneath our feet." As courageous as it was beautiful, the prayer ended as follows: "We are filled

with sorrow and affliction. Standing silently before our God, we express what is on our souls. May this mute prayer go forth and be heard above all other sound."[14]

But the noise of the prayers of the *Deutsche Christen* and Teutonic pagans, both on behalf of Hitler, was too great: the "mute prayer" was not heard.

This was before I had come to Berlin. After my 1939 flight from the country, Baeck told the SS trying to insert a stooge in the *Reichsvertretung*, now itself a stooge and renamed *Reichsvereinigung*, that they could force a Kareski on him but they could not force Baeck himself to remain president. His fortitude would have impressed others, including those in what once was a German *Rechtsstaat*, but not the Eichmanns or Himmlers of the SS. But while I was at the Berlin *Hochschule*, Baeck inspired us, his students. Both his fortitude and his faith.

Baeck taught midrash and homiletics. One midrash he taught was on Song of Songs 2:7: "O daughters of Jerusalem, I adjure you / Do not awaken Love until it is ready."

This may be a secular love song, but for the midrash, the Love is between God and Israel. Baeck taught this midrash in Berlin, perhaps also in Theresienstadt. By a Gestapo error he survived, but the pious had waited for divine love too long, and then came Auschwitz and Treblinka.

I visited Baeck in London, after all was over, and he told me how he and another had discussed Plato and Isaiah while pulling a heavy wagon in Theresienstadt. He did not speak of Nazis, and I did not dare to ask him. But he did make a few comments in Hans Adler's *Theresienstadt 1941–1945*, just in the one page preface, for him that was enough. Theresienstadt was a place for Jewish dying, not for Jewish living, and it was designed to force or manipulate Jews into crime, in order then to "punish" them.

I remember just one lesson from Baeck's homiletics class: a word never to appear in a sermon is the word "I," Ego. Regarding this advice, he practiced what he had taught to the end: he took dreadful facts he knew, silently, to his grave.

He wanted Jews, Judaism, Jewish faith to survive.

Baeck died in 1956. In 1961 Raul Hilberg's monumental *Destruction of the European Jews* appeared, and we were slow to absorb it. But now, another quarter of a century later, I ask, at my one time *Heimatstadt Universität*, how long silence is possible, even permitted. When I spoke here five years ago, I submitted two lecture topics, "Judaism in German

Philosophy," an easy one, for one can always fall back on the German proverb that it was "so long ago it is no longer true," and a hard one, "Auschwitz as Challenge for Philosophy and Theology"; at the time I was glad the hard one was chosen. But the challenge must have been too hard, for I have yet to hear of someone taking it up.[15] At his Jerusalem trial, Adolf Eichmann claimed that in obeying Hitler he had followed Kant, but I know of no philosopher—he can only be German—yet to ask, let alone answer, how the Hitlerization of Kant's "categorical imperative" was possible. I also said that Isaiah's "hut of cucumbers" (Isa. 1:8) did not "barely stand" but fell at Auschwitz, the Jewish one but also the Christian one. But I have not heard of any theological response to this charge either. (This speech was given in 1998, before 1999, after reflecting on my three months in Kassel and writing the two chapters of my memoirs, "Return to Halle" and "Before and After My Return to Halle.")

I also learned five years ago that my uncle, Adolf Goldberg, was carted off to Buchenwald in December 1941, and that he died—it was not known where and how—in March 1942.[16]

I then wrote an article for the *Mitteldeutsche Zeitung*, "The Thank You of the *Vaterland.*" [But although I found out only later *where and how* he died, even then I went on as follows.] I thought of my uncle sometimes then, but now I do every day. And the first thing I must do is tear up the "existential" conviction on which I had built my life. I did not, after all, go on these trips "existentially" *as I* wanted but *as they* wanted—*rette sich wer kann,* "save your skin." I say this, not because of my parents and my brother Alex, who, we could hope, would follow, but because of Uncle Adolf. A one-legged veteran, what country would take him? (There was not yet an Israel.) I could not have saved him either, *but no day should have passed without my thinking of him.*

This is the century of genocide. Stalin, then Pol Pot, now Africa. But *nowhere else* did a country murder veterans who had risked their lives for it and then were heavily wounded.

Another thought comes to me—whether I want it or not—for it comes relentlessly. Why has it taken me so long to recognize the fact, when it was always so obvious? My Uncle Willy, my mother's only sibling, was killed in the Great War before I was born. Uncle Adolf was a presence in my childhood and youth. My Aunt Trude's husband, who survived Theresienstadt, was war blinded.

The answer is shockingly simple: *the fact was obvious, but too much to bear.* I could write about quite a few German philosophers and theologians, Jewish and Gentile, many of whom I knew personally, who simply did not live long enough. Hegel's "Owl of Minerva" wants patience for philosophy and also, one assumes, for theology, but for this—wait for the late afternoon, till the day of action is over—it is not nearly enough.

This evil lasted for twelve years, but much more time is needed, even for facing it.

Thus it has taken me to my eighties to be sure of the right to exaggerate wildly. The "why" of the Holocaust, in Hitler's mind, in Goering's, Goebbels's, Himmler's, Heydrich's? Each a will o' the wisp, each cheating the hangman. Perhaps the sole purpose of the *sprachlich und inhaltlich jammervolles Machwerk* (a linguistically and substantively pathetic creation, Wilhelm von Sternbuch's brilliant, if untranslatable, assessment of *Mein Kampf*)—"Aryan," "blood," even "racist"—Weltanschauung was just one, to murder, as they did, my Uncle Adolf.

I do not quite know why I have burst out like this, but if not now, in my eighties, in my one time *Heimat,* at a *Universität* wanting sincerity and truth, *when and where?*

I was glad to learn that streets in Halle have been named after Jews who once lived here. Some were famous before, others famous afterward. But two of those Jews never left, were not famous, yet have streets named after them. Both were relatives, one my great-grandfather, Wilhelm Fröhlich, once a rabbi in Halle, the other Adolf Goldberg.

Perhaps one day Adolf Goldberg Strasse will become famous. A recent Canadian affair has honored Raoul Wallenberg, a "righteous Gentile" who saved Jews. Were it to become famous, two facts would be different about Adolf Goldberg Strasse. First, it commemorates a Jewish victim, innocent by all standards anywhere, including those once German and, second, since it would be made famous by the nation that committed the crime, it would teach the world that the Holocaust *was* unique, must *remain* unique, never again to happen anywhere.

E

"Idle" Messianic Hope and "World-Historical" Return: Thoughts on Hegel and Jerusalem, Lecture on Receipt of an Honorary Doctorate in Philosophy

Martin Luther-Universität, Halle/Wittenberg, May 12, 1999

When I returned from Sachsenhausen in February 1939, I no longer telephoned any "Aryan" friends. (Only one was left anyway, Jürgen Wenzlau; it had become dangerous for him.) But Adolph Lörcher phoned me: if I did not come to say goodbye to him, he would not forgive me. Between 1933 and 1935, most teachers in the Halle *Stadtgymnasium* had not been Nazis; but he alone protested bravely, outspokenly, on behalf of Germany and Christianity. Until the 1935 matriculation, he was more important for me than Hitler. Just on his account I would never be anti-German or anti-Christian. I went to see him, of course.

He had two copies of Martin Buber's *Königtum Gottes*, one for me, the other for himself. This is a custom among friends of the classics when they part. Lörcher had been my Greek teacher at the *Gymnasium*.

After he gave me the book, he said: "Since 1933 I have told you 'Do not leave, the Nazi disease must pass.' Now you must leave. But promise me to come back. Germany will be destroyed"—by the Nazis, he meant, not by Englishmen, Americans, Russians—"and we shall need you to rebuild her."

I replied: "I have never contradicted you, but now I must. Two or three years ago I still might have said, 'I will come back.' But now I know that the Jewish people and Judaism need me more. Others will have to rebuild Germany."

I did not want to burden Lörcher with my KZ experience, and I mention it only briefly now. After we arrived in the camp, we had to stand and run through the night. In the morning came an "interrogation." We had to stand in rows, while an SS officer walked back and forth in front, leisurely; at length he stopped in front of someone and asked about his profession. On hearing "doctor," he burst into screams and began beating the unfortunate victim, "You *Judenschwein*, you have seduced German women." Then he moved on, still in leisurely fashion, and repeated his question; whatever the answer—"lawyer," "businessman," and so on—again came the beating and the screaming: "You have perverted German law," "You have cheated German customers," and the like.

Then he came to someone who said he was a bricklayer, and one look showed he was. At that the SS man became apoplectic: "You liar, you are a banker!" It almost felt like laughter, but the bricklayer was so naïve, he didn't realize that the beating might stop had he "confessed." He was the kind who had not thought of emigration or hiding, the kind whom, later, the Nazis would find easily and transport to Auschwitz or Treblinka, with the victim having no idea where he or she was or why.

Why am I speaking of long ago, of my "yes," "no," of Lörcher's "Rebuilding"? It may have been "long ago," but it "is still true": for Europe's Jews the "Final Solution" was carried out *by enemies;* for German Jews, by people with whom, as it were, *they had gone to school.*

And why speak of it here and now? If not in *my eighties,* and in my *Heimatuniversität,* then never; and if you want *to honor me, you have to listen.*

Since 1933 we had known that an unprecedented attack on Jews and Judaism was underway. For this I needed but to look at the swastika flag, displayed by the church opposite our house. Hence after matriculation I went to Berlin to study at the Hochschule für die Wissenschaft des Judentums with Leo Baeck, to find out what Jews and Judaism were. This was in 1935, but by 1939—when I saw Lörcher for the last time—the strong word "unprecedented" had become too weak, for all Germany was poisoned: two hundred synagogues burned; Jewish store windows smashed, Jewish property stolen; and more than twenty thousand Jews in concentration camps. And the few who, like Lörcher, had protested were now helpless and powerless. But with my KZ experience, I just had to say no to Lörcher; and, with what came afterward, Lörcher himself would not have asked me to return.

I had decided that Jews and Judaism "needed me more," but what did I do subsequently? For many years I taught two subjects at the University of Toronto, one, German philosophy in its Golden Age, from Kant to Hegel, inclusive of Kierkegaard, the other, Judaism as interpreted by Jewish philosophy. Of all subjects possible, why just these two? Like it or not, they belong together: no Hermann Cohen without Kant; and without Schelling and Hegel, no Franz Rosenzweig. The Golden Age in German philosophy had influenced Jewish thought profoundly. But, alas, that age has passed.

Hence Hitler's Germany was *doubly* catastrophic: generally, for German Judaism and Germany; but also, in particular, for the Golden Age in German philosophy and its influence on Jewish thought. This duality must find philosophical expression: it must not happen, if only through neglect, that Hermann Cohen and Franz Rosenzweig are forgotten, and for their true recovery another is needed, that of the Golden Age in German philosophy. In both cases one should think of Kierkegaard's "repetition."[17]

For my wife and me, Toronto was almost at an end in 1967, for the Jewish state was in danger: in our thoughts we were already in Israel. Once Hegel had written that the Jews had defended their state with "the most inspired courage," but that, when they lost, they also lost their courage, and that after the "most gruesome, human misery . . . the dispersed remnant of the Jews . . . had not abandoned the idea of its state, but had never returned to the flag of its courage, but only to that of an idle messianic hope."[18]

After a "misery"—its "gruesomeness" unimaginable to Hegel: Nazi Germany, Nazi Europe, Auschwitz—and, *with no more "idle" but* desperate *hope,* the Jewish "remnant" recovered its "courage" and restored its state; besieged since birth but, from 1967 and ever since, it exists in manifest danger, ever—new danger.

Hence German Catholic theologian Johann Baptist Metz has said that the Jewish state is a "house against death" and that it is the "first Christian duty . . . at long last to listen to Jews."[19] In 1983 we moved to Jerusalem, in the hope of Jewish life and of Christian listening. And also of a philosophical one.

Later Hegel became a philosopher of "world history," that is, of history as the "true theodicy," of "justification of God." He says this at the end of his *Philosophie der Weltgeschichte,* although perhaps only for his own time.[20] Elsewhere he writes of its end as the "reconciliation of *every* contradiction," of its being "raised to reality and self-conscious Reason," this surely transcendent of time *altogether,* that is, systematically complete.[21]

Perhaps someone should have told Hegel even then—as a Christian but also as a philosopher—that he was only half listening to Jews, for to Hegel Jewish history, to be sure, had "world historical significance and importance," but only because the "higher" had evolved from it, that is, Christianity in the "Germanic world."[22] But Hegel failed to listen to Jewish experience: Jews could not forget Jerusalem (Ps. 137), yet only two tribes "laughed" and "sang," when they returned (Ps. 126). Had *all* been "lost" in Babylon—if *nobody* had returned to Jerusalem—then, by Hegel's own standards, *Weltgeschichte* would have been a fragment, Scripture never codified, and Christianity in—the—Germanic world bare *Geschichte. The Jewish return to Jerusalem was not only no "idle" hope, but hope fulfilled.*[23] And since Islam hardly exists in Hegel's thought, *the Jewish return to Jerusalem—with or against Hegel—is weltgeschichtlich;* not always *does World Spirit move West.*

And now there is a second Jewish return to Jerusalem, not after seventy years but after nearly two thousand, not from one country but from all the world; and this has happened after Hegel's *Weltgeschichte* was ruptured, at least in three histories, the Jewish, the Christian, the German: "theodicy, "justification of God in history"—all in Hegel's sense—is no more.

Had Hegel experienced Auschwitz, it would have shaken him, not only humanly but also philosophically.[24]

Hegel's philosophy of world history was "righteous," but post-*Hegel mortuum* (Rosenzweig) it was trivialized, even made chauvinistic.[25] Kaiser Wilhelm II abused it in the First World War—terrible for Europe, for the world—and Martin Heidegger lapsed into chauvinism as well.[26] After Greek, philosophy can speak only German? Without such German *Quatsch* words as *Aufbruch,* Heidegger might not have followed Hitler so easily; and if the post-Auschwitz world needs the "overreaching" (Hegel) unity of *two* activities.[27] English has one word for it, "recovery," whereas two are needed in German, *Erholung* from a sickness, *Wiederholung* of a tradition.

The Jewish remnant finds recovery—despite and because of Hitler— if the second return to Jerusalem strengthens it, enough to reach Abraham, his faith without question; Christians if, as "the peoples" in Psalm

126, understand "the Lord" as "acting greatly," through Jerusalem; Germans if they recover their Golden Age in philosophy, through a Hegel listening in righteousness.

Hegel once said that the wounds of Spirit heal without leaving scars. He could no longer say this. But what I have called a "destructive recovery" is possible.[28]

F

The Holocaust and the Book of Job: Reflections on Theology and Philosophy

Jerusalem, December 2, 2002

People concerned with the Holocaust should write about the Book of Job. So one would think, but few seem to have done so, and to explain it is not difficult. Having found a just and omnipotent God always escapist, "pie in the sky," "secularists" see Him now as a grim joke, for while one can look up, timidly, to "the stars above" (Immanuel Kant), for some sort of order-in-Nature, History—which alone counts for humans, Job included—looks forward to disaster. Once one could argue—again with Kant—that "eternal peace" is possible, if two equally armed powers want it, at least "cold peace," for the greater their armaments, the likelier is a war that destroys both. (Now, what with nuclear arms-plus-terror-anywhere, it is not "both" but "the world.") Kant, if we have a Kant, should think again.[29]

✝

Returning to "Holocaust and Job," normally pious readers are impatient, since Job had to live so long till he got back sheep and camels, more than he had before, new children, whereas such readers have bad luck much younger and want justice, Divine or other, *now*. Moreover, if their piety is abnormal, that is, genuine, they are upset with Job dying happily, "full of days" when he got new children, for the old are still dead. (A Christian rightly protests that children are persons, i.e., irreplaceable.)

Let me give two recent relevant examples. The late Nahum Norbert Glatzer collected a book of selections on the Book of Job. (Though a good scholar, he published mainly anthologies, to save what he could after Hitler.) But his book was not a success.[30]

In contrast, another book, also Jewish, written by a rabbi, was called *When Bad Things Happen to Good People,* was a success mainly because of its title, for people thought "Why" instead of "When": this we all would like to know if we could.[31]

✝

Two wrote seriously about Job and the Holocaust. Rudolf Otto's *The Idea of the Holy* (1917) directly, Martin Buber's *I and Thou* (1923) indirectly. One was Christian, the other a Jew. Both stressed religious experience.

Since Otto's interest is not theology, only religious experience, he has little use for friends who argue that either Job must have sinned, hence deserves punishment, or should give up his faith; and with his wife egging him on *to curse* God: with such friends, such a wife, who needs enemies! In contrast, Otto *truly pounces* on chapters 38–42:6 of the Book, beginning with *God Himself* coming on the scene, "out of the whirl-wind," ending with Job's own *mere humanity*—"I am dust and ashes": these are beginning and end: *The Tremendum* is between them.[32]

The last nine verses of the Book, Job's full-of-days-death, at an age higher than Moses' *meah v-esrim,* 120, his own 140 are insignificant for Otto: they are merely "extra payment, after quittance already made." Thus Otto *the scholar*; but for him as *theologian,* Job-as-person is merely pre-Christ ahead, a symbol of the "mystery" of the "Old" Testament, the "suffering of the innocent," whereas in Christ Job's suffering is both re-vealed and overcome.[33]

For a Jew, this is, of course, an ancient story, new-told; however, in this of all centuries, the twentieth, Martin Buber has long been forced to modify his *I and Thou,* by an "eclipse of God." He needs this metaphor, for he cannot conceive of God as ever *not* speaking, being "absent," let alone His "death." However, speaking in New York, the "center of the Diaspora," Buber had to be much more extreme, bold enough to cite not Job but, of all biblical texts, a *Hallel* psalm: "'Call on Him, for he is kind, for His mercy endures forever': dare we quote this text to the sur-vivors of 'Auschwitz'"?

For Otto this question does not arise, nor did it for Karl Barth, fearless anti-Nazi though he was, because "Auschwitz" was just another, more—*most?*—terrible "Good Friday," but, like all the others, "after Easter."[34]

But Buber gives up his theology, his *I and Thou*, yet stubbornly stays with God: "Though His coming appearance resemble no earlier one, we shall recognize again our cruel and merciful God."[35]

‡

Unlike Otto, Hegel read the Book of Job to the end, understanding Jews, a "collective Job." Did Hegel ever go to a Jewish funeral and hear mourners recite Job? Did he ever get Kaddish translated, no mention of the dead, only about God's holiness? But, whether he did or not, even in his own time, he found Jewish stubborn faith "admirable"; after what has happened, he would surely find it more so today.

Documents

REGISTRAR FOR STUDENTS

המזכירות להוראה

Jerusalem, **כד' בטבת תרצ'ט** ,ירושלים
15.1.39

א ש ו ר – ק ב ל ה

מאשרים אנו בזה, כי

מר אמיל פ ק נ ה י י ם

נתקבל כתלמיד מן המניין לאוניברסיטה העברית.

א. אבן–זהב
מנהל המזכירות להוראה

d.

(*Translation*)

CERTIFICATE OF ADMISSION

This is to certify that

Mr. Emil F a c k e n h e i m

has been admitted as a regular student to the Hebrew University.

A. Ibn-Sahav
Registrar for Students

Certificate of admission, January 15, 1939.

I was accepted by Hebrew University but did not get the British visa. In 1935 or 1936 the *Hochschule* accepted students waiting for their visa to Palestine and, while waiting, they studied Judaism, and this was part of their preparation, as members of a *Hochschule* group. I got friendly with one whose name I've forgotten, who thought I was a younger Rosenzweig.

15 Widener Library
Jan. 20, 1939

Dear Dr. Fackenheim:

I enclose herewith a
letter for your son Emil of Berlin in
which he is officially informed of his
appointment to the position of Assistant
Librarian at the Jewish Institute of Religion
in New York.

With best wishes and in the hope of
seeing your son here soon, I am

Sincerely yours,

H. A. Wolfson

Dr. Julius Israel Fackenheim
Wettinernerstrasse 17
Halle/Saale

Letter by Professor H. A. Wolfson, Harvard University, to Dr. Julius Fackenheim, Widener Library, January 20, 1939.

The late Professor Wolfson was the most famous expert in Jewish philosophy in his time. I owe it to his action that I was released from concentration
camp, where it was thought that my proposed job in America would get me a
nonquota visa. This was wrong, however, for only professors and ministers, not
library workers, were entitled to them. Hence my friend Fischel had been right
in joking that we had no problem in concentration camp, only after we got out.

JEWISH INSTITUTE OF RELIGION
WEST SIXTY-EIGHTH STREET
NEAR CENTRAL PARK
NEW YORK

January 20, 1939

Mr. Emil Fackenheim
Berlin, Germany

Dear Mr. Fackenheim:

I take great pleasure in informing you on behalf
of the Board of Trustees and the Faculty of the Jewish
Institute of Religion that you have been appointed to the
position of Assistant Librarian of our Institute for the
space of two years at an annual salary of Two Thousand
Dollars ($2000.).

Will you please let me know when we may expect
your arrival.

Very faithfully yours,

Henry Slonimsky
Dean

HS:GS

State of New York)
) SS:
County of New York)

On this twentieth day of January 1939, before me personally
appeared Henry Slonimsky to me known and known to me to be
the Dean of the Jewish Institute of Religion and the individual who signed the above letter.

Kate V. [signature]

Kings County . . .
New York County Clerk's No. . . .
New York County Register's No. . . .
Term Expires March 30, 1939

Letter by Henry Slonimsky, Jewish Institute of Religion, January 20, 1939, with
testimonial note below.

This is the document that got me out of concentration camp. The Gestapo assumed that I would get a visa, but special visas were given only to professors
and clergymen. It got me out of concentration camp, but not into the United
States.

PALÄSTINA-AMT BERLIN
der JEWISH AGENCY FOR PALESTINE

Vom Herrn Reichsminister des Innern durch
Verfüg. v. 25.7.1924 Nr. 6174 B als gemeinnützige
Auswanderer-Beratungsstelle anerkannt.

BERLIN W 15, MEINEKESTRASSE 10

משרד ארצישראל

TELEGR.-ADR.   FERNSPRECHER: POSTSCHEC
ORGHIP PALAMT   SAMMEL-NR. 91 90 31   BERLIN 167 0(

ABTEILUNG

IHRE ZEICHEN   IHRE NACHRICHT VOM   UNSERE ZEICHEN   TAG:
                                                                     24.1.39

BETRIFFT: Im Antwortschreiben sind anzugeben:
                 Abteilung, Zeichen, Datum und Betrifftvermerk

B e s c h e i n i g u n g.

Hierdurch bescheinigen wir, Herrn Emil F a c k e n h e i m,
dass er durch Zulassungsurkunde der Hebräischen Universität Jerusalem vom 15.1.1939 als Student registriert worden ist. Er wird nunmehr der Einwanderungsbehörde von der
Universität gemeldet und darf damit rechnen, dass er sein
Einwanderungszertifikat im Frühjahr 1939 erhalten wird.

Jewish Agency for Palestine
Palästina-Amt

Certificate by Palästina-Amt Berlin der Jewish Agency for Palestine, January 24, 1939, confirming that Emil Fackenheim, already registered as a student of the Hebrew University of Jerusalem, will now be registered by the university with the office of immigration and may expect his immigration certificate in spring 1939.

The term *Frühjahr* (spring) was vague. After release from Sachsenhausen on February 8, 1939, I was given by the Gestapo a deadline of six weeks. Extending these six weeks I managed to leave Germany on May 12, 1939, with the Gestapo phoning my parents a week later. When told I was in Scotland, the man replied: "Da hat er Schwein gehabt."

האוניברסיטה העברית
THE HEBREW UNIVERSITY

Jerusalem,   29.I.39.   ירושלים,

Mr. Emil Fackenheim
B e r l i n .

Dear Sir,

This is to certify that you have been
admitted to the Hebrew University.

Application for an Immigration Certificate
will be made for you as soon as students' certificates
will be available, which should be in April or May, 1939.

Yours faithfully,

A. Ibn-Sahav
A. Ibn-Sahav
Registrar for Students

Certificate signed by A. Ibn-Sahav, Hebrew University, Jerusalem, January 29, 1939.

   I was admitted to Hebrew University. When I, at last, got there as a professor in 1981, I waved this certificate at my students saying, "At last I made it."

University of Aberdeen.

PROF. A. C. KENNEDY, B.D.

DEPARTMENT OF SEMITICS,
KING'S COLLEGE,
ABERDEEN.

7th February 1939

Dear Herr Fackenheim,

It will give me great pleasure
if you will make your home with us here during your
stay in Scotland. I have applied to the Home Office
for the necessary authorisation and hope to hear from
the International Student Service when you are at
liberty to come to Aberdeen.

With every good wish, I am

yours sincerely

A. C. Kennedy

REGIUS Professor of Hebrew and Oriental Languages
47 Queens Road, ABERDEEN, SCOTLAND.

Letter by Professor A. C. Kennedy, B.D., University of Aberdeen, Department of Semitics, February 7, 1939.

Professor and Mrs. Kennedy were very friendly to us, including too my parents when they came to Aberdeen. This would have been unnecessary, for he was only the guarantor required by the British government. But Aberdeen, both town and gown, was lovely for the year I was there and for my parents until they died.

I knew all the time that my stay in Scotland was only temporary and it must have been friends in Scotland who persuaded the government to make the stay of my parents permanent. The U.S. Consul had already stated that I would be able to immigrate in two years, and I had already sent my books to a distant cousin in New York.

Certificate of Rabbinical Ordination, Berlin, March 8, 1939.

I passed my rabbinical exams just one month after being released from Sachsenhausen and within the six weeks I was to leave Germany given me by the Gestapo (it turned out a few weeks longer), but this is a good reason why I passed my exams only with a B.

Herr Rabbiner Dr. Baeck:

Religionsgeschichte, Homiletik und Methodik des Religions-

unterrichts,

Herr Rabbiner Dr. Wiener:

Religionsphilosophie,

Herr Dr. Sister:

Sprach- und Bibelwissenschaft,

Herr Dr. Guttmann:

Talmudwissenschaft.

Herr Fackenheim hat die Prüfung mit dem Gesamt-

prädikat

gut

bestanden.

Auf Grund dieser Prüfung wird Herrn Fackenheim

mittels dieser Urkunde die Befähigung,

als

Rabbiner, Prediger und Religionslehrer

zu wirken,

zuerkannt.

Gleichzeitig wird Herrn Fackenheim von dem Dozenten für

die talmudischen Disziplinen, Herrn Dr. Guttmann, eine

Hattarat Horaa

ausgestellt.

Dies bekunden wir mit unserer Namensunterschrift unter

Beidrückung des Amtssiegels.

Unsere

The document shows the emergency not only for me but also for my teachers. Sister had already been grabbed by the Gestapo, Elbogen already in America, and of the three who actually signed it, only Baeck and Wiener used the compulsory word *Israel*; Guttmann did not have to, for his nationality was Hungarian.

At right, testimonial by Max Wiener, President, Hochschule für die Wissenschaft des Judentums, Berlin, March 23, 1939.

Wiener had replaced Julius Guttman, who was already in Jerusalem, but I was happy with Wiener since he was concerned also with what Jews could believe and not only, as Guttman, with the history of what they had believed. In this respect, Guttmann had been a much greater scholar. But Wiener was more relevant for our time. When I got the Steinthal prize under Wiener's direction, he made two comments in public when awarding it, one of which I listened to immediately: Had I written my thesis in English it would have been much clearer. The second it took me a long time to accept. He said that in criticizing Luzzato's criticism of Maimonides, I had shot at a sparrow with a cannon. Only later I learned to ignore sparrows and shoot, if necessary, only at giants.

BERLIN N 24, den   23. März 1935
Artillerie-Straße 14

Herr Emil F a c k e n h e i m verlässt die Lehran-
stalt für die Wissenschaft des Judentums mit dem abgelegten Rabbiner-
examen, zu dem er zugelassen war, obwohl er die vorschriftsmässige
Zahl der Semester nicht erreicht hat. Dies geschah nicht nur wegen
der ausserordentlichen Zeitumstände, sondern weil Herr Fackenheim
mit grösster Hingabe und ernstem überdurchschnittlichen Verständnis
seiner Arbeit nachgegangen ist.

Fackenheim hat besondere Begabung auf dem Gebiet der
Philosophie bewiesen, und es wäre dringend erwünscht, wenn ihm die
Fortsetzung und Vertiefung seiner wissenschaftlichen Arbeit gerade
in diesem Fach ermöglicht würde. Obwohl ihm nur noch zum Teil ein
Universitätsstudium offenstand, hat er mit sichtlichem Erfolge durch
Selbststudium sich Wissen und Kenntnisse angeeignet, und gehört
zu denjenigen Schülern aus dieser letzten Studienzeit unseres In-
stituts, auf die das Lehrerkollegium mit besonderer Erwartung blickt.
Man darf ihn unter diejenigen rechnen, die bei nur einigermassen güns-
tigen äusseren Umständen die geistige und wissenschaftliche Tradition des Judentums von Deutschland in einem anderen Lande fortzusetzen
geeignet sind.

Das Lehrerkollegium
der Lehranstalt für
die Wissenschaft des Judentums.

Dr. Max Israel Wiener

Vorsitzender

Mrs. Cowan
Canadian Jewish Congress
Toronto , Canada

My dear Mrs. Cowan,
I was informed that you want some notes about Rabbi Emil Fackenhei
of the Shulwoke Refugee Camp . While he was a student of the
Hochschule für die Wissenschaft des Judentums , Berlin Germany,
he not only attended my classes but had many talks with me about
his studies and his private affairs so that I won an intimate
knowledge of his personality . During my forty years' career as
academic teacher I had but few pupils of his standing . Fackenheim
was a brilliant boy with a broad range of interests , equally gift
ed for Philosophy as for Philology . When he started his studies,
he knew but little Hebrew , and after a short time he wrote and
spoke Hebrew fluently and was versed in the modern Hebrew literat-
as well as in the old classic one . He was an extremely healthy
boy - physically as well as mentally and morally . Although being
a bookworm , he loved music and was a well -trained sportsman ,
and after a full day's work he was able to cook a meal for himself and his friends.
Within a short time he prepared for his final examination and took
a rabbinical diploma. That he was later admitted to the University
of Aberdeen and entrusted by his professor with a very difficult
thesis , may already be known to you. You will likewise know that
in Aberdeen he lived in the house of a Protestant minister , and
that the latter's family was very fond of this well educated young
man.
His closest friend is Rabbi Heinz Fischel of the same Camp . He al
made amazing progress in his studies , he won a price for a valuable essay on a biblical subject which is being published in the
Hebrew Union College Annual. He also received a rabbinical diploma
and was admitted to the Ph. D. examination at the University of
Edinburgh , Scotland . I will not fail to remark that Fischel is
an excellent pianist.
It is highly desirable that these bright young men get enabled to

---

Letter by Ismar Elbogen to Mrs. Cowan, Canadian Jewish Congress, on behalf
of his former students, November 27, 1941, and, *following left,* a testimonial by
the chairmen of the Jewish Community, Refugee Camp, Sherbrooke, P.Q., December 16, 1941.

continue their academic studies.

If you need further informations , I am always at your disposal.

Yours very sincerely

J. Elbogen

(Dr. I. Elbogen)

Mrs. Cowan was then in charge of the Jewish community trying to find homes for students and jobs for workers when, at last, the authorities would let us out from internment camp. The reason for that was that, with the war, unemployment was no longer a problem. Professor Elbogen was not only the head of the Hochschule but also behaved like a father to us all. He knew every student personally and worried about them all. In view of the fact that the students were there for many reasons, some just for no better reason than waiting and hoping the Nazis would go away, this was a formidable task. As much as Baeck, Elbogen knew we were in an unprecedented crisis situation.

Jewish Community, Refugee Camp,

SHERBROOKE, P.Q.

Canada.

December 16th 1941.

T e s t i m o n i a l.

To whom it may concern:

          Rabbi E.Fackenheim founded our Refugee Congregation
even during our passage across to Canada in July 1940 and has
been leading it as rabbi to this day through a grave time and
amidst difficult conditions.-

          His extensive and profound knowledge as well as his
true piety gained for him high respect and unconditional devotion
and confidence on the part of the congregation. His sense of
humour, his humane faculties, his energy and the force of his personality made him everyone's friend and beyond the bounds of the
congregation, a prominent figure of the camp.-

          Rabbi Fackenheim maintained a comprehensive and un-
selfish activity; aside from the sermons, and his administrative
and representative tasks, he gave courses and lectures on all
branches of Jewish knowledge, such as the Bible, Talmud, Jewish
Theology, History, Modern Hebrew and Arabic, which were of particular importance in view of the prevailing circumstances.-

          The gap torn by his release is a great loss for us
which fills us with real regret, at the same time, however, with
joy that he is now looking towards a better future for which he
is accompanied by the best wishes of all.-

                    G. Soln H.R.Cohn. Moriger
                  (The chairmen of the community)

Refugee Camp,
SHERBROOKE,P.Q.
C a n a d a.

December 16th 1941.

This is to certify that

Rabbi Emil F a c k e n h e i m

has been acting as a Rabbi and leader of the Jewish Community in
this camp from October 1940 till December 1941.-

        During this time he was in charge of all the various
activities of the Community, comprising the religious services,
instruction in all branches of Jewish knowledge, organizing,
administering and representing the community.

        His services have been appreciated by the whole
Jewish community.

(K.Hellmann, Camp Speaker)   (Dr.S.Orgel, Chairman)

Witness:

(C.B.Leggo,Lieut. Assist.Adjutant and Paymaster)

Certificate signed by K. Hellmann, Dr. S. Orgel, and C. B. Leggo, all Refugee
Camp, Sherbrooke, P.Q., December 16, 1941, stating that Emil Fackenheim
acted as Rabbi and leader of the camp's Jewish community from October 1940
until December 1941.

    This document is typical for my uncertainty even in Canada. I never needed
this document.

UNIVERSITY OF TORONTO
BURSAR'S OFFICE

TORONTO 5 _____ JUN 1 4 1948 _____

To Mr. E. L. Fackenheim,

108 East Avenue S.,

Hamilton, Ontario.

Dear Sir or Madam:

The Board of Governors have appointed you to the

position of Lecturer

in the Department of Philosophy

Faculty of Arts

~~Commencing on~~ for the academic year 1948-49

Ending not later than

at a Salary of Twenty-four Hundred Dollars ($2,400.)

If you accept this appointment kindly sign and return to me the **duplicate** sent herewith. If such an acceptance is not received within

Ten days it will be assumed that you have declined the appointment.

Yours truly,

C. E. HIGGINBOTTOM,

Bursar,
(*Secretary to the Board.*)

AEC/

_____19____

The Bursar,

University of Toronto.

Sir:

I hereby accept the above appointment

Signature _____

Appointment of Emil Fackenheim as lecturer in the Department of Philosophy by the University of Toronto, June 14, 1948, for the academic year 1948–1949.

My salary in Hamilton had been small enough, but I was happy to take this job even though the salary was little more than half of it. In between the two jobs I visited my brother in England and my parents in Aberdeen, Scotland.

16 May 1948

Dear Dr. Fackenheim

I've read your paper with great care and attention — and I may say, now that I've gone through it a second time, with increasing enthusiasm and admiration. It really is superb in thought and presentation. Perhaps part of my enthusiasm is due to the fact that I agree with it so XXXXXX thoroughly, but only part; I am sure that anyone at all competent to pass judgment would agree with me substantially.

To tell you the truth, I did not believe any Jewish thinker writing in English today was capable of such a grasp of the problem and of such profund: profundity of treatment. Certainly, my reading hitherto had not led me to expect it. Your book, when you complete it, will take rank, I am conviced, with the best of contemporary Protestant theology in America (Niebuhr, Tillich) and that, I think, is very high rank indeed.

But you must complete your book at all costs! It is all right to think of separate publication of what you already have done — but not if such publication becomes a substitute for completing the entire work.

As to separate publication, I would very strongly advise it. The part I have read constitutes very much a whole by itself. But where? As to Jewish journals, since you are already going to have something in Commentary, The Menorah Journal seems to be the only one left. You might try that. As to general journals, I think Ethics, published at the University of Chicago, might find it of interest. Or perhaps the Review of Religion, published at Columbia University. XXX There are others, but these occur to me first. What do you think?

Thank you ever so much for letting me — and my wife — read your extraordinary XXXXXX paper. I hope we will maintain our correspondence and that some day before very long I will have the opportunity of meeting you.

With best personal greetings,

Will Herberg

Your letter on my first Commentary article is the one comment on it that seems to understand best what I was driving at. It is certainly unfortunate that it was never published.

I enclose some reprints I have available of my own writing. Perhaps you might find them of interest.

Letter by Will Herberg, New York, May 16, 1948.

I got to know Will Herberg well enough, so much as to agree on general theological principles. But we parted company not only geographically but also ideologically when we moved to Israel: his idea that Jews who no longer believed in God should cease to be Jews had become unacceptable to Rose and me.

Mr. Erwin A. Glikes
President and Publisher
Basic Books, Inc.
10 East 53d Street
New York, new York 10022   March 3, 1973

Dear Mr. Glikes:

    To the best of my knowledge Emil Ffackenheim is among
the american Jews the one best equiped by virtue of his
devoutness and his knowledge to pave the way for future
Jewish thought through encounters between Judaism and modern
philosophy. The Judaism which he courageously defends is traditional,
rabbinical, non-mystical Judaism as authoritatively
interpreted in the most profound Middrashim: before the
tribunal of that Judaism modern philosophy must make good
its claim that it has done or can do justice to Judaism,
for it has hardly ever seriously tried to do so, although
it always laid claim to universalism, to universal justice.

    Fackenheim calls his work""A Preface to Future Jewish Thought":
the time has not yet come for what one might call a new
Jewish philosophy. Maimonides is indeed the greatest Jewish
philosopher, yet his way is closed to Fackenheim for the
simple reason that Fackenheim cannot accept, as Maimonides could,
a divine presence as a publically verifiable phenomenon.
In simplistic terms: the historical consciousness demands a
radical revision of traditional theology; in somewhat more
precise terms, Jewish thought after Auschwitz and the birth
of the state of Israel can never be the same as it was before
these shattering events.

    Fackenheim assigns the highest place among modern philosophers,
very understandably, to Hegel - very understandably given Hegel's
intellectual greatness, spiritual freedom, and nobility of
character. He discusses also quite a few writers of a lower
rank. The contemporary thinker who attracts and repells
him most is, not suprisingly, Heidegger. No word beyond what
Fackenheim says need or can be said about Heidegger's siding
with Hitler. But one cannot hold it against Heidegger as
Fackenheim does that Heidegger's Sein und Zeit is still silent
on "das Volk": in that work Heidegger was still on his way
from Reason to Language. Furthermore, however nauseating
Heidegger's conduct in 1933 was, we must not overlook the

Letter by Leo Strauss, St. John's College, to Erwin A. Glikes, President and Publisher of Basic Books, Inc., March 3, 1973.

    This letter by Leo Strauss is valuable in that he influenced me to such a degree that I wrote my Ph.D. thesis on medieval Arabic philosophy. It is also valuable in what he says about Hegel as well as Heidegger. The former her respected whereas the latter he took seriously without respecting him.

fact that both the young and the old Heidegger remind one of
an altar-boy who, without the slighest qualms, piously,
if perhaps not altogether unhypocritically, officiates
at an auto-da-fe. This is not the place to discuss whether
this phenomenon would become more intelligible by the
admission that there are demons, especially before the question
"what is a demon?" has received a satisfactory answer.

Yours sincerely,

Leo Strauss

Books by Emil L. Fackenheim

Paths to Jewish Belief (New York: Behrman, 1960).

Metaphysics and Historicity (Milwaukee: Marquette University Press, 1961).

The Religious Dimension in Hegel's Thought (Bloomington: University of Indiana Press, 1967; Boston: Beacon, 1970; Chicago: University of Chicago Press, 1982).

Quest for Past and Future (Bloomington: University of Indiana Press, 1968; Boston: Beacon, 1970; Westport, Conn.: Greenwood Press, 1983).

God's Presence in History (New York: New York University Press, 1970; New York: Harper Torchbooks, 1970; Northvale, N.J.: Jason Aronson, 1997).

Encounters between Judaism and Modern Philosophy (New York: Basic, 1973; New York: Schocken, 1980; Northvale, Conn.: Jason Aronson, 1994).

La presenza di Dio nella storia, trans. Cornelius A. Rijk (Brescia: Editrice Queriniana, 1977).

The Jewish Return into History (New York: Schocken, 1978).

La presence de Dieu dans l'histoire, trans. Marguerite Delmotte and Bernard Dupuy (Paris: Verdier, 1980).

To Mend the World (New York: Schocken 1982, 1989; Bloomington: University of Indiana Press, 1994).

The Jewish Thought of Emil Fackenheim, ed. Michael Morgan (Detroit: Wayne State University Press, 1987).

What Is Judaism? (New York: Summit, 1987; New York: Collier McMillan, 1988).

Al Emunah V'Historia: Masot B'Yahadut Zmanenu (Jerusalem: Ha'Sifriah Ha'Tzionit, 1989).

The Jewish Bible after the Holocaust (Manchester: Manchester University Press, 1991; Bloomington: University of Indiana Press, 1991).

Fackenheim: German Philosophy and Jewish Thought, ed. Louis Greenspan and Graeme Nicholson (Toronto: University of Toronto Press, 1992).

Judaisme au present, trans. Gabriel Roth (Paris: Albin Michel, 1992).

The God Within: Kant, Schelling, and Historicity, ed. John Burbidge (Toronto: University of Toronto Press, 1996).

Jewish Philosophers and Jewish Philosophy, ed. Michael Morgan (Bloomington: University of Indiana Press, 1996).

Jewish Philosophy and the Academy, eds. Emil Fackenheim and Raphael Jospe (Madison, N.J.: Fairleigh Dickinson University Press, 1996).

Was ist Judentum? trans. Gudrun Holtz (Berlin: Institut Kirche und Judentum, 1999).

La presencia de Dios en la historia: Afirmaciones, judías y reflexiones filosóficas (Salamanca, Spain: Ediciones Sígueme, 2002).

Notes

Introduction

1. Hegel would have been the one philosopher—not Jewish, a German no less—to grasp that the Holocaust left Jews but two choices, eventual extinction or return to Jerusalem. On this issue, see addresses C and E to Germans in the appendix; also my *Religious Dimension in Hegel's Thought*, 157–58; *Encounters between Judaism and Modern Philosophy*, chapter 3; and especially "Hegel and Judaism: A Flaw in the Hegelian Mediation" (*The Legacy of Hegel* [The Hague: Martinus Nijhoff, 1973], 161–85).

Chapter 1. Childhood and Youth in Halle

1. Leo Strauss, "Preface (to the English edition of Leo Strauss, *Spinoza's Critique of Religion*)," in Judah Goldin, ed., *The Jewish Expression* (New Haven: Yale University Press, 1977), 345.

2. Primo Levi, *The Drowned and the Saved*, trans. Raymond Rosenthal (London: Abacus, 1986), 37.

3. Gerhard Engel, *Heeresadjutant bei Hitler, 1938–1943*, ed. Hildegard von Kotze (Stuttgart: Deutsche Verlags-Anstalt, 1974), 31–32; quotation taken from Raul Hilberg, *Perpetrators Victims Bystanders: The Jewish Catastrophe, 1933–1945* (New York: Harper Collins, 1992), 6.

4. When I wrote this passage in 1993, Heidegger was on my mind. But when I reread it in 1999, I recalled that in 1933–1935 I had been thinking mostly of Buber. Compare two addresses in April 1933, *Die Stunde und die Erkenntnis* (Berlin: Schocken, 1936), 13–17. These few pages stun the reader today because of the clash between Buber's

advice to German Jews in April 1933 and the murder camps. What was essential, Buber had written, was not what was happening to Jews but how they would respond in the *Heimsuchung*, the "visitation" when God *sucht* us, "seeks us." I must have read it at eighteen: it took me a long time to accept mass murder, longer to accept that it was disguised carefully, longest to accept *why* they did it—too suddenly, unexpectedly for Jews to respond then with *Sh'ma Yisrael*, "Hear, O Israel, the Lord our God, the Lord is one" (Deut. 6:4), the Jewish confession on death.

Yehuda Bauer has made the distinction, for historians, between what one hears, reads, has telegraphed, even experiences—between all that *and its sinking in*. This distinction applies also to theologians and philosophers.

5. North Sea holidays were out for Jews, hence Baltic ones, among them Binz, were heavy with Jews, but even there was an annual battle of flags. On arrival you would rent a *Strandkorb*, a covered deck-chair, dig a sand-wall around it, and plant your flag, black-red-gold for the Republic, black-white-red for the *Kaiser-Reich*. The battle was sometimes crude. (An "argument" on the *Kaiser* side was that Weimar's gold looked like mustard.) But it was friendly until—in 1931, I seem to recall, not 1932—the first Nazi flag appeared, and my father, followed by others, stormed to the mayor's office and had it removed. Next year there were so many it was hopeless.

Chapter 2. Halle under Nazism

1. Quotation taken from Ian Kershaw, *Hitler, 1889–1936: Hubris* (London: Penguin Press, 1998), 377; see also Robert Payne, *The Life and Death of Adolf Hitler* (Toronto: Popular Library, 1973), 251.

2. Albert Speer, *Spandau: The Secret Diaries*, trans. Richard and Clara Winston (London: Collins, 1976), 63. The case of Karl May is more important than it may seem. Novels such as Gustav Freytag's *Soll und Haben* (Debit and credit) are often cited in explanations of how Germany became nazified, *but this is in retrospect*. Neither I nor my fellow-students read Freytag, but we all veritably lived in the world of May, author of no fewer than sixty *Reiseerzählungen* (travel stories), always fancying himself as traveling, fighting against black slavery in Africa, against the Ku Klux Klan in America, and above all, as being no racist, at least where American Indians are concerned. Today he would be liked by environmentalists and liberals. In his most famous novel,

Winnetou, the hero, in the Wild West always known as "Old Shatter-hand," is nothing less than Winnetou's "blood-brother."

Karl May's books have plenty of stereotypes, of course, above all that Germans he meets are always brave, always honest; but he died in 1912, before the Great War. A nasty Jewish stereotype appears in only one novel, and even here the evil traitor is a German, and the Jewish swindler is no worse than "Trapper Geierschnabel," who outwits him. When Hitler told Field Marshal von Manstein to deal with Soviet sab-oteurs as "Old Shatterhand" would with hostile Indians, he recog-nized no Winnetou. I used to think of Nazism—until the crises at Mos-cow and Stalingrad—as a huge relapse into "Old Shatterhand" male adolescence.

3. When I was in Halle in 1998 I received the list. Eighty-three Halle Jews had served in the First World War; thirty-two had fallen.

4. On November 10, 1938, Paul Schmitthenner, rector of Heidelberg University, wrote to the Baden minister of education in Karlsruhe that, in view of the struggle of world Jewry against the Third Reich, it was intolerable that names of members of the Jewish race remain on plaques of the war dead.

5. I wrote this passage in 1993. In 1999 I remembered that we had read Stefan Zweig's *Jeremiah.* Looking at it now, I find it a great book still and further recall that later, in Berlin, Jeremiah was my fa-vorite prophet; I also recall that—perhaps based on Zweig or on Jer-emiah himself—not just pacifists like Hanff, but all of us thought re-visionist Zionism close to fascism. But then came Kristallnacht and Sachsenhausen.

Chapter 3. "Finish Studies First, Emigrate Later"

1. I once spent a whole year on the *summum bonum* in Kant's second *Critique,* trying to understand how he can honestly believe, not just in "Freedom," but also in "God" and "Immortality"; in my view, he was too honest to write just for the censors and too alive to be senile (see *God Within,* chap. 1). I found myself dissenting with Hermann Cohen; he was a "neo-Kantian," accepting Kant only when it suited him. Later I found the neo-Hegelians guilty of the same.

2. See further Albert H. Friedlaender, *Leo Baeck: Teacher of Theresien-stadt* (New York: Holt, Rinehart & Winston, 1968), and especially Her-bert Strauss and Kurt R. Grossman, eds., *Gegenwart im Rückblick* (Hei-delberg: Lothar Stiehm, 1970), a short but grimly true record of what

Nazism had done to Berlin Jewry and also of a Jewish *Neubeginn,* a "new beginning" of the Berlin Jewish community twenty-five years afterward. I stress this book because even for Heinz Warschauer (of whom I will say more later), born and raised in Berlin, a *Neubeginn* was unthinkable; he would do no more than get the book. To me, having been in Berlin just over three years, and then not really there, attending did not even occur. After his death, I inherited the book, marked up by him in places he considered crucial. Baeck, who died in 1956, never returned to Germany to live.

3. Max Wiener, *Jüdische Religion im Zeitalter der Emanzipation* (Berlin, 1933).

4. In his "Philosophy in the Age of Auschwitz: Emil Fackenheim and Leo Strauss," Kenneth Blanchard Jr. offers an able defense of Strauss that understands him. In *Remembering for the Future* (Oxford: Pergamon, 1988), 1815–29. On Strauss, see my *Jewish Philosophers and Jewish Philosophy,* chap. 7.

5. Martin Buber, *I and Thou,* 2d ed., trans. Ronald Smith (Edinburgh: T&T Clark, 1966), 109.

6. Buber, *Werke,* vol. 1 (Munich: Lambert Schneider, 1962), 170. At that time and place it must have taken sheer defiance of evil for evil's sake for Buber to make this statement; but Buber was not always defiant. When Ernst Simon urged him, just before his death to write or dictate his memoirs, Buber "rejected the idea categorically," since "[i]t is beyond my power." (Ernst Simon, "Comments on the Article on the late Rabbi Baeck," *Yad Vashem Studies* 4 [1967]: 134.)

7. Martin Buber, *Der Jude und sein Judentum* (Cologne: Joseph Melzer Verlag, 1963), 621–27.

8. Martin Buber, "A Letter to Gandhi," in *A Land of Two Peoples: Martin Buber on Jews and Arabs,* edited with commentary by Paul R. Mendes-Flohr (New York: Oxford University Press, 1983), 117. Mendes-Flohr gives Buber's letter to Gandhi (February 24, 1939) at length. See also Buber, "The Land and Its Possessors: An Answer to Gandhi," in *The Writings of Martin Buber,* selected, edited, and introduced by Will Herberg (New York: Meridian, 1956), 281; Buber, "The Land and Its Possessors," in *Israel and the World: Essays in a Time of Crisis* (New York: Schocken, 1948, 1963), 227. For the German text of the letter see Buber, *Der Jude und sein Judentum:*

Ein Land, von dem ein heiliges Buch den Söhnen dieses Landes erzählt, ist niemals bloss in den Herzen, ein Land wird nie zum blossen Symbol. Es ist in den Herzen, weil es in der Welt ist; es ist

ein Symbol, weil es Wirklichkeit ist. Zion ist das prophetische
Bild einer Verheissung für die Menschheit; aber es wäre nur eine
schlechte Metapher, wenn es den Zionsberg nicht wirklich gäbe.
Dieses Land heisst "heilig," aber es ist nicht die Heiligkeit einer
Idee, es ist die Heiligkeit eines Stücks Erde; was Idee ist und
nichts anderes, kann nicht heilig werden, aber win Stück Erde
kann heilig werden, wie ein Mutterleib heilig werden kann (632).

See also Buber, *Der Jude und sein Judentum:* "Sie sagen, Mahatma
Gandhi, für den Ruf nach einem nationalen Heim, der Sie 'nicht sehr
anspreche,' werde eine Beglaubigung (sanction) 'in der Bibel gesucht.'
Nein so ist es nicht" (633). Here, in Herberg's selection, Buber writes:
"You say Mahatma Gandhi, that to support the cry for a national home
which 'does not appeal to you,' a sanction is sought in the Bible. No that
is not so" (282). Mendes-Flohr translates the passage: "You say, Mahatma Gandhi, that to support the cry for a national home which 'does
not make much appeal to you,' a sanction is sought in the Bible. No—
this is not so" (118).

   9. See chap. 11 of *What Is Judaism?*

   10. Buber, *Der Jude und sein Judentum,* 630 (translation by Emil L. Fackenheim, the italics are mine). See also Buber, *A Land of Two Peoples,* 115.

   11. Paul Arthur Schilpp and Maurice Friedman, eds., *The Philosophy
of Martin Buber* (London: Cambridge University Press, 1967), 720.

   12. Buber, *Writings of Martin Buber,* 289.

   13. Schilpp and Freidman, *Philosophy of Martin Buber,* 716 n.10; see
also 289. Friedman has a section on Buber's "replies to critics," but the
passage just quoted appears by itself, at the end of a chapter, without my
response (*Martin Buber's Life and Work,* vol. 3, *The Later Years, 1945–1965*
[New York: Dutton, 1983], 168, 246–79). Buber told Friedman that I
understood him (257), which I had tried hard to do (*Jewish Philosphers
and Jewish Philosophy,* chap. 4). In retrospect, Buber's reply to Gandhi
was much longer than necessary. But he could not bring himself to accept that even Gandhi—although revered, justly, to this day—was then
playing politics: the great Indian leader would not admit that something worse existed than persecution of Indians. Perhaps he was unable
to do so.

   14. *Nachlese* (Heidelberg: Lambert Schneider, 1965), 259. This book
was Buber's very last; the cited passage is the last in the book itself, but
it was written before 1933, in 1927. Buber was still able to proofread before his death. He died on June 15, 1965.

   Buber's inability to confront radical evil—just when confrontation
was needed most—also had political implications. Ichud, of which

Buber was the most prominent member, wanted a binational state, in which Jews would never exceed Arabs in number. Even if the Arabs had agreed (of which there was no sign), this arrangement would have been problematic: in the postwar world survivors were welcome practically anywhere, while the binational Jewish-Arab state alone would have had a *numerus clausus*. On this moral contradiction Ichud ran aground.

15. But for attempts at such understanding, see chapters 13 and 20, as well as chap. 2 in *The God Within*, and the epilogue of this book.

16. For my writings on Buber, see *Jewish Philosophers and Jewish Philosophy*, chaps. 4 and 5, and *The Jewish Bible after the Holocaust*, chap. 1; on Rosenzweig *Jewish Philosophers and Jewish Philosophy*, chap. 6, and *Jewish Bible after the Holocaust*, chap. 1.

17. In 1933 our organization called itself Bund deutsch-jüdischer Jugend (BdjJ). By 1935 this self-definition had become impossible and the organization called itself Ring. But, when in 1935 they restored the German army and classified Jews as *Ersatz Reserve II* (without meaning it, of course), we still wondered whether it was our duty to serve the country or, if by volunteering, we would be caving in to Hitler.

In that year, in Berlin, I was called up to the army, went, was uncomfortable for everyone who came in, and said *Heil Hitler*. The group was waiting until a sergeant made us stand up stiffly and put us in a row for the officer. The officer came, saying: "Good morning, gentlemen!" The group was stunned and said nothing. The officer repeated sharply. "If I address you with 'Good morning,' I expect to hear, 'Good morning, Officer!'" This, as far as I experienced it personally, was the extent of the army's revolt. Only much later did I read how the army had caved in. For this see also Guido Knopp, *Hitler's Krieger* (Munich: Bertelsmann, 1998), the chapter on Rommel, "Das Idol," 15–93.

18. See *The Jewish Thought of Emil Fackenheim*, 21–25.

Chapter 4. Last Chance in Halle

1. Metzger's books are now forgotten: *Phänomenologie und Metaphysik* (Halle: Niemeyer, 1933) and *Freiheit und Tod* (Freedom and death) (Tübingen: Niemeyer, 1955).

Chapter 5. Six Months of Collapse

1. Although Jewish emancipation was not complete till the Weimar Republic, a *Rechtsstaat* for all had existed since Bismarck. See Karl

Dietrich Bracher, *The German Dictatorship: The Origins, Structure and Effects of National Socialism*, trans. Jean Steinberg (New York: Prager, 1970), 210, 219, and 225: "The catalogue of laws proclaimed by the Cabinet on the all-important day of July 14, 1933, is an extensive one. Celebrated in France as the anniversary of the storming of the Bastille, as symbol of rebellion against absolutism, this day formally sealed the establishment of the National Socialist dictatorship in Germany. . . . [a] whole series of major laws" was enacted by a regime seeing itself as the "antithesis of the ideals of 1776 and 1789."

Joachim Fest also notes the date but writes "there was at that date no sense of break or rupture; it simply marked the legal end of the Weimar Republic." In *Plotting Hitler's Death* (New York: Henry Holt, 1996), 33.

But before that "mammoth session," Bismarck's *Rechtsstaat* had already been abolished for my father and my uncle, on April 1, 1933.

2. My 1975 article is still worth reading ("Sachsenhausen 1938: Groundwork for Auschwitz," in *The Jewish Return into History*, 58–68). Stefan Kley wonders to what extent, if any, Hitler was involved; whether Goebbels (who hated Jews) acted on this occasion (i.e., Kristallnacht) because his love affair with Linda Baroova had caused trouble with his wife, hence, with Hitler; is surprised that a Himmler document distanced itself from the pogrom; and had Goering (a known rival of Goebbels) use Kristallnacht to accuse him, of all people, of stupidity. Written by a young scholar, Kley's otherwise excellent article is limited by records, raising this huge question for all Holocaust scholars: *if the records do not show who was responsible for Kristallnacht—the most public of all Nazi anti-Jewish crimes—how do they fare with the Holocaust, the most secret?* (But in any case the Nazis knew well enough that the problem was serious, not only because they used code words, but because the most terrible orders were verbal, never written down.) (Stefan Kley, "Hitler and the Pogrom of November 9–10, 1938," *Yad Vashem Studies* 28 (2000): 87–113.)

In contrast, I had personal experience, corrected, moreover—after much thought and many years—by a document written by one with the same experience, but who was older and more perceptive. *We both knew*—never mind Himmler's document!—that the SS had arrested us, was handling us; that otherwise honest *Bürger* had looted Jewish stores after the windows were smashed; and that Goering was involved when the synagogues burned.

3. Joseph Ackermann, *Heinrich Himmler als Ideologe* (Göttingen: Musterschmidt, 1970), 162–63. This is an outstanding work.

4. Weinberg, *Germany, Hitler and World War II* (Cambridge: Cambridge University Press, 1995), 2, front page.

5. Winter and Baggett, *The Great War and the Shaping of the Twentieth Century* (London: Penguin, 1996), 399.

6. Ibid., 398.

7. Weinberg, *Germany, Hitler and World War II*, 33.

8. Understandably a young scholar of Hungarian ancestry, Daniel Jonah Goldhagen, in his *Hitler's Willing Executioners* (New York: Alfred Knopf, 1996), thinks of "'ordinary Germans' as Jew-eliminators." But it is not my story nor can it be that of any Jew of German origin.

9. On the prayer, see Leonard Baker, *Days of Sorrow and Pain: Leo Baeck and the Berlin Jews* (New York: Macmillan, 1978), 207.

10. Ibid., 205–53, 264. Photographs of the four are following chapter 10.

Chapter 6. Scottish Interlude

1. I now think better of Chamberlain, less because of Gerhard L. Weinberg's massive *A World at Arms* (Cambridge: Cambridge University Press, 1994) than because of its sequel, *Germany, Hitler and World War II* (Cambridge: Cambridge University Press, 1995). First, Weinberg stresses, rightly, that Chamberlain, if hesitantly, declared war when England was not directly threatened, for he knew Hitler was untrustworthy, even if, unlike Winston Churchill, he did not regard him as evil. (Needless to say, Chamberlain also lacked Churchill's indomitable resolve in the desperate Dunkirk situation, but he still supported, if weakly, Churchill's "nations which went down fighting rose again, but those which surrendered tamely were finished" [Tim Clayton and Phil Craig, *Finest Hour* (London: Hodder & Stoughton, 1999), 117].)

Second, Weinberg stresses Hitler's regret about the Munich pact: had he not yielded to Chamberlain's "peace in our time"—as it were, fallen for his "umbrella"—and started war a year earlier, Germany might have won: Hitler would never again make the mistake of making a limited demand, out of fear that it might be accepted.

Chapter 8. "His Majesty's Guests" in Canada

1. Eric Koch, *Deemed Suspect: A Wartime Blunder* (Toronto: Methuen, 1980).

Chapter 9. University of Toronto

1. In 1989 I was asked about *Heimat* and replied it no longer exists, that I cannot use the word, that, like so much else, the Nazis have destroyed it (Herlinde Koelb, *Jüdische Portraits: Photographien und Interviews* [Frankfurt: S. Fischer, 1989], 66). Koelb has photographed and, with extraordinary perspicacity, interviewed each and every individual who appears in the book, about a hundred Jewish refugees, all from Nazism. With some, like Bruno Kreisky, I have nothing in common. I admire Jonas and Levinas, but my situation has been different from theirs. And with Yeshayahu Leibowitz I am in vigorous disagreement, politically and, above all, theologically.

Even before Oslo, Peace Now activists have advised withdrawal from "occupied territories," regardless of whether doing so would be safe; Leibowitz was a rare Orthodox supporter of this position. To me his God resembles a sergeant major, whose orders must be blindly obeyed but who, unlike that officer, does not protect his men.

Once, Claude Lanzmann was in Tel Aviv for a symposium on his *Shoah*, which hundreds of listeners were supposed to have seen. The chairman called on Leibowitz first, who went on about his theological politics, of which everyone was already aware; this made Lanzmann, the third one on the symposium, deeply irritated. When he was called on, he asked Leibowitz only one question: "Where were you during the Holocaust?" Leibowitz replied "in Palestine" and added that if Rommel had destroyed the Yishuv, he would not have changed his opinion. With Lanzmann saying no more, I raised my arm: "This must surely be a grim joke, for there is no Judaism without Jews." I was booed by his leftist supporters and never spoke to Leibowitz again.

2. This quote is taken from the *laudatio Enskat* delivered on May 12, 1999, when I was presented with an honorary doctorate from Halle University on the sixtieth anniversary of my expulsion from Halle and Germany. Guido Knopp's *Hitlers Krieger* (Munich: Bertelsmann, 1998) shows how Rommel, von Manstein, Paulus, and other generals, although not Nazis themselves, fought Hitler's wars and in some instances became implicated in Nazi crimes. Dietrich Bonhoeffer's "those who do their duty end up doing it for the devil" applies to these military figures, more so, of course, to Höss, who at Auschwitz murdered more people than any mad tyrant ever. But their number—let alone their names—will never be known, for the victims were often murdered on arrival: they never were registered.

3. See *To Mend the World*, 282, where the term is used to eliminate Jew-hatred in the religion of love.

4. Allan Gould, *What Did They Think of the Jews* (Northdale, N.J.: Jason Aronson, 1991).

5. Ayer, *Language, Truth, and Logic* (London: Gollancz Ltd., 1936, 1946).

6. Ibid.

7. R. J. Collingwood is no empiricist. His *Idea of History* (Oxford: Oxford University Press, 1946) finds an explanation for Caesar's crossing the Rubicon, not in psychology or "psychohistory," but in the purpose in his mind. One wonders what he would have done with an event a few years before publication of his book. Hitler was having lunch with General Rommel. Discussing enemy propaganda, the general suggested fighting it by appointing a Jewish *Gauleiter*. After Rommel had left, Hitler expressed vast astonishment: "He did not understand the Jews are the cause of this war." Historian Guido Knopp explains: "This indeed Rommel had not understood" (*Hitlers Krieger*, 54).

8. The main cause for this change, of course, has been the Holocaust. In Toronto I taught philosophy of history, taking up Collingwood, as well as "positivists" for whom historical explanations, like scientific ones, imply laws (such as "poverty creates revolutions" and "defeat in war inflames nationalism") except that freely acting human beings make "lawlike" explanations precarious and predictions impossible. I used to argue that lay historian Churchill was better at predictions than all the professionals. More, if the Depression in America produced Roosevelt, in Germany it produced Hitler; to explain *him* one would have to multiply laws so badly as to have Hitler, like God in old-fashioned metaphysics, in a class with only one member. But if Hitler is other than Roosevelt, is he like Caesar, crossing the Rubicon?

If I were teaching still, I would have students read Fest on Hitler, Winter and Baggett on the wars, and Klaus Fischer's *Nazi Germany: A New History* (New York: Continuum, 1996), and philosophize *thereafter*. Perhaps three books are too many; maybe just Fischer is enough.

9. As late as 1967 I still criticized Heidegger in the light of the *philosophia perennis*; see *God Within*, chap. 9.

Chapter 10. Second Rabbinate, Hamilton

1. *Brichah* is the Hebrew word for flight and became the name of a movement in which "Between 1944 and 1948, after their liberation from

the Nazis, some 250,000 Jews fled from Eastern Europe to the countries of Central Europe—Germany, Austria, and Italy. Their goal, generally speaking, was Palestine." Yehuda Bauer, *Flight and Rescue: Brichah* (New York: Random House, 1970), vii. For the Morgan incident, see 194–98, 243–44.

Chapter 11. "At Home in Toronto," or "Wearing Two Hats"

1. My 1893 *Klassiker-Ausgabe* praises Heine's Jewish activities prior to his conversion, while having only contempt for Gans, whose conversion was *an der Spitze* (at the helm) (*Heinrich Heines sämtliche werke*, ed. Ernst Elster [Leipzig: Bibliographisches Institut, 1893]). But in 1918 Rubaschaff could only lament that these gifted Jews were lost to the Jewish people. However, he could not have guessed that by 1933 the *Loreley* was still on a concert program but the *Dichter* (poet) was now *unbekannt* (unknown).

2. Herbert Marcuse, *Reason and Revolution: Hegel and the Rise of Social Theory* (New York: Oxford University Press, 1941).

3. In July 1999 in Berlin, when I was giving a one-week course for Peter von der Osten-Sacken's *Kirche und Judentum*, a well-versed student reminded me that Hegel's *Aufheben* means *three* things, "abolition" as well as the two others mentioned in the text. It was a good reminder. Two months earlier, in Halle on May 12, I had already asserted that Hegel fails to "abolish" the Jewish return to Jerusalem: *that* failure was built into my Berlin lectures. (See the epilogue of this book and also "'Idle' Messianic Hope and 'World-Historical Return,'" in the appendix.)

4. Hegel quoted in *Phänomenologie des Geistes*, ed. Georg Lasson (Leipzig: Duerr, 1907), 22. Translation by Emil L. Fackenheim. See also *Religious Dimensions in Hegel's Thought*, 82.

5. See Barth, *Against the Stream* (London: SCM Press, 1954). See also Andreas Pangritz, *Karl Barth in der Theologie Dietrich Bonhoeffers* (Berlin: Alektor, 1989). Apparently, the relations between Barth and Bonhoeffer were more complex; but if our friend David Demson or my wife, Rose, both Barth students, had read Pangritz's book, called a "necessary clarification"—at a time, when *all* Christianity was in question—they would have been frustrated by these discussions of theological minutiae.

I found among Rose's books *The Anatomy of Anti-Semitism* by James Daane (Grand Rapids: Eerdmans, 1965). This theologian, who had bothered with the subject at all, could still write in 1965 that "God alone may punish the Jews for their rejection of the crucified and resurrected Christ; the church may not. God may punish His enemies; the Church may only love its enemies and pray for them" (30). Rose had underlined that passage and placed an exclamation point beside it.

In 1949 not much had penetrated even to great Christian theologians. Israel had been founded a year before, but Rudolf Bultmann could still describe Jewish existence as a "self-contradictory phenomenon," that is, at once empirical and eschatological; see "Prophecy and Fulfillment," in *Essays: Philosophical and Theological* (London: SCM Press, 1955), 203. From a Jewish perspective, one might ask Christians whether, after the Holocaust, the Jewish state's *very existence* does not manifest this self-contradiction and also its transcendence but as *empirically present.* Christians are now said widely to believe that the divine promise to Israel is not superseded, but they have yet to face its implications, especially vis-à-vis Jerusalem. See also the following note and the epilogue of this book.

6. By the 1990s there was already a well-established "Texte & Kontexte" in an *Exegetische Zeitschrift* of Kloster Denkendorf, a Protestant institute committed to Jewish-Christian dialogues in Wuerttemberg, which not only brings rabbinic interpretations of Hebrew Scripture to Christian believers—taking seriously the belief, both Catholic and Protestant, that the election of Israel is not superseded—but also texts that relate them to the Shoah. Compare, for example, Andreas Bedenbender, "Die Bindung Isaaks nach dem Midrasch Bereschit Rabba: Mit einer Einfuehrung in die rabbinische Literatur," *Texte & Contexte* 65/ 66 (May 1995). In that work Andreas Bedenbender quotes me: "Like Abraham of old, European Jews sometime in the nineteenth century offered a human sacrifice, by the mere minimal commitment to the Jewish faith of bringing up Jewish children. But unlike Abraham they did not know what they were doing, and there was no reprieve" (55). This passage did not appear until 1967, in *Commentary,* and a German translation not until the early 1980s. See Fackenheim, "Jewish Faith and the Holocaust," in *Philosophy in the Age of Crisis,* ed. Eleanor Kuykendall (New York: Harper & Row, 1970), 464–82, here 467; "Jewish Faith and the Holocaust: A Fragment" in *Jewish Return into History,* 25–43, here 30. For further places of publication and translation of this article see *Fackenheim: German Philosophy and Jewish Thought,* edited by Louis Greenspan and Graeme Nicholson (Toronto: University of Toronto Press, 1992), 305 n.23.

7. Norman Podhoretz, *Ex Friends* (New York: Free Press, 1999), 167, 176.

8. Daniel Pipes, "Israel's Moment of Truth," *Commentary* (February 2000): 19–25; letters to the editor, *Commentary* (May 2000): 6, Pipes's response is on 6 and 8.

9. Efraim Karsh, "Were the Palestinians Expelled?" *Commentary* (July–August 2000): 29, 32, 34.

10. Midrash *Rabbah, Shir Ha-Shirim,* V 16 # 3, quoted in *God's Presence in History,* 15.

11. See *Religious Dimension in Hegel's Thought,* especially chap. 4.

12. The German original text reads: "Und wie es einen Enthusiasmus zum Guten gibt, ebenso gibt es eine Begeisterung des Bösen." F. W. Schelling, *Das Wesen Der Menschlichen Freiheit: Mit Einleitung, Namen- und Sachregister neu herausgegeben von Christian Herrmann* (Leipzig: Felix Meiner, 1925), 44. Translation by Emil L. Fackenheim.

13. Ibid. The German original text reads: "Nie kann das Tier aus der Einheit heraustreten, anstatt dass der Mensch das ewige Band der Kräfte willkürlich zerreissen kann. Daher Fr. Baader mit Recht sagt, es wäre zu wünschen, dass die Verderbtheit im Menschen nur bis zur Tierwerdung ginge; leider aber könne der Mensch nur unter oder über dem Tiere stehen." Translation by Emil L. Fackenheim. In his *The Ages of the World* (New York: Columbia, 1942), Schelling wrote: "The godhead sits enthroned over a world of horrors" (156).

Chapter 12. Between Toronto and Jerusalem

1. In *To Mend the World* I had to think more radically about the Shoah. But the Easter Purim 1967 event was opposed to the belief—my own and that of friends and colleagues—in Sinaitic Judaism. Thus Michael Wyshogrod had me "replace Judaism with Auschwitzism." In Berlin in 1997, I think we clarified our real difference, between Michael's Hasidic "with faith there are no questions, and without it there are no answers," and my inability to accept either. Wyshogrod was not the only person who reacted negatively to my 614th commandment. Schwarzschild did also. He must have regretted twisting my arm.

2. See R. Thalman and E. Feinermann, *Crystal Night* (New York: Coward, McCann & Geoghenan, 1974), 33.

3. *God's Presence in History,* 84.

4. The facts below I remembered only after the manuscript was finished.

Our first trip to Israel in 1968 followed the New York Symposium in 1967. Elie Wiesel had suggested that the Israeli government invite me, a Jewish philosopher. In Israel we met Levi Eshkol, Ya'acov Herzog, who asked us, "Why aren't you coming [to Israel, i.e., on aliyah]?" It was one of the two big questions I had no answer to at the time. (The other had been in 1938: "What does Judaism say to us now?" That I answered as late as in 1987. Herzog's question we answered much sooner, in 1983, when we came.)

The other trip to Israel was in 1970, with the World Federation of Bergen-Belsen Survivors. I, no survivor, was invited as a judge on Holocaust literature, a prize that was given to Manès Sperber among others. I had never written about the Holocaust, was reluctant when Schwarzschild first asked me for the 1967 symposium; he must have been sorry later he did, for we derived opposite conclusions, even though both of us are German Jews: Schwarzschild relied on Hermann Cohen, I, of course negatively, on Martin Heidegger, and positively, on Franz Rosenzweig.

For me the greatest speech in Bergen-Belsen was by Norbert Wollheim, a German Jew like myself.

5. I got involved in theopolitics because, as I think of it now, it has always been impossible to separate theology from politics, at least in Judaism. The Biblical Gideon was asked to be king, but replied that only God was King. Everybody understands that now it (i.e., such a response) is impossible, in Christianity and Islam as well.

On March 26, 2000, Pope John Paul II called on the "God of our fathers, you chose Abraham and his descendants to bring your name to the Nations." But in the book *Good and Evil after Auschwitz* (published with this dedication, which the Pope made in Jerusalem on the occasion of his visit to the Western Wall), as well as during the conference on this topic in Rome in 1998, Jews and Christians were present, Muslims were not.

6. Rose did not stay well long enough to understand Franklin's thirty-year-struggle arising from the German *Kirchenkampf* (church struggle). Littell views the Shoah as the "most traumatic" event in Christian history. Also, he holds, rightly, that Jewish-Christian cooperation is essential also for Jews, that without it, the Shoah "will slide into the pathology of Jewish victimology or the banal flattening of the

Shoah into an immoral equivalence of many 'Holocausts.'" Late in 1999, in a letter to friends, he wrote: "This was my thirty-seventh trip to Israel. I am not one of those who visit the 'Holy Land' without setting foot in a restored Israel."

This is not just written in a book, but realized in conferences. In 2002 is the 32nd Annual Scholars' conference on the Holocaust and the Churches: The Genocidal Mind, March 2–5, 2002, at Union, New Jersey.

The quotation is from personal conversation, but is of a profundity that it should be in this book.

7. Eva Fleischner, ed., *Auschwitz: Beginning of a New Era?* (New York: Ktav, 1977), 417–19. The book was published as a result of this conference, which was on Christians as well as Jews. Later there were others, e.g., *Good and Evil after Auschwitz: Ethical Implications for Today,* ed. Jack Bemporad, John T. Pawlikowski, and Joseph Sievers (Hoboken, N.J.: Ktav Publishing House, 2000). This conference was attended by Protestants, Catholics, and Jews.

8. I had already reached the same conclusion with Martin Buber, who made the word "dialogue" famous, but not its content, regarding Kristallnacht—dialogue with German Christians. My parting with Buber had been traumatic. I use that word rarely, but I had to take radical evil seriously and found out gradually that Martin Buber could not.

For any Jew reading Jonah on Yom Kippur, Rosemary Radford Ruether and Herman J. Ruether's very title—*The Wrath of Jonah: The Crisis of Religious Nationalism in the Israeli-Palestinian Conflict* (San Francisco: Harper & Row, 1987)—is enough: she has Jonah wrathful because God cares about Gentiles. But on Yom Kippur every Jewish child knows he was wrathful because God made a fool of him, and that on Yom Kippur Jews read him, repent, ever learn again that God loves even Nineveh. As a child myself I loved how the book ends: God cares even about cattle.

I had come upon "Christians and Jonah" once before, when the Ontario government introduced a course on Christianity—illegal in the United States, but not in Canada—and had ministers prepare an Old Testament course; as an afterthought of their own, the ministers asked me to look at their text. I made the same criticism about Jonah and Yom Kippur. Ruether never apologized, nor did she scrap her book.

The Greenbergs are friends, with whom we once stayed for the Pesach Seder. When Greenberg published his *The Jewish Way* (New York: Summit, 1988), he gave it to us for our "precious friendship"; when his wife, Blu, published her *How to Run a Traditional Jewish Household* (New

York: Simon & Schuster, 1983), she presented us with a copy with "friendship we treasure."

9. In Salaspils the Soviets advertised Nazi genocide: in Rumbula only Jews were murdered. The Soviet guides volunteered to take us to Salaspils; but they had to be pressured to take us to Rumbula.

10. On this, see further below, especially the epilogue, and my address in Halle included in the appendix: "'Idle' Messianic Hope and 'World-Historical' Return." An indispensable book is Eliyahu Tal, *Whose Jerusalem?* (Jerusalem: International Forum for a United Jerusalem, 1994). See also his *You Don't Have to Be Jewish to Be a Zionist* (Jerusalem: International Forum for a United Jerusalem, 2000). In view of the worldwide fuss about Jerusalem, which began just after its appearance, this book is prophetic.

11. "Abortive spawn of fire and dirt!" Johann Wolfgang von Goethe, *Faust, I.*, trans. Philip Wayne (London: Penguin Books, 1949). In April 1970 the World Organization of Bergen-Belsen Survivors asked me to serve on their committee for prizes they were giving to writers about the Holocaust. They invited my wife and me to join them for a pilgrimage which would take us first to Bergen-Belsen and then to Jerusalem. The committee then met in London.

12. I had Wollheim in mind, but not him alone, when I wrote "The Rebirth of the Holy Remnant," in *Major Changes within the Jewish People in the Wake of the Holocaust:Proceedings of the Ninth Yad Vashem International Historical Conference* (Jerusalem: Yad Vashem, 1996), 649–58. There I myself call the Shoah victims *k'doshim*. Nor was this the first time. Before I had quoted Wollheim's sentence, "*k'doshim* was the name given those who did not survive by those who did," and commented that "*k'doshim* is the legacy bestowed by *amcha* on future theological thought" (*Jewish Philosophers and Jewish Philosophy*, 225).

13. *Holocaust and Rebirth: Bergen-Belsen, 1945–1965*, ed. Sam E. Bloch (New York and Tel Aviv: Bergen-Belsen Memorial Press of the World Federation of Bergen-Belsen Associations, 1965).

14. A Hebrew word for messenger. Israel has a Law of Return, surely because of the Holocaust, that Jews having a home nowhere else have a home in Israel. Toronto had been the home for Rose and me; but when Israel was in danger, we felt obliged to move to Jerusalem. There is a *Shaliach* in every North American city having a large Jewish population. They must have a *Shaliach* in Buenos Aires. True, there is an official *Shaliach*, usually a retired politician. But Peli was not one of them, he just was a personal friend. If I call him a "philosopher" this is intentional,

although his profession was not philosophy, but two events were central to his thought, the Holocaust and Israel. This is true of few professional philosophers, even Jewish ones.

15. Bernhard Postal and Henry W. Levy, *And the Hills Shouted for Joy: The Day Israel Was Born* (Philadelphia: Jewish Publication Society of America, 1975), 193. Tom Segev criticizes Israeli leaders as manipulative about the Shoah. But his chapter title "What Is There to Understand? They Died and That's It" is itself manipulative (*The Seventh Million* [New York: Hill & Wang, 1993], 468–69). Ben-Gurion was uttering these words in despair, yet was unable to yield, for he had to prepare the state. I have read *The Seventh Million* from cover to cover, also Segev's *Soldaten des Bösen* (Hamburg: Rowohlt, 1995), his account of the *KZ Kommandanten* (concentration camp commandants), and, though critical of him, I take Segev seriously.

16. See, for example, Alvin Rosenfeld, *Imagining Hitler* (Bloomington: University of Indiana Press, 1985), 94 on Nazi apologist H. Kardel, author of *Adolf Hitler: Begründer Israels;* see also Ron Rosenbaum, *Explaining Hitler* (New York: Macmillan, 1998) on George Steiner's *The Portage to San Cristobal of A. H.,* chap. 17.

17. Events since Intifada II have made this view unduly optimistic. But I still differentiate Arab, even Palestinian, antisemitism from the Nazi version.

18. I come back to this Hegelian term, *weltgeschichtlich,* crucially in the epilogue and in the lectures B and D in the appendix, and I hope yet again in future writings.

19. Readers should see photographs in Jürgen Stroop's *The Stroop Report* (New York: Pantheon, 1979), which documents the bureaucratic diligence *and its supporting photographs;* the latter were meant for German *Weltgeschichte*—for example, pictures of "bandits" jumping from burning houses rather than yielding to Wehrmacht arrest—and must be *seen.* To read *about* it is not enough.

20. *God's Presence in History,* 102. I wrote this in 1970, because Kant did not ask Jews to become Christians. But by 1990, Paul Lawrence Rose had become much more exacting: Kant wanted the euthanasia of Judaism, because it was an immoral religion, if a religion at all. (*Revolutionary Antisemitism in Germany: From Kant to Wagner* [Princeton, N.J.: Princeton University Press, 1990], 93–97).

21. This Hegel passage is a motto of the crucial chapter 3 in *Religious Dimension in Hegel's Thought.* The italics are mine.

22. Georg Wilhelm Friedrich Hegel, *Phaenomenologie des Geistes*

(Leipzig: Verlag Dürr'schen Buchhandlung, 1907), 22. Translation by Emil L. Fackenheim.

23. Claude Lanzmann, *Shoah* (New York: Pantheon 1985), 109.

24. Ernst Klee, Willi Dressen, Volker Riess, *Schöne Zeiten: Judenmord aus der Sicht der Täter und Gaffer* (Frankfurt: S. Fischer, 1988). The blurb quotes one perpetrator as follows: "Hatred of Jews was so great, revenge was wanted, and we wanted money and gold. We should not pretend anything else, but from the 'Jewish actions' there was something to get." The book shows that nobody who refused to murder Jews was punished.

25. C. R. Browning, *Ordinary Men* (New York: Harper, 1992), 133–46. Edward Alexander asks whether Browning is "too charitable" when stating that, since they were not sophisticated, these policemen expressed no moral revulsion about murdering Jews: does one need to be Bishop Berkeley to understand "thou shalt not murder" (*The Jewish Wars* [Carbondale: Southern Illinois University Press, 1996], 121).

26. Hannah Arendt, *Ich Will Verstehen* (Munich: Piper, 1996). Arendt's main work on this subject is, of course, her *Eichmann in Jerusalem* (New York: Penguin, 1992). Among the many critics of Arendt, including her much-too-glib "wish to understand," is a solid one, Michael R. Marrus, *The Holocaust in History* (Toronto: Lester & Orpen Dennys, 1987), 110–11; cf. Marrus also on Leo Baeck, 123.

27. Joachim Fest, *Plotting Hitler's Death* (New York: Henry Holt, 1996), 297–303.

28. Fest, *Hitler* (New York: Vintage, 1973), 681. Fest would surely admit this *huge* difference: *Hitler hated the July 20, 1944, "traitors," but Jews were hated in his Weltanschauung.* As everybody reports, he had no reason to hate Jews personally. For this insight alone, terrible as it is, but in my opinion tenable, I value Fest's book, which is probably the best on Hitler, if only because later books, though necessary for a final judgment of history, can no longer be "from inside." But his *Hitler* is also most disturbing, for "if you *explain* evil, it is *ipso facto* less than radical," and his blurb on Klaus Fischer's *Nazi Germany* (New York: Continuum, 1996) as "contributing to the understanding of what no one can fully understand" seems to admit it. (I wrote this paragraph before reading Ian Kershaw.)

But he admits more: Fischer cites the very passage in Fest that troubles me but ascribes Hitler's "silence" and "secrecy," not to his Weltanschauung, but to "some psychological need to maintain the atrocity at a distance" (498). Fest never explains, first, why, if the conclusions following these "premises" are "absolutely inevitable," anyone should grant these premises, indeed why Hitler himself was *unerschütterlich* (unshakable) about them; second, why Germans in general accepted them, including generals, who became war criminals. Fest seems himself to be under Hitler's "shadow" when he ascribes the Holocaust to a late "lost reality," when the Jew hatred was there already in the 1920s. I must admit that the bit about Hitler's "bourgeois morality" stopped me for years from reading Fest's *Hitler* with the care it deserves.

29. Although *Hitler: Legend, Myth and Reality* (New York: Harper & Row, 1971) is accurate, its author, Werner Maser, is not a respected historian. In describing Hitler's Weltanschauung, he is so close to this view himself that, under "intellectual background," he speaks of "books" when referring to pamphlets, and includes a chapter titled "The Ailing Führer" that comes close to excusing Hitler's "mistakes," including the Shoah.

Afraid of this trap, Germans often have preferred Hermann Rauschning, for whom Hitler was just a nihilist seeking power. (Perhaps for this reason even Ralph Manheim, the translator of *Mein Kampf*, did not retain the German term Weltanschauung [now a good English word] in chapters 1 and 5 of the second part, but translated it, incorrectly, as "philosophy.") Thus Eberhard Jaeckel virtually had to reestablish the fact that Hitler did have a Weltanschauung.

30. Fest, *Hitler*, 9.

31. Gitta Sereny was very brave when she interviewed Franz Stangl, the commandant of Treblinka, and his wife for seventy hours—but, Treblinka being absolute evil, she was perhaps too patient in listening.

32. Albert Speer, *Spandau: The Secret Diaries*, trans. Richard and Clara Winston (London: Collins, 1976), 87.

33. Richard Gutteridge describes Kristallnacht as "a unique and a last opportunity to speak out in protest," but also that the "Church kept a stunned and fearful silence," that "no one ventured to take the initiative in organizing a protest," thus leaving it to a "humble village pastor, Julius von Jan of Oberlingen in Wuertemberg, to speak out fearlessly and for the whole church" ("German Protestantism and the Jews," in *Judaism and Christianity under the Impact of National Socialism, 1919–1945*, ed. Otto Dov Kulka and Paul R. Mendes-Flohr [Jerusalem: Historical Society of Israel and Zalman Shazar Center for Jewish History, 1987], 239–40).

This is, of course, a criticism *after* the 1938 *Gleichschaltung* that must have made "organizing" impossible, but one need only study the fuss they made about *one* Lichtenberg to understand that *spontaneous* Lichtenbergs were not. To U.S. Catholics visiting in Jerusalem, I once said his prayer "for Jews and non-Aryan Christians" saved, if nothing else, Christianity.

In 1995 I could speak on "Holocaust and Hope," in Toronto to the United Church College, only after stressing Raul Hilberg's *Hoffnungslosigkeit* (*Unerbetene Erinnerung* [Frankfurt: Fischer, 1994], 174). I quoted Hilberg, quoting H. G. Adler, the author of the massive *Theresienstadt 1941-45* (Tübingen: Mohr, 1955): "Am Ende bleibt nichts als die Verzweiflung (despair) . . . Für Hilberg gibt es nur ein *"Erkennen"* (scholarship), vielleicht auch noch ein *Begreifen* (comprehension), *aber bestimmt kein Verstehen."*

The difference between *Begreifen* and *Verstehen* is subtle, best understood philosophically as between "understanding-the-internal-logic-of-another" and "sharing-by-'mediation.'" Alone in Western philosophy, Hegel shares every "other" by "overcoming," either by making it accidental vis-à-vis the "essential" or, if radical, through the ultimate "Identity of Identity and Non-Identity"; but vis-à-vis "Planet Auschwitz" both are impossible.

34. *To Mend the World*, 247

35. There is a biography of Rudolph Höss, the Auschwitz Kommandant (Manfred Deselaers, *"Und Sie hatten nie Gewissensbisse?"* [Leipzig: Benno, 1997]). Höss, of course, was long dead, and the author could just interpret Höss's book. He accepts both his pleas (i) that he only obeyed orders and (ii) that his repentance was genuine. This is a classic case—considering who Höss was, perhaps *the* classic one—of "evil being somewhere else." Hitler, Goering, Goebbels, Himmler, Heydrich, all escaped the hangman and never repented: they not only relished what they were doing, but *the very concept* "repentance" did not exist for them. Deselaers saves his Christianity with much too little *Betroffenheit* (a term explained below, roughly, stunned or shaken). He told me at a Rome conference that Auschwitz needs a church, and in that wish this Catholic is not alone. He deserves credit, however, for doing more than most Christians, even living for a while in Auschwitz.

But Deselaers is much more *betroffen* than Winter and Baggett about Höss and *Arbeit Macht Frei*. (See note 25 for this chapter.) Other students have stressed how, without pity for the Gypsy children he would murder—perversely but, for Nazis, typically, "normally"—Höss lapsed into self-pity. (See Martin Broszat in *To Mend the World*, 242).

36. Fackenheim, *To Mend the World*, 242.

Chapter 13. On Icons and Radical Evil

1. *God Within*, 51–52.
2. Ibid., 33
3. Winter and Baggett, *Great War and the Shaping of the Twentieth Century*, 402. Winter and Baggett's book is important if only because it gives the horrors of the Great War in photographs. Has their Höss's *Arbeit Macht Frei* been taken out of context? But the context in which Winter and Baggett present it is *itself scandalous:* in their book, Höss and Niemoeller—one a Sachsenhausen guard, the other a privileged prisoner—have much in common. By the same token, Hitler and de Gaulle are treated as Great War victims. Churchill is not the World War II hero stopping Hitler, but the reckless Gallipolli warrior; and the U.S. president who counts in the twentieth century is not Roosevelt, who avoided involving the United States in the war as long as possible but waged it when necessary, but rather the ineffectual Herbert Hoover, who, to counter war and communism, sent food to Reds and Whites in Russia.

Winter and Baggett *do* make moral judgments, but they are not unbiased ones. They have no fewer than seven pages on Lawrence of Arabia, whom they describe as seeking a "national future for an oppressed people" and blame Britain for "abandoning" him (124). In contrast, they see Weizmann mainly as supplying acetone to Churchill and do not even mention Herzl.

At a minimum, these judgments derive from a naïve "all peace is good, all wars bad, and the Great War is catastrophic" viewpoint: any peace-war-irony-in-history is missing. As for the Jewish victims of Auschwitz, they are dead "icons." Had either Winter or Baggett *been there*, as Rose and I were in Bergen-Belsen, the survivors' "Holocaust and Rebirth" would not have escaped them and the "Rebirth" would not necessarily have been peaceful.

4. Shocking proof of how far they got, in merely twelve years, is given by Jay W. Baird, *To Die for Germany* (Bloomington: University of Indiana Press, 1992). The title says all: Germany was replacing God—not only "the God of philosophers," but also the God of "Abraham, Isaac and Jacob," that is, of Jews, of Christians, of Muslims. The mothers shock one especially: they do not mourn their fallen sons but celebrate that they died for Germany.

As Goebbels expressed it: this total war is *Gottesdienst* (worship service of God).

5. I could cope easily with reviews of my Hegel book that argued that the young "revolutionary" author of the *Phenomenology* had become a passively pious Christian: before his death Hegel had planned to reissue the *Phenomenology*.

But it was harder to cope with Hegel and "Planet Auschwitz." That Auschwitz was a "planet" had been clear ever since the writer *Yehiel (K. Zetnick)* used that word at the Eichmann trial and then collapsed. What the term would mean to Hegel, the philosopher-of-the-whole came to me on reading—this beyond Browning's "ordinary men" and Goldhagen's "ordinary Germans"—that when the "harvest" was "celebrated" in Poland, it was not so bad to murder Jewish children, since without parents they would not survive anyway: for this "planet," it is true that the whole is more than the sum of the parts.

6. Fischer, *Nazi Germany: A New History*, 499, 502. Admitting "our inability to define evil or malignant destructiveness," Fischer lists for Hitler no fewer than seven categories—all quasi-medical, none adequate, either apart or together—but also applies them to those "attracted to Hitler," the attraction having been "no accident" (301, 305).

7. Heidegger's *Schellings Abhandllung über das Wesen der menschlichen Freiheit* (Schelling's treatise on the essence of human freedom) (Tübingen: Niemeyer, 1971) "proceeded from his own question" (Werner Marx, *The Philosophy of Schelling* [Bloomington: University of Indiana Press, 1984], 93) and hence posited Being as prior to Good and Evil: thus he trivialized evil.

That the philosopher "proceeded from his own question" is true also, if differently, of Heidegger on Hegel's *Phenomenology*. Having written that, for Hegel, the "leap" into "the whole of the absolute is all that is left," Heidegger further "rightly understood, this issue is in itself the question: what should man do as an existing being?" (Martin Heidegger, *Hegel's Phenomenology of Spirit* [Bloomington: University of Indiana Press, 1988], 149).

But Hegel *does not ask* Heidegger's question but rather *has answered* it: his own age is ripe for "Science." Is Heidegger different only in that, unlike Hegel's, *his* "age" is "indigent," a *dürftige Zeit*, that cannot be transcended? Heidegger's own question was how existing man gets to Being. He never wrote the promised second part of *Sein und Zeit*, but got stuck with this question, whereas Schelling asks how pantheism is compatible with human freedom, which causes him more and more to focus on the latter, hence to think more deeply about Good and Evil. See Annemarie Gethmann-Siefert and Otto Poeggeler, eds.,

Heidegger und die praktische Philosophie (Frankfurt: Suhrkamp, 1989), 62–63.

Chapter 14. To Jerusalem

1. Frank Talmage, *Disputation and Dialogue: Readings in the Jewish-Christian Encounter* (New York: Ktav, 1975) remains an important book. I think that what Father Kelly did had something to do with Talmage's courage to publish his book. The foreword was written by Reverend Edward A. Synan of the Pontifical Institute of Medieval Studies in Toronto.

Chapter 15. A New Job

1. An ulpan is a specifically Israeli institution for learning Hebrew fast, eight hours a day.

2. The joke that Hebrew University was German was not entirely inappropriate: the further past events were, the more scholarly was the scholarship. In contrast, contemporary events were despised, only for journalists. Moshe Davis's Institute for Contemporary Jewry broke with this tradition for two reasons: the Holocaust does need scholarship, if only because of its extreme secrecy; both the Holocaust and the Jewish state are epoch-making.

3. "Civilization" is now much more common that a Harvard professor, Samuel P. Huntington has written about "The Clash of Civilizations" (*The Clash of Civilizations and the Remaking of World Order* [New York: Simon & Schuster, 1996]), but "Jewish Civilization," Israeli or Diaspora, is still a step-child.

Kaplan's merit was that he stressed living people—Yiddish, kosher food, at least lighting of candles on Shabbat—against abstract theology, but it was weak—I thought hopeless—in theology itself. The prayers in his prayer books seemed to be addressed "To whom it may concern." His concept is becoming more real in the clash between Sefardi (Spanish) and Ashkenazi (German) Jews, but what unites them more and more is a shared destiny and shared dangers.

4. See, for example, Moshe Davis, *My Formative Years 1937–38* and *America and the Holy Land,* both published under Israeli government auspices. Before his death in 1995, Moshe published a work on a subject of which he was the acknowledged master, *Teaching Jewish Civilization* (New York: New York University Press, 1995). The "civilization" covered by the book is worldwide, or almost so.

5. From a later writing it is obvious that he thought more of Wiesel than of me, i.e. the contradiction that Wiesel finds the Holocaust incommunicable yet tries to communicate it. As a philosopher I see nothing wrong with this contradiction.

6. Rosenbaum, *Explaining Hitler,* vii and chap. 16. Rosenbaum's dedication is "To those who survived, and to those who did not" (v). As a Jewish philosopher, I republished twice my 1988 essay "Holocaust and Weltanschauung: Philosophical Reflections on Why They Did It" (*God Within,* 174–85, and *Jewish Philosophers and Jewish Philosophy,* 146–58.) As a philosopher, I seem to be virtually alone on the Holocaust, to say nothing about exploring the concept of Weltanschauung. In German philosophy, I may have shocked, for different reasons, both Germans and Jews, by connecting the "golden age" in German philosophy with the "philosopher Hitler." Now I think the connection needs even deeper, more painful reflection. But I would no longer describe it as yet another case of *corruptio optimi pessima,* but, as I did in my 1997 Kassel inaugural lecture, as a unique rupture. See also my lectures in Bochum, May 20, 1998, and in Halle, May 12, 1999, in the appendix.

The deepest point is the difference between history that explains everything and between philosophers such as Leo Strauss who disagree emphatically.

7. Rosenbaum, *Explaining Hitler,* vii.

8. These *Hashomer ha Tzair* members were nonreligious, left-wing, if "left" means (as it still does in Israel) that if Palestinians are treated well they will be accommodating in turn. "Right-wing" Israelis do not share this optimism about Palestinians. For details on the history of the *Hashomer ha Tzair* movement see *Encyclopaedia Judaica* (Jerusalem: Keter, 1971).

9. See *Lam.R.* 3:60, on 3:43 (cf. *Midr.Ps.* on 65:5 [157A § 4]) (cf. 1105).

10. It was alright to teach the historical fact that medieval philosopher Yehuda Halevi had said that Jerusalem will be redeemed only if Jews love her stones and dust; to talk ideology, that students were here and so were dust and stones was not. But as the dean had said, I could get away with it because I was a scholar also on non-Jewish subjects such as Hegel.

11. I had lunch with John almost daily, but we never talked philosophy, for he was into Wittgenstein, and I into Hegel. Bob was into aesthetics but he, the most conscientious Canadian professor I knew, had volunteered at the beginning of the war, was captured at Dieppe (Northern France, raid on Dieppe, August 19, 1942), and knew the Nazi

enemy better than anyone else. A story of his I kept asking him to tell me was this: he and others were interned on a hill above the Rhine with six or seven grand pianos. One day, an officer told them they would move, and with a smile: would they leave those grand pianos to the Nazis? Their rights included what to do with their property. So they shoved the pianos from above into the Rhine. Heinrich Heine would have enjoyed it in his grave.

12. I've said elsewhere I had to send her to a home in the end, but until then, she would always accompany me to my lectures.

13. Frank Cunningham (Professor of Philosophy and Principal of Innis College at the University of Toronto) established a relationship with Holy Blossom Temple and I was friendly with him.

Chapter 16. Mostly Unfinished Business

1. Gerstenfeld, *Israel's New Future* (Jerusalem: Jerusalem Center for Public Affairs, 1994), 218.

2. With a cheap shot, Edward Said drags in "a woman, a Jew, a child of Holocaust survivors" as a witness to Palestinian misery, thus blotting out the Holocaust. His other shot, equally cheap, has a long history: blotting out "Zion" in Zionism by making Jerusalem "the heart of our [i.e., Palestinian] predicament" (*Peace and Its Discontents: Essays on Palestine in the Middle East Peace Process* [New York: Vintage, 1995], 47, 29). This is in a tract, supposedly timely, about compromise solutions of an admittedly tragic conflict between "right" and "right."

In the five years since 1995, Said's bias—against Israel, against the Holocaust, for pan-Arabism-at-any-price, his wishful thinking included—has not changed. In a *Los Angeles Times* article, reprinted in the *Jerusalem Post* of June 4, 2000, he attacks "Holocaust memories, cynically exploited"—for him *all* Holocaust memories are cynically exploited—while expressing his "conviction," undocumented and purely private, that, not Muslim fanaticism, but "secular opposition to it" will win in the Arab world.

This was before the worldwide "religious" fuss about Jerusalem, with Arafat seeking help with Egypt (with which we have peace) and Saudi Arabia (with which we do not). A Saudi king once received Henry Kissinger, not "as a Jew," but as a "human being." Sarcastically, Kissinger replied: "Some of my best friends are human beings."

Recently Said threw stones at Israeli troops withdrawing from Lebanon, explaining that these were stones of joy; he had not known there were photographers present.

3. *Azure: Ideas for the Jewish Nation* 6 (Winter 1999): 83–84.

4. For the reader, I repeat that these memoirs were finished in 2000. Only one essay at the end of this book was written in 2002.

Chapter 17. Germany

1. Jürgen Wenzlau's older brother is said to be alive still in Braunschweig; I have never contacted him to ask how Jürgen died. In 1999 in Halle I was phoned by Rossmann, who in 1933 did not want the "damn thing," the swastika. I was happy to hear he was alive but have yet to write what happened to the others. I have tried to find out how Jürgen died, but after more than fifty years did not succeed. I contacted a Wenzlau in Braunschweig but he is no relative.

2. Wilhelm Breuning and Hanspeter Heinz, eds., *Damit die Erde Menschlich Bleibt* (Freiburg: Herder, 1985), 14.

3. Marquardt, *Von Elend und Heimsuchung der Theologie* (Munich: Chr. Kaiser, 1988).

4. Henrix got into trouble with a Jewish resident in Germany, Edna Brocke, much later, when the Vatican beatified Edith Stein. In beatifying Bernhard Lichtenberg, the Vatican chose the right person. (I have mentioned him earlier.) In contrast, Edith Stein was a convert to Christianity and murdered, not for of her Christian faith, but because of her Jewish birth. The Vatican moves slowly, but the truth of more than half a century ago should by now have sunk in.

It is hoped that Henrix will argue against the beatification of Pius XII, at least until the Vatican records are opened and scrutinized. Yehuda Bauer has declined being on a scrutinizing committee: he thinks the records will not be fully open.

5. From a Christian who viewed Jews as "brothers" in 1523, Luther had become a Jew-hater in 1543. Stöhr confronts this later Luther: for him "eternal salvation" or "eternal damnation" was at stake. Luther is "ultimately serious" when claiming the "Old Testament" for Christianity alone (W. D. Marsch and K. Thieme, eds., *Juden und Christen* [Mainz: Gruenewald, 1961], 131).

Stöhr's effort (and von der Osten-Sacken's, which I will mention later) were anticipated on Luther's birthday, November 10, in 1932, in *Martin Luther: Theologie des Kreuzes* (Theology of the cross) (Leipzig: Kroener, 1933). Its preface cites Luther: if Germans "do not stop their sins till an external enemy wipes out their madness," they will receive "just punishment for forgetting and despising the word of God." The book appeared in 1933; its editor, Georg Helbig, must have long since died, either of natural causes, or if Deutsche Christen (German Christians) insisted on denouncing him, of SS murder.

Stöhr does not shrink from political implications: "Israel may be strong vis-à-vis the Palestinians, but hopelessly inferior to the sum of Arab countries, supplied with arms by East and West. Israel cannot lose a war. Arab Christians overlook the fact that time works against Israel" (Klaus Mueller and Alfred Wittstock, eds., *Drein Reden* [To interfere] [Wuppertal: Foedus, 1997], 321).

6. And now they have honored Ernst Nolte, who had started the Historikerstreit—honored him for something else, of course. For a German to argue that the Holocaust was "only" Hitler's response to the Gulag is ipso facto to diminish it; *the very fact* of debate is obscene, including, alas, even those who, like Jürgen Habermas, attack Nolte or who, like Hans Ulrich Wehler's *Entsorgung der deutschen Vergangenheit* (A cleansing of the German past from care) (Munich: Beck, 1988) expose it. If this is still a German problem I had just as soon stay away.

7. Schmied-Kowarzik, ed., *Der Philosoph Franz Rosenzweig* (Freiburg: Alber, 1988).

8. Schmied-Kowarzik, *Vergegenwärtigungen des zerstörten jüdischen Erbes* (Kassel: Kassel University Press, 1997).

9. Münz, *Der Welt ein Gedächtnis Geben* (Gütersloh: Chr. Kaiser, 1995).

10. Otto Hermann Pesch has rightly warned against *"falsches Betroffenheitspathos"* (Birte Peterson, *Theologie nach Auschwitz?* [Berlin: Institut Kirche und Judentum, 1998], 10). But there is nothing false about Eva and Burkhard; I stayed with them for three months. Eva has reminded me that Kassel was the first time I used the "beloved, hated" German language; also that when we went shopping I, too, taught her something: "philosophical astonishment" that lullabies I learned as child still exist.

Chapter 18. Return to Halle

1. Dietrich Bonhoeffer said that the person doing his *Pflicht* (duty) ends up doing it even to the devil. In *Hitlers Krieger* Guido Knopp has shown not only that this was true in the case of Eichmann but also that with the "military elite" this prophecy was "dreadfully fulfilled." But only such as Menzer understood Kant himself on the subject of *Pflicht*. Kant says that one must always treat human beings as ends in themselves, not as means only. (Eichmann failed to understand Kant and defied that principle both in his victims and in himself.)

2. *German Philosophy and Jewish Thought*, 255

3. Shlomo Aronson, *Reinhard Heydrich und die Frühgeschichte von Gestapo und SD* (Stuttgart: Deutsche Verlags-Anstalt, 1972).

4. Ibid., 121 ff.

5. Saul Friedlaender, *Nazi Germany and the Jews*, vol. 1 (New York: Harper, 1997), 200.

6. Joachim Fest, *The Face of the Third Reich* (London: Penguin, 1972), 165, 501.

7. *Die Judenpolitik des SD 1935 bis 1938*, ed. Michael Wildt (Munich: Oldenburg, 1995) speaks of SD as a *wahrhaft satanisch ausgeklügelte Organisation*, a "truly satanically calculated organization."

8. Fest, *Face of the Third Reich*, 169, 152, 190.

9. Ibid., 152

10. Fred K. Prieberg, *Musik im NS-Staat* (Frankfurt: Fischer, 1989), 352–53.

Chapter 19. Before and After My Return to Halle

1. Eberhard Bethge, "Bonhoeffer und die Juden," in Ernst Feil and Ilse Todt, eds., *Konsequenzen: Dietrich Bonhoeffers Kirchenverstandnis heute* (Munich: Chr. Kaiser, 1980), 171–215. Bethge, "Nichts scheint mehr in Ordnung," in *Ethik im Ernstfall* (Munich: Chr. Kaiser, 1982), 30–40, especially 34, where the title of the article is repeated: "nichts scheint mehr in Ordnung."

2. See Bethge, "Bonhoeffer und die Juden," 173: "Bonhoeffer hat sich den fast nahtlosen (seamlessly) Anschluss an 1932 von Theologie und Kirche nach 1945 überhaupt nicht vorzustellen (unimaginable) vermocht." See also 171, 209.

3. The translation of excerpts from the resolution are mine. The original reads: "Wer ist betroffen von diesem ungeheuerlichen Ereignis?"

4. The original reads:

Jüdische Antworten haben es schwer wegen der eigenen Betroffenheit. Juden weigern sich mit Recht, mit schnellem Trost das Undenkliche fassbar und das Unaussprechliche sagbar zu machen, und damit den Ermordeten noch gleichsam ihren Tod zu stehlen.

Christliche Antworten haben es schwer, wegen der Gefahr, aus der Verwicklung in das Geschehen zu entfliehen. Diese Gefahr ist gegeben mit jeder vorzeitigen Sinngebung und Erklärung oder, mit einem eilfertigen Kreuzesschema oder einer billigen Auferstehungsthese, der nicht eine lange, tätige Busse vorangegangen ist, oder mit einem kurzschlüssigen "Dennoch" glauben ohne vergleichbare Leidenssituation.

5. The original reads: "Theologische Antworten auf die Theodizee-frage haben darauf zu achten, dass sie weder Gott die Wahrheit seines Gott-seins rauben, noch den Ermordeten die Wirklichkeit ihres Ausge-liefertseins verfälschen."

6. *Auschwitz als Herausforderung für Juden und Christen* (Auschwitz as a challenge to Jews and Christians), ed. Günter B. Ginzel (Heidelberg: Lambert Schneider, 1980), 385–87. See also chapter 3. Bethge is one "father." The other probably is Friedrich-Wilhelm Marquardt. His *Von Elend und Heimsuchung der Theologie* (Munich: Chr. Kaiser, 1992) is the most thorough explication known to me of the Rheinland "resolution," explicit also on why there must be both *Betroffenheit* and *Erschütterung*, hence silence, theological and other kinds.

7. *Warsaw Diary of Chaim Kaplan* (New York: Collier, 1973), 400.

8. David Patterson, *Along the Edge of Annihilation: The Collapse and Recovery of Life in the Holocaust Diary* (Seattle: University of Washington Press, 1999), 3.

Chapter 20. A Political Decision by a Jewish Philosopher

1. Greenspan and Nicholson, eds., *Fackenheim: German Philosophy and Jewish Thought* (Toronto: University of Toronto Press, 1992).

2. The case of the philosophers is different from that of German theologians. Traumatized *during* Hitler's regime and his war, theologians Martin Niemoeller and Ernst Tillich became pacifists *after it*, neither giving much thought to Holocaust survivors having no home yet or having to defend their newly found Jewish state.

Epilogue

1. Karl Jaspers, *The Question of German Guilt* (New York: Capricorn, 1947), 34, 71–73.

2. James Parkes, *The Conflict of the Church and the Synagogue: A Study in the Origins of Antisemitism* (New York: Atheneum, 1969).

3. Hegel, *Vorlesungen über die Philosophie der Weltgeschichte, Bd. 2*, ed. Georg Lasson (Hamburg: Meiner, 1966), 82.

4. Hegel, *Philosophie der Weltgeschichte, Bd. 2*, ed. Georg Lasson (Leipzig: Meiner, 1919), 727–30.

5. Op. cit., 98, also 79.

6. *Hegels Theologische Jugendschriften*, ed. H. Nohl (Tübingen: Mohr, 1907), 225. Translated by T. M. Knox, *Early Theological Writings* (Chicago: University of Chicago Press, 1948), 159. Hegel would have viewed the Arab-Jewish conflict as tragic, between right and right. And a just solution possible only by compromise on both sides.

7. Tom Segev's *Die Soldaten des Bösen* (Hamburg: Rowohlt, 1995) is much more profound than his popular *The Seventh Million* for, concentrating on evil, it makes it as intelligible as possible, by showing how quantity was deliberately turned into quality. Joseph Kramer began with a slap in the face as adequate punishment, but ended up as the "beast of Belsen" (44).

8. Sebastian Haffner, *Anmerkungen zu Hitler* (Franfurt: Fischer, 2002), 162.

9. In Hans Erler, ed., *Erinnern und Verstehen: Der Völkermord an den Juden im politischen Gedächtnis der Deutschen* (Frankfurt: Campus Verlag, 2003).

10. The first time Hitler is known to have referred to the "Jewish problem" was in 1919, when he said the Jews must be *entfernt*. He did not yet say what "removal" was necessary.

11. Buber, *Der Jude und sein Judentum* (Köln: J. Melzer, 1963), 557.

12. See my *Metaphysics and Historicity*.

13. See chapter 4 in my *The Religious Dimension in Hegel's Thought*.

14. Zalman Rubaschoff, "Erstlinge der Entjudung: Drei Reden von Eduard Gans im Kulturverein," *Der Jüdische Wille* 1 (1918): 198.

Appendixes

1. *Editor's note*—Strictly speaking, this sentence is not accurate. Nonetheless, the sentence is retained as it appeared in the notes for the last revisions. The confusion arises because the essay "Post-Holocaust Antisemitism in Europe" was included in two places. One is as the first part of the revised epilogue; the second is as the political essay mentioned here, which would have been Appendix G. I have printed the essay as the first part of the epilogue. Appendix F, "The Holocaust and the Book of Job: Reflections on Theology and Philosophy," is the theological one to which Fackenheim here refers.

2. I had taught German students in Jerusalem for several years. Now I was asked to give this *laudatio* for the organization in Germany on the occasion of the annual award of the Buber Rosenzweig Medaillen

handed out by the Deutscher Koordimerungsrat der Gesellschaft für Christlich-Judische Zusammenarbeit, a highlight of the week called Woche der Brüderlichkeit, which takes place in March every year.

3. My inaugural lecture in Kassel when, for the first time in my life, I conducted a whole term for German students.

4. Friedrich Schleiermacher, *On Religion: Speeches to Its Cultured Despisers,* trans. with an introduction and notes by Richard Crouter (New York: Cambridge University Press, 1988), 211.

5. Hermann Cohen's Kant-influenced Judaism cites Ezekiel 18:21–23. For a harsher post-Holocaust critique of Kant's "euthanasia" of Judaism, see P. L. Rose, *Revolutionary Antisemitism in Germany: From Kant to Wagner* (Princeton: Princeton University Press, 1990), 93 ff.

6. For Fichte's German *Urvolk,* see "Reden an die deutsche Nation" [1807/8], in *Sämmtliche Werke VII,* ed. by Immanuel H. Fichte (Berlin, 1846), 257–508, here, 359. For his *Zwingherr,* see "Staatslehre" [1813], in *Sämmtliche Werke IV,* ed. by Immanuel H. Fichte (Berlin, 1845), 369–600, here, 437–442; as well as "Excurse zur Staatslehre," in *Sämmtliche Werke VII,* 574–613, here, 576.

For Heidegger, see his *Einführung in die Metaphysik* (Introduction in metaphysics) (Tübingen: Max Niemeyer, 1953), 29. The book was published only in 1953, but the lecture had been given already in 1935.

7. Alvin H. Rosenfeld, ed., *Thinking about the Holocaust: After Half a Century* (Bloomington: Indiana University Press, 1997).

8. Anita Shapira, "The Holocaust and World War II as Elements of the Yishuv Psyche until 1948," in Rosenfeld, *Thinking about the Holocaust,* 67 and 81 giving full information on Fishel Schneerson. See also Fishel Schneerson, "Writers' Convention at Ma'aleh Hahamisha, 25 Elul 1945," *Moznayim* 21 [Tishrei-Adar 1945–1946]: 255–57.

9. Viktor Frankl cites Nietzsche, "What does not kill me makes me stronger." But Lawrence Langer asks, "Will it make me stronger if they kill my wife, my children?" Langer also stresses that the filmmakers did not tell us that Anne Frank, simply because she was Jewish, had her "merry spirit" extinguished at Bergen-Belsen (*Admitting the Holocaust* [Oxford: Oxford University Press, 1995], 26, 160).

10 Hegel, *Early Theological Writings,* trans. T. M. Knox (Chicago: University of Chicago Press 1948), 159.

11. *Secret Conversations, 1941–1944,* trans. Norman Cameron and R. H. Stevens, with an introductory essay by H. R. Trevor-Roper (New York: Farrar, Strauss & Young, 1953), 269.

12. *Hitler: Sämtliche Aufzeichnungen 1905–1924* (Collected notes), ed.

E. Jaeckel and A. Kuhn (Stuttgart: Deutsche Verlags-Anstalt, 1980), especially 119–20. This massive work of nearly thirteen hundred pages—all with material written before 1924!—leaves no doubt about either Hitler's "relentless" Jew-hatred or how perfectly it fitted into his yet-incomplete Weltanschauung. In *Mein Kampf* this is developed further. But he claimed to the end that he had nothing to change and nothing to learn.

13. Primo Levi, *The Drowned and the Saved* (London: Abacus 1988), 37.

14. Leonhard Baker, *Days of Sorrow and Pain: Leo Baeck and the Berlin Jews* (New York, London: MacMillan, 1978), 206.

15. The address was published in *Die Zeichen der Zeit* (1993), 122–29.

16. *Drei Hundert Jahre Juden in Halle* (Three hundred years of Jews in Halle) (Halle: Mitteldeutscher Verlag, 1992), 120.

17. Some sort of repetition was intended by the International Franz Rosenzweig Conference, held in Kassel in 1986. See *Der Philosoph Franz Rosenzweig (1886-1929)*, 2 vols., ed. Wolfdietrich Schmied-Kowarzik (Freiburg: Alber, 1988).

18. Hegel, *Early Theological Writings*, 159.

19. Metz, *Gott nach Auschwitz* (God after Auschwitz) (Freiburg: Herder, 1979), 143.

20. Hegel, *Philosophie der Weltgeschichte*, ed. G. Lasson (Leipzig: Meiner, 1939), 938. On the preceding page Hegel had written: "[T]hus far consciousness has come."

21. Hegel, *Rechtsphilosophie* (Philosophy of law), §358. In §270 *Anmerkung* he argued that, since Jews are, "first of all, human," they are entitled to civic rights.

22. Hegel, *Philosophie der Weltgeschichte*, 727–30, 757–67.

23. Brevard Childs, *Introduction to the Old Testament* (Philadelphia: Fortress, 1979) is a breakthrough. Written after the *Shoah* and in obvious response to it, the work pays attention to Jewish as well as Christian commentaries, thus showing that, for a canonizing of the Hebrew Bible, the Jewish return to Jerusalem was essential: divine promises had proven trustworthy. Contrary to Luther's hatred of Esther, Childs stresses that inclusion of the book in the Christian canon was a "check against all attempts to spiritualize the concept of Israel—usually by misinterpreting Paul" (606). See also my *The Jewish Bible after the Holocaust*, 118–19.

24. The "evil" of Eichmann was supposedly "banal," within "Planet Auschwitz." But who produced that "Planet" except these Eichmanns? A magisterial thinker-of-the-whole such as Hegel could not have

ignored the Planet's wholeness; it would have been a radically upsetting *factum brutum*, its comprehension to be resisted just as radically. See further my *To Mend the World*, 247–48.

Dorothy Sölle "could never understand how 'theology-after-Auschwitz' could be the same as before"; but this led her to a "politization of conscience" of other victims elsewhere, but not on behalf of the surviving Auschwitz remnant, to say nothing of Israel, the Jewish "state against death" (*Wie ich mich geändert habe* [How I have changed] [Gütersloh: Chr. Kaiser, 1997], 31, 33, 37).

25. Leo Strauss thought differently from Hegel, but once told me that Hegel's "righteousness" was admirable.

26. The kaiser described the First World War as one between two philosophies: "either the Prussian-German-Teutonic world-philosophy wins—justice, freedom, honor, ethics—or the Anglo-Saxon worship of the golden calf. In this struggle one philosophy must perish. We are fighting for the victory of German philosophy."

27. "Das Vorlaufen zum Tod wurde für Heidegger 1933 zum Opfer Albert Leo Schlageters, der nach Heidegger den 'schwersten Tod' starb und allein, während seine Nation erniedrigt wurde, 'aus sich das Bild des kuenftigen Aufbruchs des Volkes zu seiner Ehre und Grösse sich vor die Seele' stellte. . . . Nach 1945 hat Heidegger kein Wort über die Vernichtung der Juden und anderer gesagt" (*Heidegger und die praktische Philosophie*, ed. Annemarie Gethmann-Siefert and Otto Pöggeler [Frankfurt: Suhrkamp 1989], 62). In the above, Otto Pöggeler writes that Heidegger in 1933 called Schlageters's death hardest, because he was alone, but never said a word about the annihilation of Jews and others.

28. See my *To Mend the World*, 282. The expression refers there only to the recovery of the religion of love by the destruction of the Jew-hatred in it. Now I would use it also for the Golden Age in German philosophy.

29. I have written about Kant for Germans, soon after the war, in "Kant's Concept of History," *Kant-Studien* (1956–57): 381–98.

30. *The Dimensions of Job* (New York: Schocken, 1969).

31. Rabbi Harold Kushner's book was responsible for a symposium at the New York 92nd Street YMCA in 1982, with Rabbi Walter Wurzburger and myself participating, along with the rabbi himself.

32. This title by Arthur A. Cohen is no "interpretation of the Holocaust" but the lack of any.

33. *The Idea of the Holy* (New York: Oxford, 1958), 78, 173. The translation, even of the title, is poor. The German is *Das Heilige*. "Idea" makes it part of that very idealism Otto and Buber wanted to overcome.

34. His "The Jewish Problem and the Christian Answer" rightly admits the Holocaust as "the greatest catastrophe in [Jewish] history" (*Against the Stream* [London: SCM Press, 1954], 196), but the thought of its being a Christian catastrophe does not arise.

35. *At The Turning* (New York: Farrar, Straus and Young, 1952), 62.

Index